*Slavery
and the
Meetinghouse*

# Slavery and the Meetinghouse

## THE QUAKERS *and the* ABOLITIONIST DILEMMA, 1820–1865

## Ryan P. Jordan

INDIANA UNIVERSITY PRESS
BLOOMINGTON AND INDIANAPOLIS

This book is a publication of
*Indiana University Press*
601 North Morton Street
Bloomington, IN 47404-3797 USA
http://iupress.indiana.edu

*Telephone orders* 800-842-6796
*Fax orders* 812-855-7931
*Orders by e-mail* iuporder@indiana.edu

© 2007 by Ryan P. Jordan

*All rights reserved*

*No part of this book may be reproduced or utilized in any form
or by any means, electronic or mechanical, including photocopying and
recording, or by any information storage and retrieval system, without permission
in writing from the publisher. The Association of American University Presses'
Resolution on Permissions constitutes the only exception
to this prohibition.*

*The paper used in this publication meets the minimum
requirements of American National Standard for Information Sciences—
Permanence of Paper for Printed Library Materials, ANSI Z39.48-1984.*

MANUFACTURED IN THE UNITED STATES OF AMERICA

**Library of Congress Cataloging-in-Publication Data**

Jordan, Ryan P., date
Slavery and the meetinghouse : the Quakers and the abolitionist dilemma, 1820–1865 /
Ryan P. Jordan.
p. cm.
Includes bibliographical references and index.
ISBN 0-253-34860-9 (cloth : alk. paper)
1. Antislavery movements—United States—History—19th century. 2. Abolitionists—United States—History—19th century. 3. Slavery and the church—Society of Friends—History—19th century. 4. Slavery and the church—United States—History—19th century. 5. Slaves—Emancipation—United States. 6. Quakers—United States—Political activity—History—19th century. 7. Quaker abolitionists—United States—History—19th century. 8. Pacifism—United States—History—19th century. 9. Society of Friends—United States—History—19th century. 10. United States—Church history.
I. Title.
E449.J775 2007
326.089′96073—dc22       2006027587

1 2 3 4 5   12 11 10 09 08 07

*For Dad, Kevin, and Aaron*

# *Contents*

PREFACE IX
ACKNOWLEDGMENTS XIII

Introduction: Quakers, Slavery, and
the "Peaceable Kingdom"   1

1. Quaker Gradualists and the Challenge of Abolitionism   24

2. Slavery, Religious Liberty, and the "Political" Abolitionism of
the Indiana Anti-Slavery Friends   41

3. Friends and the "Children of Africa": Quaker Abolitionists
Confront the Negro Pew   67

4. "Progressive" Friends and the Government of God   81

5. Quaker Pacifism and Civil Disobedience in
the Antebellum Period   104

Conclusion: "Fighting Quakers," Abolitionists,
and the Civil War   122

NOTES 135
BIBLIOGRAPHY 155
INDEX 163

# *Preface*

This book explores the manner in which the Society of Friends (Quakers) translated their critique of state-sanctioned force into political practice when confronting the antebellum American movement for immediate emancipation. The Society of Friends, both in the United States and in Great Britain, had represented the vanguard of opposition to slavery during the late eighteenth and early nineteenth centuries. But the implications of their religious beliefs remained unclear as the American abolitionist movement became more radical in the 1830s. Because Quaker pacifist and anti-slavery beliefs closely approximated the agenda of the American Anti-Slavery Society, some reformers expected Friends to support their cause to divorce the American government and Constitution from slaveholding. At the same time, other politicians and ministers feared that the Quakers might lend their backing to a movement considered by many to be seditious. Although they were pacifists, Quakers had no desire to be revolutionaries: leaders of the church feared that their dislike of slavery might in fact instigate armed conflict. As a result, the Society of Friends in the United States followed the larger trend of American society in opposing the American Anti-Slavery Society's campaign for immediatism, while leading Friends defined the abolitionists within their church as heterodox radicals working toward the destruction of civil and religious liberty.

The following account of the abolitionist controversy within Quaker meetinghouses recovers the largely forgotten negative reactions to the immediatist movement from denominations that otherwise agreed with the abolitionists' campaign to purge American churches of slaveholding. While historians have spent much time examining the motivations and views of the 250,000 or so Americans who supported the American Anti-Slavery Society, they have written almost nothing about the views of the several hundred thousand Christians who belonged to churches with views that seemed to agree with aspects of the immediatist agenda, but who did not support it. Historians have also left unexplored the serious scrutiny received by anti-slavery and pacifist groups such as the Friends from political leaders in the antebellum era regarding the potentially dangerous implications of their critiques of state-sanctioned force. This book therefore provides an important new perspective on viewing the radicalism and unpopularity of the abolitionist movement by explaining why the movement could not count on support from a religious group long associated with efforts to divorce Christianity from slaveholding.[1]

In addition to revealing the extreme unpopularity of abolitionism among avowedly anti-slavery churches such as the Friends, the story of the Quakers and abolitionists symbolizes the dilemma of liberal religion within a slaveholding republic. The argument between abolitionists and Quakers concerning the role of religious dissent in American civil society occurred at a time when many Protestant Americans debated the meaning of the separation of politics and religion implied by clerical disestablishment, and many clerical leaders and politicians actually congratulated the Friends for their skepticism toward abolitionist principles. In the opinion of nearly all Protestant clerical leaders, groups such as the abolitionists tested the limits of acceptable forms of religious speech by attacking the government's complicity with slavery. As Catharine Beecher explained, the "rights of free discussion [rooted] in the gentle spirit of Christianity" were in danger of being destroyed by "ungoverned factions" such as the American Anti-Slavery Society.[2] When they confronted abolitionist demands for emancipation and greater racial equality, American church leaders often attempted to contain anti-slavery beliefs in the "private" world of the individual conscience. According to the Reformed Presbyterian minister Gilbert McMaster, for example, "ecclesiastical society" (represented in this case by the American Anti-Slavery Society) must not "mingle in the affairs of state." Christianity, continued McMaster, was to be "applied to civil society" by converting "public sentiment" with God's means, and not man's. In this regard, McMaster and others often contrasted the means and ends of abolitionism unfavorably with those of the much more popular temperance movement.[3]

The argument over the political meaning of Quaker opposition to slavery in the antebellum United States helps to reveal how a discourse regarding the limits of religious liberty defined limits for citizenship in American civil society.[4] This study's examination of how Quaker leaders tied religious liberty to *anti*-abolitionism offers insights for many students of early America who have studied the construction of a white, male, Protestant identity that proscribed those who were nonwhite, female, and religiously heterodox.[5] Anglo-American Protestant values inherited from the

English Reformation and Civil War were often mobilized to oppose radical efforts at racial egalitarianism, and this fact further problematizes the meaning of religious liberalization or democratization in the early republic.[6] The process of religious democratization threatened many, and ostensibly liberal concerns about the mixing of politics and religion could be mobilized for illiberal ends such as the continued compromise over slavery's future in the United States.

The radical Quaker abolitionists and their allies realized how religious discourses—including ones surrounding the separation of church and state—bolstered racial prejudice. Between the late 1830s and early 1850s, these men and women began a sustained attack on what they termed "pro-slavery" Christianity. In response to clerical hostility to their cause, many Quaker abolitionists in the United States began to build countercultural church communities that actively dissented from the complicity of America's religious institutions with slavery. Abolitionist "comeouters" rejected flatly the complaint of church leaders that the politics of antislavery had no business in Quaker meetinghouses. Because, as the abolitionist Stephen Foster wrote, "judgement of national crimes [must] begin at the house of God," it was a necessity for church communities to oppose the national evil of slavery.[7] In the opinion of abolitionists, churches were obligated to organize petition drives and lectures or make other public statements in favor of immediatism. Seeking to reconstruct human authority in accordance with the "government of God," abolitionists sought to revamp existing structures of clerical authority to "introduce perfectionism"—meaning human progress toward God's kingdom—"into the social system," in the words of William Goodell.[8] The abolitionist "comeouter" vision of American churches was far different from that of the majority of Christian churches in antebellum America. Yet the abolitionists believed that institutional religion possessed, in the words of Frederick Douglass, "the power of life and death" over the success of efforts to advance emancipation.[9]

Because it was through church institutions that millions of people in the free states understood the cultural system of American Protestantism, this project takes seriously the abolitionist claim that the social and cultural power of institutional Christianity could in fact revolutionize American public opinion regarding race relations. Furthermore, the following study treats the religious vision of reformers as the primary mode through which they articulated their understanding of an alternative social and racial order.[10] Yet the pervasive failure of that countercultural vision, and the subsequent marginalization of Quaker abolitionist "comeouters" provide an instructive context for understanding the insurmountable obstacles facing the American movement for immediate emancipation in the antebellum period.

This book is also a cautionary tale regarding the assumption that personal pacifist beliefs lead inevitably to public or political practice. Although there were many vocal and visible abolitionists and women's rights reformers who adhered to the Quaker faith in the nineteenth century, these high-profile activists in no way represented the typical "Friend," even among the supposedly more radical Hicksite branch of Quakerism. In fact, Quaker dissent from a slaveholding state came at a price, and many in the church could not abide the stinging radicalism of certain activists within their church when urban mobs or slave-hunting posses threatened communities of Friends. This book seeks to reconstruct how members of America's leading anti-slavery church experienced the dilemma between liberty and union that confronted so many who were living in a nation on the brink of civil war. This story hopes to balance the ultimate justice of the radicals' claims with a fair consideration of how difficult it was even for progressive whites to support the abolitionists in antebellum America.

This book lays out a narrative unfolding of events and begins with an introduction to the history of Quakerism, as well as to the church's pacifist and anti-slavery beliefs, before the birth of immediatism in Britain in the 1820s. Chapter 1 describes the first reactions of American Friends to the founding of the American Anti-Slavery Society in the 1830s and details the opposition of Friends to the congressional petition campaign launched by abolitionists in 1834. Chapters 2 through 5 explain the different rationales and events behind abolitionist "comeouter" efforts to redefine the social and political meaning of Friends' worship. Chapter 2 describes Quaker abolitionist support for the Liberty Party and the creation of the Indiana Yearly Meeting of Anti-Slavery Friends in 1842. Chapter 3 details abolitionist critiques of the "Negro pew" and of racial prejudice within Quaker meetinghouses. Chapter 4 explains the formation of the "Progressive" and "Congregational" Friends in the years after 1848, groups that extended abolitionist critiques of slavery to include attacks on gender and class inequities in American society. Chapter 5 examines Quaker abolitionist support for civil disobedience after the Compromise of 1850 and relates how many other Quakers shied away from making pacifist beliefs synonymous with efforts to personally subvert the slave system. Finally, the conclusion of the book examines the dilemma of Quaker anti-slavery during the 1850s and 1860s, when events made the viability of any peaceful solution to the slavery issue in the United States impossible.

# *Acknowledgments*

This book dates from my time at the University of California, Los Angeles, and without the early encouragement of Joyce Appleby, I would not have thought to stick with the topic of Quakers and abolitionists as a graduate student. At Princeton, my dissertation advisor, James McPherson, made helpful comments on several drafts of this project from its earliest stages. Thanks also to Sean Wilentz, Christine Stansell, Jonathan Earle, and Nancy Hewitt for their advice and critiques concerning my work. In addition, Nicholas Guyatt offered a particularly incisive critique of an early draft of this manuscript. At Princeton, I am grateful for the many friends and colleagues who provided a special intellectual and social community to sustain me through my six years there.

The research funding for this project came from the Princeton Department of History, the Center for the Study of Religion at Princeton University, and the Shelby Cullom Davis Center for Historical Studies. During the academic year 2003–2004, I benefited greatly from the weekly seminars of the Center for the Study of Religion, where I was able to present portions of my work and receive valuable feedback from several scholars of religion.

Among the archivists I have encountered over the past several years, I would like to acknowledge Christopher Densmore of the Swarthmore Friends Collection, Thomas Hamm of Earlham College, and Ann Upton and Diana Franzusoff Peterson of the Haverford Friends Collection. Both Christopher Densmore and Thomas Hamm offered important ideas and reminders about Quaker history that shaped the writing of this book. In addition, Professor Hamm read and commented upon this manuscript in its entirety.

Another important reviewer of this book was my late father, James Jordan, who, along with my mother Pauline, supported me in many ways during my time in graduate school. My father instilled in me early on an interest in religious mysticism and social activism, and his advice and critiques helped make this project a better one. I wish to dedicate this book not only to him, but additionally to the memory of both my brother Kevin Jordan and Aaron Cornwell. Their young loss in many ways gave me greater appreciation for the Quaker search for peace at one's center in spite of the disappointments of this world.

*Slavery and the Meetinghouse*

INTRODUCTION
# Quakers, Slavery, and the "Peaceable Kingdom"

For some, the term "Quaker" conjures up images of Edward Hicks's nineteenth-century paintings depicting the "Peaceable Kingdom." Based on Isaiah's prophesies concerning the ultimate victory of the Christian "Prince of Peace," Hicks's paintings exemplified the Quaker hope in the oneness of humanity and nature with God. In the peaceable kingdom, conflict and strife caused by human frailty had been banished, and the broken conscience of the sinner had finally found its perfect reconstitution. Hicks's depiction of William Penn's treaty with the Indians, in particular, showed a foretaste of the peaceable kingdom, illustrating the Quakers' once harmonious relations with seventeenth-century Native Americans in Pennsylvania. Here was the ideal New World, the quaint picture of equality and personal virtue, where all Old World oppression had faded away. As exemplars of this virtue and morality so pivotal to the American republic, the Quakers, to many observers, could demonstrate how a distinct religious community might yoke its dissenting religiosity to a concern for the nation's broader welfare. During debates in Congress over the Missouri Compromise, for example, a congressman named Thomas Forrest was heard to exclaim, "Would to God that we were all Quakers, in order that there might be less oppression, evil, and bloodshed in the land!"[1]

But as students of antebellum American history know, the republican vision of equality and virtue was largely built with the toil of American slaves, the oppression of Europe lingered on in a racially divided America, and the idyllic scenes of Edward Hicks's kingdom were threatened by slave revolt, sectional strife, and, ultimately, civil war. Moreover, behind Hicks's images of animals coexisting peacefully in beautiful pastoral scenes was the reality that Hicks's own religious community had not been immune from controversy and schism. Edward Hicks, as a recorded minister in the Society of Friends, continued to paint scenes of the peaceable kingdom during the 1820s and 30s, decades when his own sect—led in no small part by his cousin Elias—was being torn apart by arguments over the engagement of Quakers with a changing American society. Many social and political concerns impinged upon Friends' meetings in these years, and none was more important than slavery. America's inability to end this practice peacefully would severely test the cohesion of Hicks's personal peaceable kingdom, and it would bring war to the very soil of Quaker Pennsylvania in 1863.

The nearly two-centuries-long history of Edward Hicks's denomination also belied his vision of tranquility. The term "Quaker" was born during a period of social and political revolution in seventeenth-century England and remained as an unrealized promise of the Christian hope to "shake the world to its foundations." There had been nothing peaceful about early Quakers fighting in Cromwell's New Model Army or disturbing congregations with warnings about the impending doom of an English Babylon. A mystical movement that sought out the government of God, that refused to pay tithes or swear oaths, that had acknowledged no king "but Jesus" could hardly be characterized as meek or unoffending. By 1820, those scenes had largely passed, the "Quakers" having generally made their peace with those in power, but the Society of Friends stood on the brink of having yet again to combat a radical attempt to infuse politics into religion with the rise of the "immediatist" abolition movement. All the disruption, vituperation, and disrespect for clerical authority that once won Friends the appellation "Quaker" were about to be revisited in the form of anti-slavery "comeouterism."

The tension between the autonomy of the lay person's conscience on the one hand and the need for sectarian coherence on the other had characterized the Religious Society of Friends from its early days in seventeenth-century England. Its founder, George Fox, had articulated the bold doc-

## Introduction

3

trine of the "Inner Light," that "every man" who believed in the "divine light of Christ . . . came out of condemnation to the light of life, and became children of it."[2] Set against the ritual of the "Roman" church or the theological learning of the Reformed ministry stood this simple doctrine with its faith in the individual to find salvation. The Quaker movement sought that union with God found not in external forms, but in human experience. In the silences of meeting, Quakers would simply "wait on the Spirit" to bring them closer—perhaps—to the fountain of all real knowledge beyond the "creaturely activity" of humankind.

But to avoid the excesses of spiritual libertarianism, Fox led the effort to put into place a disciplinary apparatus that would regulate the lives of the "children of light." Such an apparatus sought to turn Quakers away from the world, and the Society of Friends, after the first few decades of its existence, never again actively attempted to gain converts. What Friends came to term the "plain life" constituted the practical fruits of their seeking after the kingdom of God. Their refusal to remove hats to social betters, the plain black-and-white dress, and the strictures against the immorality of gambling, dancing, fornication, swearing, and drunkenness all characterized the Quaker ethic. So too did the demand that Quakers only marry others committed to the faith. Perhaps the most distinctive aspect of the plain life, however, was pacifism. Believing that all "carnal weapons" in the world were works of evil, Fox instructed his followers to refuse military service or any taxation to that end. Brotherly love in all things was to be a quite literal rule of behavior among Friends.[3] By the eighteenth century this distaste for violence would push Quakers down an anti-slavery path taken by few other Christians. Eventually, owning slaves would be added to the list of offenses that qualified one for "disownment," or the cutting off of a believer from his or her community.

Yet Friends were not communalists in the tradition of the Amish or Mennonites—they believed in remaining engaged with the world outside of the meetinghouse. Whether establishing mercantile operations, or founding colonies such as Pennsylvania, Quakers prospered in the world beyond their denomination. Some Quakers even partook in the slave trade. The direction of this participation, however, and its meaning for the Quaker ethic were often a source of consternation. For obvious reasons, William Penn's view of Quaker social behavior ("True Godliness doesn't turn men out of the world, but enables them to live better in it") was not really being adhered to by Quaker slave traders.[4]

As a result, Friends discovered that the sect and the world could often clash. This realization was particularly acute during the so-called Quaker reformation of the middle and late eighteenth century. When wealth lured young men away from Quaker communities in eastern Pennsylvania and at the same time the Quaker-dominated legislature compromised its pacifist principles during the French and Indian War, leaders within the Society demanded a tightening of the disciplinary code in general, and in particular began to demand that Quakers stop holding slaves. Although complaints about slaveholding among the Society dated back to at least the 1670s, it took a sustained effort on the part of reformers such as John Woolman and Anthony Benezet to wean Quakers from their dependence upon slave labor. In fact, the abolition of slavery within the Society of Friends took nearly three decades from the first admonition against involuntary servitude in 1754 until Virginia moved against slavery in 1784.[5]

During this period, the tenor of the Quaker reformers' complaints took on an increasingly "tribalistic" note. Disgusted by the worldly compromise of church members who were either marrying out of the society, rejecting the peace testimony, or shirking the material simplicity of the "plain life," certain leaders began to demand a return to sectarian purity. During the American Revolution, reformers demanded that the sect's testimony against war be upheld by disowning many young men who fought either for the patriot cause or for the British. Individual Quaker pacifists suffered greatly for their adherence to the sect's nonviolent directives. James Pemberton of Philadelphia, along with several other men, was arrested by the patriot government as a "security risk" and put in jail. Many Quaker meetings therefore referred to the Revolution's test of pacifism as a "mark of divine displeasure" and saw a warning in the war regarding compromise with the world.[6] Even in these years of trial and travail, however, the demand to assert sectarian purity never wholly eclipsed Quaker involvement in the world. The impetus behind Quaker leadership in the colony of Pennsylvania, or in the desire of Friends to build mercantile empires could not be stomped out by sectarian reform. The reformers simply tempered and redirected worldly involvement, allowing Quakers to participate in a broader move to curtail sinful behavior in the society at large.[7]

The campaign against Quaker slaveholding coincided with a larger Anglo-American awakening that slavery was inconsistent with Enlightenment ideals of personal autonomy and economic development. Men as disparate in their ideologies as Edmund Burke, Adam Smith, the Abbe Raynal, and the monarch of Prussia were in agreement on the evils of both slavery and the slave trade. During the American Revolution, Rhode Island Quakers sought to limit the slave trade, and in the aftermath of pa-

## Introduction

triot victory, Philadelphia Friends revived the Society for the Relief of Free Negroes Unlawfully Held in Bondage that had been suspended during fighting. Out of this society would grow the world's first abolition society, the Pennsylvania Society for Promoting the Abolition of Slavery, headed by Benjamin Franklin.

The founding of this abolition society marked the first of many societies organized from Massachusetts to North Carolina to petition state legislatures for the gradual abolition of slavery. "Gradual" abolition usually meant that only certain slaves would be freed after a certain number of years, and there were often complex laws and fines ensuring that said slaves would not become a "charge" on the community. Success in gradual manumission, however, did occur in six northeastern states, largely with Quaker involvement. But in the years of the Confederation and during the ratification of the Constitution, Friends had their hopes dashed for a strong national stance against slavery. In deference to compromise, the authors of the Constitution—hardly willing to force abolition on Southern states—allowed the slave trade to continue for twenty years, and included an infamous provision that affirmed the right of slaveholders to recover their "property."

Realizing the danger of building a nation with an acceptance of slavery's legal legitimacy, in 1783 the Friend David Cooper hoped the Continental Congress would support manumission as "advocates of freedom" and "lovers of mankind." He implored, "Now is the time to demonstrate to Europe, to the whole world, that America was in earnest" when she pled "that all mankind came from the hand of their Creator equally free."[8] Of course, the young republic as a whole did no such thing. And at nearly the same time, African slaves throughout the New World began attempts to achieve freedom on their own terms; taking the American Revolution's enlightened sentiments of freedom and equality to heart, they revolted. Beginning in 1792, slaves in Santo Domingo initiated an ultimately successful and bloody rebellion against their French masters, a rebellion that would give the New World its first black nation. Fears of slave insurrection would from this time forward remain vivid among slaveholding whites in the United States, making manumission that much more difficult. When, a year after the Santo Domingo revolution began, the Philadelphia Quaker Warner Mifflin tried to petition Congress to end the slave trade and to support manumission efforts in the states, his views were termed "fanatical" by Southern legislators who felt Mifflin's words would "excite" slave "insurrections" and destroy the "present excellent harmony of the union."[9] Confronting defensive planters in the halls of a newly formed American Congress, white anti-slavery reformers—such as the Quakers or Methodists—found that excising human bondage from the public life of the American republic could be a difficult undertaking.[10]

American Quakers, now citizens of a slaveholding republic, learned early on the necessity of compromise when attempting to promote the American Revolution's promise of human brotherhood and equality. In the early 1800s, members of the manumission and abolition societies offered only modest proposals for gradually ending slavery that normally included the prospect of some type of colonization for freed blacks. As an idea, colonization dated back to the days of Anthony Benezet, who could not realistically envision abolition occurring on a large scale without former slaves being given land of their own away from their former masters. This "realistic" approach to ending slavery also won support among slaveholders themselves, and in 1817, the American Colonization Society was formed with the high hopes of convincing slaveholders to send their manumitted slaves to the coast of west Africa. There, in Liberia, philanthropists hoped former slaves would enlighten and civilize the "dark continent."

Liberia, however, also existed as a mere safety valve against slave revolution. As would always be the accusation, a significant motivation for colonization came from slaveholders who simply wanted to rid themselves of freed slaves and thus maintain the future security of slavery. Later critics would note, for example, how the president of the society, Henry Clay, never offered to colonize his own slaves. The fact that the largest "anti-slavery" organization formed between 1800 and 1830 was predicated on the expulsion of African slaves from American soil exemplified the inability to tackle slavery head-on during the middle period. In many ways, the desire of Quakers to become "peaceable" citizens of the United States caused them to eschew more radical attacks on the legality of slaveholding.

Besides this lack of initiative to end slavery, the prospect of slavery actually expanding across the American continent only produced more problems for Quakers active in anti-slavery efforts. Far from being a contained institution presided over by masters willing to put the practice on a gradual road to extinction, human bondage proved to be alive and well with the nation's admission of Missouri as a slave state in 1820. Hinting at the agitation of the years ahead, Quakers Elisha Tyson and William Newbold organized protest meetings against the "Missouri Compromise" in Baltimore, Maryland, and Trenton, New Jersey, respectively.[11] Elihu Embree and Charles Osborn also criticized Missouri's admission in their anti-slavery journals.

Introduction

Occasionally, then, during these years of anti-slavery moderation, such voices in the wilderness could be heard heralding a rebirth of abolitionist fervor. Among the Quakers, the aforementioned Elihu Embree and Charles Osborn, as well as Elias Hicks, gave eloquent defenses of racial equality and of the ultimate justice of abolition. In his pamphlet *Observations on the Slavery of the Africans and their Descendants,* Hicks stated that every legislature in the country must "entirely ... abolish slavery." Hicks also chided the belief that Africans are "inferior in nature and understanding" as representing "manifest futility" on the part of white thinking.[12] Through his paper the *Emancipator* in 1820, Elihu Embree encouraged his fellow Tennesseans that notwithstanding the apparent "gloomy ... prospect" for abolition in the South, "providence" gives "signal deliverance to the oppressed" and should spur all on with "reanimated exertion" to break the yoke of oppression.[13] Nor were Quaker men the only voices of protest in these years. In the 1820s, a young Quaker woman named Rachel Leonard appeared before the North Carolina Manumission Society to read her own address against slavery.[14] The text of the speech does not exist, but that a woman addressed a "mixed assembly" testifies to the role women played in the abolitionist movement. Quaker women also formed societies in the 1820s, such as the Female Society for the Encouragement of Free Labor, to advance a boycott of merchandise made with slave labor.[15] Such involvement in protesting the coercion of slavery would, in time, move some women to protest not only the coercion of slavery but of gender relations as well.

A minority of Quakers also worked to build an interracial America in the 1810s and 20s. Perhaps the best known was the Baltimore Quaker Elisha Tyson, a tireless defender of manumission and freedmen's protective legislation in Maryland. A "great crowd of colored people" attended his funeral out of the belief that the community had lost a rare, unflinching defender.[16] In a social circle that included both Benjamin Lundy and, later, William Lloyd Garrison, anti-slavery Quakers in Baltimore listened to African Americans tired of a colonizationist movement that reinforced racial prejudice, and William Lloyd Garrison encouraged militant black voices to editorialize in the *Genius of Universal Emancipation.* These Quakers, along with other whites such as Garrison, watched with concern as local whites in places like Philadelphia met the increasing free black population with calls for a crackdown on further black emigration. The opposition to the rights of free blacks contributed to the radicalization of many anti-slavery Quakers. Yet it would take several more years of frustration over the intransigence of both slaveholders and their northern allies before those committed to a more perfectionist version of anti-slavery reform would find their place on the national stage.

One of the real challenges that would face abolitionist reformers within the Society of Friends was the climate of hostility, mutual recrimination, and disunity that characterized the American Society of Friends in the years after the War of 1812. The explosion of caustic religious debate, the proliferation of lay religious preaching, and the impulse to create sects out of churches believed to be "dead as wood" typified the American religious landscape in the first half of the nineteenth century. The Society of Friends was not immune from these developments, and because of them anti-slavery efforts hardly constituted the largest concern for most members of the Society of Friends in America during the 1820s and early 30s. Indeed, the theological acrimony culminating in the "Hicksite" separation of 1827–28 held the attention of Quakers throughout the Unites States, for a time, seemingly to the exclusion of any other concern. Yet the debates largely generated by Elias Hicks's preaching were not wholly unrelated to the Quakers' later confrontation with immediate abolitionists, as they addressed the problem of sectarian involvement in the public sphere of voluntary associations.

In the years after the American Revolution, the political culture of the United States was irrevocably altered by numerous associations of American citizens congregating to effect social and political reform. Old authorities felt under siege with the explosion of mechanic associations, fire societies, Masonic lodges, missionary associations, tract societies, benevolence associations, and a hundred other associations for the promotion of a thousand different causes. The noted French observer of early American society, Alexis de Tocqueville, wrote that while in his home country one would inevitably find the government behind every enterprise, in America "you will find an association." American society, continued Tocqueville, was not remarkable "for the marvelous grandeur of some undertakings" but for the "innumerable number of small ones."[17] Such voluntary "undertakings" were not limited to upper-class or genteel white men, either; women formed literary associations, and African Americans formed library companies. Previously unheard groups within American society began to make their presence felt, thus signaling the liberating potential—if not always the reality—of new platforms for civic participation.

Often responsible for the rise of voluntary societies was evangelical Protestantism. With the demise of state-supported religion, thousands of preachers vied for the allegiance of American souls. Along with the explosion of frontier Methodism, there were powerful movements such as the

New Light Presbyterians, Freewill Baptists, Universalists, Campbellites, Disciples of Christ, Mormons, and Seventh-Day Baptists that in varying degrees envisioned a Christian restoration: the church militant must return to an age unpolluted by tradition and priestly authority. But even as these groups represented the "democratization" of American Protestantism, they were suspicious of the very combinations of associations such democracy produced.[18] Anti-Masonic, anti-sabbatarian, and anti-mission campaigns testify to the often negative (even paranoid) nature of democratic evangelism, an evangelism that disliked new religious institutions often led by an emerging mercantile elite. Those with political clout in the young republic hardly stood by and watched "democratization" sweep away their power. The rising tide of theological orthodoxy expressed in the sabbatarian movement, for example, demonstrated the ability of an upper-class, urban, Protestant cadre to adapt its methods for influence in a new "democratic" age. Seeking to rein in a nation that appeared to be quite literally going to hell, the new world of voluntary associations, then, could give new expression to old ideas regarding the rule of the godly. In this way, both the forces of change and reaction could be served by a developing public sphere. As a result, the free exchange of knowledge, the "marketplace" of religious competition, the reams of circulars and pamphlets, newspapers and broadsides being generated by a robust participatory culture hardly unified the country. In many ways, it accomplished the exact opposite.[19] And it changed the Society of Friends forever.

In the years after the War of 1812, some Friends in Philadelphia began to gravitate toward organizations belonging to the so-called "benevolent empire." Such benevolence sought to spread correct knowledge of Christian faith in Jesus Christ, encourage daily reading of the Bible, and otherwise speak out against the vices of immorality and irreligion in American society. They also desired the conversion of the "heathen" in far-off lands. Serving these ends, Bible societies, tract associations, as well as missionary and Sunday school unions soon came into being. By the 1810s, certain Quaker leaders were offering financial support for the Bible Society of Philadelphia, and the Quaker John Warder served on the board of managers of the American Bible Society, founded in 1816 in New York. That same year Philadelphia Friends founded the Tract Association of Friends to disseminate pamphlets that would "enforce the doctrines of the Christian religion."[20]

Viewing these developments with increasing alarm, a well-regarded Quaker minister from Long Island, Elias Hicks, began to preach against attempts by evangelicals to "promote, merely by human wisdom and animal force, morality and virtue." Beginning in 1816, Hicks traveled around the Northeast and Midwest visiting Quaker meetings and letting his thoughts be known on the dangers facing Quakerism. No one can "love enemies, and pray to God for them," declared Hicks, "while he is either directly or indirectly exercising force on a rational fellow creature."[21] Articulating the vision of Christian mysticism that all "must come back to that of God in our own souls . . . for Jesus declares 'the kingdom of God is within you,'" Hicks found many Christian institutions defiling the progress of mankind with coercive measures.[22] The elusive goal of promoting people's desire to seek after the Holy Spirit in silence, to find within themselves the light of Christ, was being ignored by more orthodox Quakers. Hicks believed that one of the great dangers hindering the advancement of God's kingdom was the coercion of creeds, hireling (paid) ministers, and institutions which looked for salvation in man-made "books, colleges, and schools." "They are antipodes," chided Hicks, "in direct opposition to God."[23]

Hicks's often radical anti-clericalism and his republican aversion to oppressive institutions generated sufficient controversy to be noted by many newspapers as well as by Friends in England. Leading Philadelphia Friends such as Jonathan Evans began to take exception to the Christian anarchism and gnostic spirituality hinted at in many of Hicks's sermons. Claiming that those who believed that Jesus was "the only son of God that can give us a knowledge of the Father" were "dark indeed," Hicks appeared to be denying the divinity of Christ, or at least the Christian notion that it is Christ alone who makes salvation possible. Hicks's faith in the "rational soul of man" to comprehend the "will of God," and his belief that "every enlightened person" could interpret the Bible for himself, appeared to some to be an uncomfortable nod to rationalist Christianity. Similarly, his assertion that God "prepares no place of torment for us" in the afterlife seemed a forthright acceptance of the heresy of mankind's universal salvation.[24]

A genuine sense pervaded orthodox circles that Hicks's preaching would further rend the social fabric of early America and generate a false faith in the human ability to change sinful human nature. Editorials in the *Friend,* which were strongly influenced by "orthodox" leaders, repeated the fear that Hicks's sermons regarding "spirituality and religious liberty" would only "beguile the unwary, and rob them of their faith and hope in Jesus Christ, the Son of God, and Saviour of the World."[25] "Christianity," another editorial continued, is "the foundation of good government"; the "safety of all states depends upon religion; it ministers to social order . . .

and gives security to property." Retracing the horrors of "revolutionary France" with its "morbid insensibility to morals, desecrated sabbaths, and abandonment to . . . amusements the most frivolous and dissipating," the author feared that the Hicksites were spreading the "same deadly principles among every class of society in our own country."[26] In the opinion of the paper, Quakers bore as much responsibility as any other group to guard against "a gloomy skepticism, or cold and heartless infidelity," and needed to "inculcate the obligations of the gospel" in "our neighbors."[27]

Those who felt challenged by Hicks's attacks on the organs of the benevolent empire responded that nothing less than the "progress of mankind" depended upon correct religious knowledge. The British and Foreign Bible Society, for example, was referred to as "one of the most powerful antidotes to infidelity, superstition, and priestcraft" on earth, and its founding was "one of the most remarkable events of our age."[28] Likewise, the Philadelphia Tract Association of Friends was valiantly serving the "cause of true religion and Christian morals" and, it was hoped, still more Quakers would "engage in the work with renewed zeal and diligence."[29] The laudable traits of morality and virtue would be advanced by Quaker support for evangelical benevolence.

Ultimately, all this was seen by the Hicksites as a plot to infuse religion into government. The union of church and state so feared by religious libertarians like Hicks represented nothing less than a form of slavery run by a religious "aristocracy" aiming for a "subjugation of the mind."[30] But if the orthodox could be accused of moving toward an insertion of religion into politics and of attempting to bring back a church establishment, the Hicksites, as earlier noted, could be accused of unleashing Jacobin revolution. The orthodox, therefore, were not the only ones with leaders possessing a broader social and political vision for the early republic. Even while Hicks decried Quaker involvement in the benevolent empire, many of his sermons engaged other groups with political agendas in the 1820s, most notably those of the Owenite socialists and the nascent workingman's movement. Though Hicks himself probably never took part in radical communitarian experiments or working-class politics, he seemed at times to speak their language. For example, in 1824 in Trenton, New Jersey, Hicks preached how the cities of the young republic were "made up too much of that sort of men and women who love to live by their wits instead of their labour." Mechanics who performed labor out of "productive good" should be looked up to by their better-heeled urban compatriots: "For it is a very great crime to be supported by the labour of another, or to take advantage of the labour of others, to live by it." "Perfect wisdom," continued Hicks, "will lead us to that kind of labour that will be profitable to all those engaged in it."[31] Hicks also advocated universal public education: "Thousands and tens of thousands have been forbid the enjoyment of every good thing on earth, even of common schooling and must it still be so?" He also termed speculative investments "vain and cruel pursuits."[32]

It should come as no surprise, then, that many Quakers sympathetic with Hicks's critique of orthodoxy played some role in the radical politics of the 1820s. Cornelius Blatchly, a Quaker physician from New Jersey and later a candidate on the Workingman's ticket for the New York legislature, laid out in *Some Causes of Popular Poverty* a ringing critique of the capitalist usurpation of property. Blatchly would eventually leave Quakerism, help form the New York Society for Promoting Communities, and work to expose the plight of outworker seamstresses.[33] The visiting reformer Frances Wright won support among urban Friends in New York and Philadelphia, though not without controversy. Maria Imlay, a young minister in New York, defended her attendance at Frances Wright's Hall of Science, dedicated to "throwing aside the distinctions of class": "If we find them in the practice of every virtue, may we not conclude them really gathered into the Kingdom of Heaven, however they may name it; that is under the reign of light, wisdom, and love?" Imlay was faced with disownment for frequenting the hall, and she chose her membership in Quakerism over her affiliation with Wright.[34]

Robert Dale Owen also won the admiration of radical Quakers, this time in Delaware. The *Delaware Free Press,* edited by the Quaker Benjamin Webb in Wilmington, often published articles sympathetic with Owen's communitarian schemes. The "notorious" British radical took notice, hailing the paper as a "spirited defender of freedom of speech and rights of conscience," standing firm "against spiritual tyranny." He was also pleasantly surprised at the number of "heterodox" Quakers in Wilmington, making it an ideal place for him to lecture on free inquiry and education reform.[35] Further evidence of Quaker involvement in workingmen's politics can be found in advertisements for the People's Hall in Philadelphia, as well as that town's Republican Political Association of Working Men, in which members of the McClintock and Marriot families took part.[36] On opposing poles from the agents of tract societies and Sunday school unions, Quakers could be found associating with the radical fringes of white American opinion.

The centrifugal forces being exerted on Quakers oftentimes resulted in crowds flocking to Quaker meetinghouses to hear ministers from one side or the other speak. Elias Hicks noted on several occasions how great numbers would come in and "greatly enlarge" the meetings for worship. Occasionally "hundreds assembled who could not get in" to hear him preach.[37] Papers throughout the Northeast and Midwest carried news and editorials regarding the Quaker controversy, broadcasting opinions and rumors in ways unimaginable just thirty years earlier. Depending on which side one listened to, one could hear threats of deistic revolution or priestly oppression, the flames of exaggeration fanned by a culture particularly sensitive to the threat of conspiracy. Ultimately, the Society of Friends could not withstand the eschatalogical firefight. On the heels of a Bible burning among Quaker teenagers at the Westtown Boarding School, as well as a near riot outside the Arch Street meetinghouse, the Philadelphia Yearly Meeting split in two in 1827.[38]

The fighting over competing theological understandings of Quakerism, and the concomitant social and political controversy it generated would impact Quakers for years to come. Writing in 1830 in the *Delaware Free Press,* the Hicksite Quaker Benjamin Webb, a man soon to be disowned for his heretical views among Hicksite Friends in Wilmington, Delaware, applauded the efforts of those recent followers of Elias Hicks who sought to strike at the "empty professions" and "spiritual pride" of those who occupied the "high seat of authority" within Hicksite Quakerism. Significantly, many of the individuals praised by Webb were women: Maria Imlay and Phebe Johnson in the New York Yearly Meeting fought gallantly against the "pride of spiritual dominion," and Elizabeth Reeder in the Philadelphia Yearly Meeting, many of whose sermons were published in the *Free Press,* refused to "bow down to the images . . . set up" by leaders of the Society of Friends.[39] Reeder, like Johnson, was finally disowned for her belief that "man [represented by the Hicksite elders] . . . dared to raise his power above the power of God" by cutting off from fellowship those Quakers who experimented with unpopular religious and social beliefs.[40] During one of her sermons, the male ministers actually closed the partition in the meetinghouse dividing male from female Friends and began to transact in secret the business of the meeting while Reeder was speaking.[41] This served as a dramatic reminder of how little power the female half of Quaker meetinghouses in fact possessed.

By 1831, these radical Hicksites sympathetic with Robert Dale Owen in Wilmington, Delaware, found themselves disowned by the very people who had so recently revolted against an overreaching clerisy. Benjamin Ferris, a member of the Wilmington Monthly Meeting, wrote to William Gibbons how some Hicksites excited "the younger and inexperienced part of society to free enquiry." Treating "subjects deemed sacred with great freedom," Wilmington elders had given "impetus to a ball that has rolled beyond our reach." Ferris wanted his meeting to be brought out of the Owenite "hurry and heat" of "natural zeal and reasoning [and] into a state of quiet." In the end, forty Quakers in Wilmington were cut off from fellowship.[42] When not attacking the pollution of free-thinking radicalism, other Friends, taking their cue from the Rhode Island minister John Wilbur, would continue the attempt to turn aside from non-Quaker evangelical groups. The "overactive restless spirit" of benevolence societies, one minister wrote, is like the "locust, the cankerworm, and the caterpillar, ready to eat up every green thing."[43] The "Wilburite" controversy would further divide the New England, Ohio, Indiana, and Philadelphia yearly meetings by 1845.

Those active in anti-slavery efforts, presaging later dissension, were not immune from disagreement over theological innovation. Writing in reaction to attempts by the Quaker abolitionist Joseph John Gurney to align the anti-Hicksites with the Protestant evangelical mainstream, Charles Osborn declared, "What a pity! What a pity! That for the abolition of slavery, and the spreading of the Bible, people should be turned against Christ!" [as represented by traditional Quakerism].[44] But not long after Osborn uttered these words, he himself would be criticized for abolitionist activities that too closely aligned Quaker meetings with evangelical politics and that fomented church division. Such was the dilemma of many nineteenth-century Quakers attempting in piecemeal fashion to delineate the boundaries of proper and improper involvement with the world, either rejecting or joining with some movements depending on time or context. It was clear, however, that Quaker leaders had become particularly sensitive to any movement that threatened the cohesion of their church communities. Searching for some sort of religious consensus, leading Quakers would caution against attempts to align the Society of Friends with organizations disliked by many in the church. Quaker social testimonies were meant to reflect the slow, gradual searching for unity in the Spirit supposedly characteristic of the Society of Friends. Groups that threatened the unity of Quaker communities by, for example, instigating arguments within the community over divisive political issues such as slavery would be in danger of being characterized by "weighty" ministers as innovators working for the destruction of the Society of Friends. This fact would make the abolitionist reformation of the Society of Friends all the more difficult to realize—in marked contrast to the success of eighteenth-century reformers who had eliminated slaveholding among Quakers. Ironically, the waves of democratic discontent with Quaker ministers led by men such as Elias Hicks and John Wilbur simply created one more obstacle facing those Quakers attempting to enforce a new moral code on Friends.[45]

Still another challenge for Quaker immediatists was the simple fact that previous failures to advance emancipation in the years before 1830 only confirmed the fears of Quaker gradualists concerning the impracticality of large-scale emancipation in the United States. Because Quakers organized the North Carolina Manumission Society and the Pennsylvania Abolition Society and possessed a strong influence on the New York Manumission Society, the opinion of Quakers regarding the practicality of emancipation represented something of a barometer for the success of immediatism in the United States. To a large extent, Quakers *were* the organized anti-slavery movement in the United States between 1800 and 1830.[46]

For a younger generation within the Society of Friends, however, the British movement for immediatism would prove a difficult one to translate into practice within a slaveholding nation. The vision of immediate emancipation, later destined to fire the imagination of a generation of American abolitionists including William Lloyd Garrison, Arthur Tappan, and Gerrit Smith, was not an idea native to America: it was first stated by a female British Quaker, Elizabeth Heyrick, in 1824. Her pamphlet, "Immediate, Not Gradual Abolition, or, an Inquiry into the Shortest, Safest, and Most Effectual Means of Getting Rid of West Indian Slavery," epitomized the rapidly increasing desire among Britons to see colonial slavery dealt one final, lethal blow. "Truth and justice make their best way in the world when they appear in bold and simple majesty," Heyrick declared, and those opposed to slavery must act more like "Christian combatants, and less [like] worldly politicians." Heyrick then asked a profound rhetorical question: "To which party do we really belong?—to the friends of emancipation, or of perpetual slavery?" The perpetuation of slavery was not an "abstract question" but one that implicated every subject of the crown. "We" concluded Heyrick "are all guilty."[47]

Many British Quakers, such as William Allen, James Cropper, and Samuel Gurney, carried the banner of immediate, unconditional emancipation through the 1820s and early 30s and played an instrumental role in convincing Parliament to outlaw slavery in 1833. Operating through the London Yearly Meeting, these Quakers, emboldened by the success of their "perfectly virtuous" act, called upon their brethren across the Atlantic to occupy the same uncompromising and principled ground in the United States that had felled West Indian bondage in Britain.[48] "We believe," wrote London Yearly Meeting to Quakers in America, "that a blessing has rested upon the Christian efforts which have been employed for the utter termination of slavery" in Britain, therefore "we are led to encourage you in your desires to act faithfully" for an "uncompromising" end to slavery in America.[49]

But an argument that seemed daring yet plausible in Britain was largely seen as impolitic, if not reckless, in a country that had always accommodated African servitude. Though there were supporters of Heyrick's immediatist tactics among American Quakers in the 1820s, they appeared to be largely the exception that proved the gradualist rule. An editorial in the *Berean,* a liberal Quaker journal in Wilmington, Delaware, spoke for the minority of those among the anti-slavery community who supported immediatism: "schemes for colonization on a distant continent . . . instead of ameliorating the condition of the slave at home, must only tend to add to the strength of his fetters." The editor then quoted directly from Heyrick's pamphlet: "the slave has a right to his liberty, a right which it is a crime to withhold—let the consequences to the planters be what they may. . . ."[50] Against this opinion, however, stood the best-known abolitionist before 1830, Benjamin Lundy, who, as editor of the *Genius of Universal Emancipation,* published Heyrick's pamphlet with the caveat that "he feared the consequences, if emancipation took place suddenly" and believed that abolition would only occur through the employment of all the various plans and methods which had been or might be suggested.[51]

Much of Lundy's efforts, as well as most of the interest in manumission before the founding of the American Anti-Slavery Society, existed south of the Mason-Dixon line. Several of the "abolition" or "manumission" organizations met several times during the 1820s under the aegis of the American Convention of Abolition Societies to discuss the merits of immediatism, but nothing near an endorsement ever materialized. Sometimes, these early anti-slavery groups did not seem much opposed to slavery at all: the Baltimore Society for the Protection of Free People of Color, for example, warned in 1827 that "it is *not* among the objects contemplated by this association to promote the abolition of legal slavery or to interfere with the legal rights which are exercised over the slaves."[52] Such was the often tenuous and hesitant nature of early-nineteenth-century gradualism, an approach that, in the end, failed to convince Southern legislatures to ease manumission laws or to stop the sale of free blacks by local whites who increasingly saw such blacks as a danger to the established order.

The largest organization opposed to slavery in the South before 1830 was the Quaker-led North Carolina Manumission Society. In similar fashion to its counterparts elsewhere, the society greeted the radicalization of British abolition with mixed, if not negative, reviews. Addison Coffin, a member of a great Quaker anti-slavery clan that included Lucretia Mott, retold how in April 1824 a "restless spirit" grew among many in the manumission society, a spirit that sought to organize a splinter group on the basis of "straight out unconditional Abolition" with "colonization left out."[53] But the radicals were "strongly urged" to give up their "immediate emancipation ideas as it would be disastrous to suddenly release 205,170 slaves, many of whom were yet half savage in their nature."[54] The North Carolina Manumission Society continued to support the curtailing of incoming slaves, the abolition of the internal slave trade, and freedom for slave children born after a certain date. The society also agreed to drop the word "colonization" from its mission statement. But as an organization, the North Carolina Manumission Society continued to support colonization schemes as the only plausible long-term solution for human bondage.

The resistance encountered by the more "radical spirits" among North Carolina's Quaker community did not augur a positive future for abolitionism in the United States. Difficulty upon difficulty met Southern Quakers who either attempted to establish freedom for slaves or who sought to better the environment for the prospect of future manumission. Matters were only made worse in the 1820s by the specter of slave revolution. Nathan Mendenhall, for example, took note of "an excitement in the minds of the legislature respecting the troubled state of the slaves" when David Walker's appeal for slave revolt had been discovered in the eastern part of the state. Mendenhall feared that such a climate would lead to an erosion of the "small privileges" given people of color in North Carolina and ultimately "prevent emancipation."[55] Eventually this occurred, as the years after 1830 saw the North Carolina state legislature require freed slaves to leave the state within ninety days after emancipation or face a legally binding return to slavery, and forbade both the education of slaves and black preaching. In this environment, then, colonization was often seen as a necessity by Quaker leaders. Jonas Mace, who was charged by the North Carolina Yearly Meeting with the responsibility of helping keep forty or fifty freed slaves out of bondage, reported to the clerk of the yearly meeting that it was "time . . . for them to be moved from this place as it has already been a narrow escape of there [sic] being sold."[56] This policy was largely supported by the yearly meeting itself, as there appeared to be "no prospect of [former slaves] enjoying equal privileges with their fellow men" while they remained in North Carolina. Therefore, slaves were to be "informed that they make a choice of a place" to emigrate (Liberia, Haiti, or the Northwest), and they were to be told that "if they [would] not comply that they must abide the consequences."⁵⁷

Even attempts to move free blacks to "free" states could backfire terribly on Southern Quakers and on the former slaves involved. The same spirit curtailing the rights of free blacks in the South was at work in many Northern states, such as Pennsylvania and Indiana, that received former slaves. In response to a proposal to land North Carolina free blacks in Philadelphia, a local Quaker leader sent an ominous warning south that any blacks sent to the city of brotherly love would "share the fate of the Boston tea."⁵⁸

Edward Bettle blamed this state of affairs on the "Southampton massacres" of Nat Turner, and he despaired that "the public mind . . . even amongst respectable persons" had become greatly "soured" against free blacks—more so than he could remember.⁵⁹ Ignoring such reports and determined to avoid watching free blacks be once again reduced to servitude, North Carolina Quakers David White and George Swain organized the migration of ninety-two free blacks on board the *Julius Pringle* to Philadelphia in 1832. But, as predicted, a mob formed at the dock, a major riot was feared, and the boat was forced to stay out on the Delaware. The crew and passengers were then shuttled to Red Bank, New Jersey, where they awaited assistance from the American Colonization Society to send the hapless former slaves off to Liberia. After events like this, it was reported that many free blacks under Quaker protection flatly refused to leave North Carolina for Africa.⁶⁰

Another defeat for the anti-slavery cause of Southern Quakers in the early 1830s stemmed from their support for the gradual abolition of slavery in Virginia in 1831 and 1832. The Virginia Yearly Meeting was clear in its memorial to the state legislature that slavery constituted "an evil in our country—an evil which has been of long continuance, and is now of increasing magnitude." And in keeping with the gradualist consensus among Friends, the yearly meeting sought the "passing of an act declaring that all persons born in the state, after some period to be fixed by law, shall be free" and that the state of Virginia "provide some territory . . . for the formation of a colony for people of colour."⁶¹ Fearing for "the fate of their female descendants," Quaker women in Virginia also threw their support behind gradual emancipation, stating humbly that their domestic prosperity was threatened by "the increasing evils of slavery."⁶² But these voices of protest against slavery—moderate when compared to the more strident immediatists—ultimately lost out to those who could not envision emancipation without colonization and who could not imagine large-scale colonization because of lack of resources and government power. The skepticism of a certain Mr. Goode, quoted in the proceedings of the debate, was indicative of what the Quakers were up against: "Where were the resources for deporting half a million people? And where would we send them?" Goode believed that abolition would disturb public tranquility, and perhaps more importantly, violate "rights of property." "[This] thing is impossible," he moaned.[63] The resolve of most Virginians did not exist, and perhaps never existed, to implement seriously a plan of emancipation that would have revolutionized the racial, social, and economic order of that state. Such opposition provided yet another example to Quakers of the Sisyphean task of peacefully ending American slavery.

Perhaps of more importance for the future of Quaker abolitionism, however, was the long-standing possibility that Friends could be viewed as reckless radicals endangering the future of the republic, as in fact happened when Quakers petitioned Southern legislatures for gradual abolition. During the Virginia debates regarding abolition, for example, John Randolph said he could not "trust the Quakers of Pennsylvania" nor the "Quakers of any county in Virginia" when it came to the right of petition regarding free blacks or slaves, for "fanatics," to Randolph, were all "on a par"; the ends they sought would "put a torch to my property" and kill "all that are dear to me."[64] Randolph had clearly increased the stakes for those, like Quaker gradualists, who sought to speak out against human bondage in the slave states. The defeat of the very public Quaker attempt in Virginia to abolish slavery in the wake of the Walker scare and the Southampton massacres revealed the increasing distaste for Quaker "meddling" in the affairs of Southerners, a meddling that was seen as socially, economically, and politically lethal to many slave owners. To be sure, Friends had always found themselves criticized by some in Virginia and the Carolinas on account of their opposition to slavery. In 1797, North Carolina congressman Nathaniel Macon called Quakers "warmakers" in spite of their pacifist principles, since the church continually endeavored in the Southern states "to stir up insurrections amongst the Negroes." Similarly, Congressman Smith of South Carolina called the Quakers "an injury to the community, because in time of war they would not defend their country and in times of peace they were interfering in the concerns of others."[65] Still the frequency of such criticism grew at an alarming rate in the late 1820s and early 1830s. A pamphlet issued in Charleston in 1827, signed by an individual identified only as "Brutus," called the largely Quaker attempts to end slavery in the South one of many "usurpations of the federal government" and openly called for war, if need be, to prevent such meddling.[66] In this environment, new organizations—usually given the title Committee for Vigilance—sprang up to defend Southern whites from both black Jacobins and annoying abolitionists alike. For the Quakers, attempts to appeal politely to legislators, to convey an image of "disinterested benevolence" not only backfired, but became potentially life-threatening.

Southern white opposition to Quaker anti-slavery sentiment and the concern for free blacks accompanying it ultimately forced thousands of Friends out of Virginia, the Carolinas, and Georgia and into Ohio, Indiana, Michigan, and Illinois in the years from 1810 to 1835. The so-called "Great Migration" of Southern Quakers may have reduced the number of Quakers in the Southeast by upwards of 60 percent.[67] Always listed prominently among the reasons given for migration was slavery. By 1830, there was more reason than ever to move on account of slavery when, in reaction to fears of slave insurrection, North Carolina politicians passed a law requiring Quakers to pay military taxes. The fear of slave revolt and the resulting challenge it could pose to the Quaker peace testimony only quickened the pace of the migration. Zachariah Dicks, a minister among Friends in South Carolina, traveled around his state preaching on the impending doom of the "Babylon" of the Southeast. Believing that the scenes in Santo Domingo would be repeated on American shores, Dicks prophesied that the "Gloom and Darkness have eclipsed the Day!" and advised Quakers to find a less dangerous home in the West.[68]

Many other Quakers in North Carolina referred to the land of their birth as being increasingly enveloped by an "Egyptian darkness," and Philadelphia Quaker John Hunt later wrote that he had "seldom, if ever" seen "a more rapid settlement" of Southern Friends in the Ohio Valley as that brought about by slavery in the 1820s and 30s.[69] Perhaps the most significant casualty of the Quaker exodus from their American Babylon was the North Carolina Manumission Society, which disbanded in 1834; many of its members, noted Addison Coffin, could only hope to "leave the land of darkness, get from under the dark but unknown shadow, and out into the light of freedom."[70] The disastrous prospects for peaceful race relations between an increasingly defensive planter class and a restive slave population forced many Quaker leaders in the Carolinas and Virginia to give up any hope for America's interracial future. Far from embracing the immediatist vision of both their brethren in Britain and of a younger generation of abolitionists in New England and New York, Quaker leaders such as Jeremiah Hubbard, Nathan Mendenhall, and Elijah Coffin—all born in the South—clung tenaciously to the American Colonization Society's pessimistic outlook on racial equality. It was Hubbard who stated most clearly to British immediatists the reasons against their "visionary scheme," and in the process helped deepen the rift over abolition that would impact American Quakerism for decades to come.

In a letter to English Quakers written in 1834, Hubbard, a one-time clerk of the North Carolina Yearly Meeting and a man deeply involved in that meeting's various attempts to aid free blacks, declared his support for the American Colonization Society because "the safety of the whites—the ignorance and degradation of the free blacks, the comfort of the slaves, the unity of the states, the peace of the country, [and] the prospects and happiness of the African race generally" demanded colonization in Africa.[71] Hubbard further enumerated the great difficulties he and other leading Quakers had faced in North Carolina on behalf of freed blacks, and he blamed the state legislature for blocking stronger manumission legislation because of the perceived "degraded and low character of the free persons of color already in the state." Believing that the "satire and vituperation" of the immediatists only further hampered the delicate efforts of philanthropists like himself, Hubbard saw in the colonization society the only realistic attempt to ease manumission laws in the South and reduce Southern fears of rebellion. In common with many colonizationists, Hubbard believed that freed blacks in Liberia were "contented with their situation, and have no desire to return to America; they enjoy their health as well as they did in this country."[72]

British immediatists, and their growing number of counterparts in New England, were seen by Hubbard as ignorant of the peculiar situation faced by Southern whites—whether they were opposed to slavery or not. In England, argued Hubbard, because the seat of legislation was far removed from the "body of slavery," the slaves and free people of color were already safely "colonized in their own native West India Islands." This allowed Britain to abolish slavery throughout its colonies "with the dash of a pen." But had the British been subject to the same conditions as in the American South, with its "large . . . proportion of coloured people," there would be "but one voice, and that would be for colonizing them somewhere."[73]

Jeremiah Hubbard's critique of immediatism and ultimate defense of Southern intransigence on the slavery issue was not the isolated opinion of one man, but rather it reflected widespread views shared by at least two yearly meetings, North Carolina and Baltimore, with members living in slave states. In response to a London Yearly Meeting epistle calling on American Quakers to "suffer no consideration of expediency, no apprehension of commercial or political difficulties to divert you from your purpose to assert" an end to slavery, powerful Quakers in the South found themselves explaining the need for both apprehension and expediency when confronting the slavepower. The epistle sent back to London from the North Carolina Yearly Meeting, for example, cited the great "prejudice of the [white] people" in both the slave and free states for their continuing support for colonization in Liberia and as evidence of the nonexistent future of an interracial North America.[74] The North Carolina Yearly Meeting reminded the opponents of colonization that "opposition to the emancipation of slaves" in the Southeast "existed long before the colonization society was founded."[75] Yet their response to this fact was to try to meet the forces of reaction halfway: "the prevailing and still increasing aversion to manumission" left colonization as the only check against further attacks on the "spirit of gradual and universal emancipation."[76] The Baltimore Yearly Meeting further noted that the subject of abolition is "encompassed with difficulties—difficulties which we fear you cannot appreciate." It was the opinion of the community in which they lived that "the modern abolition movement . . . has more connexion with politics and fanaticism than with morality and religion." Like North Carolina, Baltimore therefore rejected immediatism as "unpropitious."[77]

In their willingness to defend colonization—even as many African Americans voiced objections to it—Quaker leaders such as Jeremiah Hubbard demonstrated the limits of the older anti-slavery approach that attempted, in the words of a sympathetic editorial, to "promote a calm and rational enquiry . . . [into] the best means for [slavery's] abolition amongst slaveholders themselves." It was slaveholders, argued the writer, who were most able to "effectually" benefit "the condition of slaves." Changing slave owners' minds "should be done temperately, ingeniously, and in a Christian spirit."[78] Yet the Southern Quaker leaders' sensitivity to slaveholders often obscured real sympathy for black slaves, evinced a willingness to acquiesce to the Southern racial order, and revealed the Quakers' own racial prejudice. "[T]he peculiarly marked difference of [African American] features and colour will always be an insurmountable barrier to general amalgamation," wrote Hubbard. "Even the Society of Friends," he continued, "have no intention of giving [black Quakers] our sons or our daughters in marriage." Although he acknowledged the potential for a black civilization in Africa, a mist "of darkness," according to Hubbard, "seems to rest upon . . . the African race" in America.[79]

Making a final statement on his hope for slavery's end in the South, Jeremiah Hubbard could no longer stand to remain in a slave state, and a colleague of Hubbard's wrote that "if times do not alter, friends will be mostly found on the other side of the Potomac and Ohio in a few years more."[80] Regardless of their professed interest in reforming slaveholders, even those willing to deal pragmatically with Southern legislatures felt unsafe, unwanted, and discouraged after decades of work on behalf of "oppressed humanity." All that was left was to vote with their feet. The great Quaker migration out of the Carolinas and Virginia in the first three decades of the nineteenth century exemplified the growing power of slaveholders in the United States to defend their property rights against the critiques of groups such as the Friends. It was against this challenging backdrop that Quaker abolitionists began their efforts to convert Northern white opinion to support a robust attack on slaveholding. The issue of abolition therefore entered national politics after many progressive whites—such as the Quakers in the South—had already failed to dislodge human bondage from its place in the social, economic, and political fabric of the early American republic.

# 1

## Quaker Gradualists and the Challenge of Abolitionism

In addition to the difficulties facing Quaker gradualists in the slave states by the early 1830s, the majority of Friends living in the northeastern and midwestern states had to contend with the widespread controversy generated by the American Anti-Slavery Society's petition and postal campaigns during the middle years of the decade. Urban riots and threats of disunion from slaveholding congressmen seemed to follow the new immediatist movement wherever it spread its doctrines, and, in response, some of the best friends of the anti-slavery cause distanced themselves from radical abolitionism. Leading Congregationalists in New England, for example, could be heard comparing the abolitionists to "the Jacobins . . . who deluged France in blood, and whelmed Europe in tears."[1] The Society of Friends also adopted a skeptical stance toward the new immediatist movement, and most leaders of the church reaffirmed the connection between anti-slavery gradualism and Quaker "quietism," or the abiding concern of church leaders that religious testimonies not foment social revolution. The terms of debate within Quaker meetinghouses over abolitionism were therefore defined by those who stressed the private, unobtrusive character of Quaker anti-slavery, and opposition to abolitionism was framed by influential Friends as a natural outgrowth of the church's theology.

The cautious stance of Quaker leaders toward radical anti-slavery reformers in the 1830s, however, was not necessarily expected by many within and without the ambit of the Quaker meetinghouse. Friends' theology, long distinguished by a commitment to pacifism, had always possessed the implication of open dissent from the laws of the American state. In the early American republic, the Society of Friends made clear their opposition to state militia drafts, as well as to any commutation fines for conscientious objection.[2] For many Friends, their opposition to war in fact meant that religious sentiments had to be translated into political practice. As a petition to the Virginia legislature read, "liberty of conscience . . . cannot be restricted to the mere liberty of thinking, or to the silent and unseen modifications of religious opinion. Religion has duties to be performed. . . ."[3] Yet the implications of Quaker dissent from state-sanctioned force could be unclear, and many Friends relayed their intention to be law-abiding citizens who respected the liberal notion that religious sentiments must not be used to undermine the American government. William Evans, for example, noted that although Quakers "cannot actively comply with laws that would violate our consciences, yet we do not rise against the Government. . . ."[4] Although potentially treasonous applications of Quaker pacifism had been feared by George Washington, he nonetheless was convinced that Friends were "one of the best supporters of the new government" because they "require moderation" in all things. Washington also claimed that Friends, notwithstanding their pacifism, possessed an "attachment to the Constitution."[5]

Quakers were not insensitive to the fear of other Americans that members of the church might abuse religious liberty in their public opposition to the instruments of war. As Benjamin Hallowell explained, Quakers must not behave like Catholics who adhered too strongly to the dictates of Rome by "placing the obligations of the citizen to a religious society above his obligations to his country."[6] Hallowell's assertion that Quakers and Catholics both needed to guard against placing their religious beliefs ahead of their duties as citizens demonstrated the tenuous and contested nature of religious liberty in the early republic. It was still unclear if groups that stood outside the Protestant mainstream—such as the Society of Friends—would in fact be good American citizens. Abolitionists working within Quaker meetinghouses would appeal to the tradition of Quaker opposition to war when attempting to win support for their movement, but the abolitionists were constantly in danger of being accused of creating seditious implications for Quaker critiques of human violence.

Rather than become discouraged by the pessimism of Quaker leadership, abolitionists pushed ahead with efforts to gain converts to the cause of immediate emancipation in the 1830s. Confidently seeking to transplant victorious British efforts at emancipation onto American soil, the American reformers believed that anti-slavery churches such as the Society of Friends functioned as a necessary lever to propel the movement of immediate emancipation to success. In 1834, long before he achieved fame as a poet, the young John Greenleaf Whittier took note of the success of immediatism in Britain and wrote to fellow Quakers in the U.S.: God "has smiled upon the cause of Emancipation. . . . Shall we not . . . rebuke our brother in his sin" and answer the "cries of the oppressed and suffering brethren in bondage?" God, continued Whittier, "hath opened our understanding . . . concerning our duty to this people; and it *is not a time for delay* . . ." for God "may answer us . . . by terrible things in righteousness."[7] Whittier angrily termed North Carolina Quaker leader Jeremiah Hubbard's defense of colonization a "testimony in favor of slavery," and he was shocked that Hubbard's position was as "clerk of a Yearly Meeting of Friends!"[8] Whittier demanded "no compromise with the iniquity—no scheme for re-acting the horrors of the 'middle-passage . . . by offering the slave the miserable alternative of *transportation*."[9]

In his aptly named pamphlet *Justice, Not Expediency*, Whittier, in typical immediatist fashion, laid out the superiority of divinely inspired moral suasion to human wisdom when confronting sin. To those, like the Southern Quaker gradualists, who asked what was propitious or politic, Whittier demanded a faith in the ultimate justice of emancipation as a weapon against slavery ten times more powerful than gradualist schemes. Quite simply, "immediate abolition of slavery" represented the "only just scheme" available to politicians.[10] Epitomizing the tactical shift being taken by immediatists, Whittier demanded that Christians stop "palliating the evil" of slavery by "voting for [the] Evil." Because all Americans were "bound by the U.S. Constitution to protect the slave-holder in his sins," all Americans must therefore demand that the Constitution reject the legality of slavery and "establish now and forever this great and fundamental truth of human liberty—that man cannot hold property in his brother." By mobilizing the public to acknowledge the illegality of slavery, the "overthrow" of the "great national evil" of slavery was possible.[11]

Along with the New England Quakers Effingham Capron and Arnold Buffum, Whittier worked with William Lloyd Garrison in founding the New England Anti-Slavery Society in Boston in 1832. This organization played a pivotal role the following year at the anti-slavery convention in Philadelphia that launched the American Anti-Slavery Society. At the founding of this national organization, the Quaker presence was strong:

twenty-one of the sixty-two delegates were members of the Society of Friends. The "radical spirits" that had previously been relegated to the sidelines in older gradualist abolition societies were now finding a platform of their own on which to stand. The American Anti-Slavery Society produced in its "Declaration of Sentiments" as principled and uncompromising a position as any abolitionist document yet produced. "The guilt of [this nation's] oppression is unequalled by any other on the face of the earth," the declaration thundered. America must "repent instantly" and "undo the heavy burden, to break every yoke, and to let the oppressed go free." "Slaves ought to be instantly . . . brought under the protection of the law."[12]

Armed with the rhetorical pyrotechnics of William Lloyd Garrison, the willingness of successful British immediatists fresh from victory in London to travel to America, and, perhaps most importantly, the funding and organizational expertise of Arthur and Lewis Tappan in New York City, the American Anti-Slavery Society began its campaign of moral suasion in 1834. Possessing the evangelical zeal of revivalists and borrowing liberally from their methods, agents of the Anti-Slavery Society fanned out across the Northeast and Midwest, armed with the pamphlets, books, and cash of godly philanthropists such as the Tappan brothers and Gerrit Smith, seeking to convert a nation to the truth of immediatism.

As William Lloyd Garrison and his agents won some converts among Quaker meetings, hope existed that immediatism would find support from America's largest anti-slavery church. After visiting Lynn, Massachusetts, where he won the support of the leading Quaker William Bassett, Garrison gladly noted how "Friends in New England are fast ceasing to be abolitionists ex officio and are becoming such in spirit and truth."[13] The Quakers, to Garrison, possessed "fundamental principles . . . more in harmony with mine than those of any other," and he therefore hoped the Quakers would "not let the example of their ancient predecessors be lost upon them" when combating slavery. "It is not enough," continued Garrison, "that we occasionally" hear a "few words" from leading Quakers criticizing so "awful and heathenish a system." Though "there are many . . . who feel and act with pristine boldness," Garrison desired that all Friends be "quickened in this benevolent work." Similarly, John Greenleaf Whittier hoped there would be "other Woolmans and other Benezets . . . on this subject" among the Friends dedicated to aligning the church with an unpopular social movement. Whittier further demanded that Friends "keep themselves aloof from all societies and all schemes which have a tendency to excuse or overlook its [slavery's] crying iniquity," and he specifically condemned Quaker involvement with the American Colonization Society.[14]

The "benevolent work" of the Anti-Slavery Society, however, proved to be extremely unpopular to many in the United States. From the start, the country's reaction was markedly negative, even violent. James Henry Hammond declared it a violation of duty to God for a Southerner *not* to kill an abolitionist invading his hometown, and mobs in cities from Philadelphia to Boston formed to intimidate abolition agents. All this violence was, to some extent, met calmly by members of an organization that stated in its declaration a willingness to "perish ultimately as martyrs in this great, benevolent, and holy cause."[15] Few other Americans thought so calmly about the prospect of mob violence. Some even felt the abolitionists purposefully provoked angry rioters. Repeating the conviction that the immediatist cause was one "worth dying for," Philadelphia Quaker Angelina Grimke courted the displeasure of other members of her meeting.[16] As pacifists, Quakers were more than shy about actively placing themselves in violent situation where self-defense might be required. Friends also shared in the conventional fear of mob violence magnified onto a larger scale of national revolution over slavery.

In the nineteenth century, the image of the "mob" posed a threat of real significance. Epitomizing the dislocated nature of Jacksonian America, the violence, frequency, and lawlessness of mobs had been on the increase since 1800 and provided an important impetus for the creation of urban police forces.[17] Particularly in major cities on the eastern seaboard, the Society of Friends sounded alarms not dissimilar from other Anglo-Saxon elites regarding the destructive capacity of urban chaos. The agitation so valued by William Lloyd Garrison as the necessary moral earthquake to crack apart the chains of oppression was simply seen by many Friends as an invitation to break up the union.

The Society of Friends was now presented with a serious challenge because of the new public space opening up between the meetinghouse on one hand and the halls of government on the other. After having lived through the traumatic consequences of the Hicksite schism, Quaker leaders demanded that reformers respect the diversity of opinion that existed among Quakers and not propose to support tactics to abolish slavery that were seen as extremely controversial. As one Quaker editorial read, "discussions between the abolitionist and colonizationist . . . might . . . endanger the existence of that Christian fellowship which is the great bond of religious communion" and "destroy that brotherly freedom and confidence" most conducive to the "promotion of truth and righteousness."[18] In the years ahead, abolitionist reformers within the Society of Friends, to the extent they offered innovative interpretations of the gradualist implications of Quaker anti-slavery, would be the ones who felt most frustrated by the lack of support for their cause from leading Friends.

The American Anti-Slavery Society therefore faced an uphill battle in its attempt to enlist the active support of Quaker meetings. Yearly meetings—Hicksite, Orthodox, and Wilburite alike—attempted to juggle their commitment to protesting slavery with their skepticism of immediatism. Some Quakers clearly sought a "third way" between immediatists and colonizationists, and they criticized zealots in both camps. The *Friend* believed that at its worst, the colonization society had succumbed to "the most vulgar of all prejudices—the prejudice of colour." "What it proposes to do is indirect and indefinite," bearing no "proportion to the pressure and extent of the evil with which it professes to deal." But if the colonization society was far behind enlightened opinion, the Anti-Slavery Society had "shot just as much in advance of the public" on the issue of abolition. Allowing nothing "to prejudice . . . to interest, or to time," the society chose "defiance" and "personal invective" against both slavery and the slaveholder. As a result, "those who would have been its best friends" are now "afraid of it." For a solution, the editorial offered that colonizationists drop their pretentions "to emancipation," concentrate on "missionary work" in Africa, and join with the "wisest and best men in the Anti-Slavery society in the cause of abolition." If such a union transpired, the "religious and generous energies of the nation would find a focus."[19]

Not waiting for cooperation on the part of conflicting activists, Quaker yearly meetings reminded their flocks of the distinct message of Quakerism, a message that had once conquered the sin of slaveholding within their sect. The opinion of the Philadelphia Yearly Meeting (Hicksite) was indicative of the call: "While all around us exhibit awful collisions, and the inflamed and angry passions of men . . . we . . . are imperiously called upon, to seek and rely upon that Almighty Power which can alone 'control the whirlwind and direct the storm.'" The meeting acknowledged that "conflicting opinions" regarding abolition "now exist in our Society," but this mandated that the meeting "dwell near the fountain of Divine Goodness" so that both "apathy and negligence" on the one hand and "intemperate zeal and creaturely activity" on the other be avoided. Only the "peaceable spirit and wisdom of Jesus" would prove effective at breaking the chains of oppression in America.[20]

By articulating the efficacy of the Quaker meeting in ending slavery, and in particular by defining the Quaker peace testimony as strictly anti-political, yearly meetings around the country laid out a defense of sectarian exceptionalism in the face of a controversy over slavery with deeply divisive potential. As would be argued time and time again, the spiritual sustenance of an autonomous Quaker community possessed the power to infuse the world with the grace needed for reformation. As the New England Yearly Meeting reminded its members in 1837, "the concern [about slavery] had its origin in a faithful attention to the convictions of religious duty, so we believe that in all our efforts to advance this cause" Quakers must seek after "Him, for the guidance of his Holy Spirit, who has declared 'without me you can do nothing.'" The Quaker concern to rid the world of slavery, however, must remain "on its original ground" of "Gospel love," working in Friends "as one body" to keep under the "benign influence" of the Holy Spirit.[21]

Yet in these statements one can discern the logic of gradualism: intemperate, "nagging" activists were making demands on meetings that were unrealistic and that might further rend the already divided Society of Friends. Quaker opposition to the ideology of the American Anti-Slavery Society would only become clearer when Quakers sympathetic with immediatism demanded that the Society of Friends petition Congress to abolish slavery wherever it had the authority to do so. Starting in late 1835, the American Anti-Slavery Society had forwarded thousands of petitions to Congress requesting the abolition of slavery in the District of Columbia and a ban on any new slave states, and not just Texas (which had applied for statehood in 1836). By 1838 the number of signatories to these petitions reached over 400,000 and had by that time sparked the famous gag rule on the floor of the House of Representatives. Fearful of arguments over slavery that generated nothing but sectional hostility and party dismemberment, a majority of congressmen voted to reject the anti-slavery petitions without reading or discussing them. Found among the Anti-Slavery Society petitions were pleas from Quaker immediatists for abolition, most notably one from the Caln Quarterly Meeting, a subordinate meeting and abolitionist stronghold within the Hicksite Philadelphia Yearly Meeting. The Caln petition, like the others, requested the "federal government . . . to secure the rights of freedom to every human being resident within the constitutional jurisdiction of Congress" as well as to prohibit the internal slave trade. Such pleas were termed by John Calhoun as "barefaced insolence," and many of his colleagues concurred regarding their incendiary character.[22]

While the *Friend* believed that Quakers should "consider whether any step can be taken with a prospect of benefit . . . to petition" Congress to end slavery in the District of Columbia, they did not openly encourage Friends to do so.[23] In fact, because they sensed the unpopularity of the petition campaign, yearly meetings of the Society of Friends proved wary of petitioning Congress directly in the same fashion as certain subordinate meetings. Quakers were called on to remonstrate with "mildness" and "prudence . . . [with] a proper regard for fitness as to the time and occasion" for public protest.[24] Even though all five northeastern yearly meetings plus Indiana published addresses to the American public denouncing slavery, they purposefully avoided action that seemed overtly political.[25] The "Address to the Citizens of the United States of America on the Subject of Slavery" published by the orthodox New York Yearly Meeting typified the style and tactics chosen by yearly meetings of the Society of Friends during the petition campaign. The meeting first pointed out that it was "abstaining, as we are known to do, from any participation in the political movements of the day," taking into account the "excitement which has been produced in the North as well as the South, by the discussion of this very important subject." The pamphlet was also quite clear that the meeting would not "suggest any mode by which the abolition of slavery should be effected" since they were aware "how closely the evil entwines itself with the relations of society at the south." But the New York Quakers' "deep sense of what is required of us as professing Christians" still entered a protest against "injustice and oppression." Referring to slavery as "among the individual and national sins, for which the American people are now sustaining severe and almost unparalleled distress," New York Yearly Meeting laid out the many injustices of American slavery. These included the internal slave trade, the illegality of black education in the South, and the existence of slavery in the nation's capital. "The Christian religion, in its purity," cautioned Friends, cannot flourish among a people "who, without compunction, claim and exercise exclusive control over the persons of their fellow men."

But this reaffirmation of the customary Quaker view of slaveholding as sin did not please abolitionists. The refusal of the orthodox New York Yearly Meeting to state the "mode" of abolition they favored, coupled with their unwillingness to address petitions to the U.S. Congress, hinted at a growing rift between the Society of Friends and Quaker members of the American Anti-Slavery Society. In the orthodox New York Yearly Meeting, for example, the Farmington Quarterly Meeting in the western part of the state had twice called upon the yearly meeting to petition the national government to abolish slavery in the District of Columbia, in 1836 and 1837, but received the response that Friends must "avoid being drawn into undo excitement" over slavery.²⁶ Only then did the yearly meeting offer its nonpolitical address to the American public. Similar disagreements over the Society of Friends' boldness in opposing slavery were evident in most if not all yearly meetings beginning in the mid-1830s. In the Hicksite New York Yearly Meeting, for example, the abolitionist David Irish went on the offensive against the moderate majority within the executive committee of his meeting, the Meeting for Sufferings. "Permit me to solicit your serious and candid attention to the subject of memorializing Congress for the abolition of slavery in the District of Columbia, the territories, and the domestic slave trade," he wrote. Being "at a loss" to find a "clearer and more responsible obligation of duty upon [this] Body," Irish asked whether or not Friends were willing "to say let it be no more where it's in our power to remedy it?"²⁷ The answer, evidently, was no. While the Hicksite New York Yearly Meeting did petition the state legislature to allow fugitive slaves trial by jury, they did nothing regarding a petition to Congress of any kind. This was hardly the bold move abolitionists within the meeting had desired.²⁸

In New England, a similar confrontation was brewing between those of a more radical bent and their cautious leaders. William Bassett, a member of the New England Yearly Meeting's Meeting for Sufferings, relayed several instances of opposition to immediatist agitation among New England Quakers. In 1837, the subordinate Salem Quarterly Meeting, of which Bassett was a member, requested that the yearly meeting "memorialise Congress for the Abolition of Slavery in the District of Columbia." They also wanted their leaders to issue a tract discussing the success of West Indian abolition. Without discussion both requests were referred to the Meeting for Sufferings, where it was determined that "no way opened to act" upon these matters. The meeting did, however, publish one of the aforementioned addresses to the American people in 1837, an address that was nonetheless found by abolitionist members of the yearly meeting to be unsatisfactory for its lack of principle. When one Friend attempted to open discussion on the address, however, it was quickly objected to, and the document was printed anyway. Further opposition from leading Friends toward the activities of Quaker abolitionists in New England only continued with time. In another incident, Bassett recounted how a document he had drafted to Friends in Virginia referring to slaves as "fellow-countrymen" and "brethren" was objected to by leading Quakers because "we must be careful what language we use, for this may not be confined to Friends, but may get out at the South." Bassett increasingly came to believe that Quakers had "lost the spirit of Him who was no respecter of persons, and who came to 'preach deliverance to the captive.'"²⁹

These developments served as discouragement to many leading abolitionists. James Birney lamented that Friends were sitting "quietly by" and beholding "undisturbed" a system that was daily destroying human bodies and human souls. Friends must call on slaveholders to "immediately emancipate their slaves" and advance the "rights" and "interests" of slaves as citizens of the United States.³⁰ After the Philadelphia Hicksite Lucretia Mott sent William Lloyd Garrison pronouncements from Quaker yearly meetings regarding slavery, Garrison commended some of their sentiments, yet complained that "in nearly all of them something is wanting." These pamphlets, in Garrison's eyes, were addressed in a style far different "from that used by Isaiah, Jeremiah, and Ezekiel." Referring in particular to one pamphlet "to a Portion of our Southern Brethren," Garrison felt "there seems to be something like an attempt to propitiate the spirit of these cruel and ungodly oppressors, in a way in which I do not like." When Quakers commented that "we are aware of the peculiar and trying situation wherein you [as slaveholders] were placed," Garrison declared that "it really looks like [Quaker leaders are] Hunting up excuses for their nefarious conduct!" God, in calling individuals and nations to repent, "always takes it for granted that they are without excuse, and calls upon them to break off their sins by righteousness without delay." When the pamphlet conceded that slaveholders believed "it lawful and right to hold" slaves in "unconditional bondage," Garrison loudly dissented: "They believe no such thing—they never did, they never can believe it!" In conclusion, Garrison felt the Society of Friends' pamphlets would never "melt ice."³¹

When making the bold claim that Southern slaveholders did not believe in the legitimacy of their slave society, or when barraging Quaker leadership for their indecision regarding abolitionism, Garrison exemplified, and in many ways gave birth to, a new style of anti-slavery agitation. Such agitation cleanly divided the world into pro-slavery and anti-slavery camps, between good and evil, and purposefully stuck to a bold, prophetic style of activism that nerved the daring supporters of immediatism even as it provoked the ire of the vast majority of more conventional Americans—Friends included. One leading New England Quaker called Garrison a "madman, a fanatic, and a radical," and no doubt spoke for thousands of cautious Friends skeptical of the tactical turn taken by American abolitionism.³²

By terming Garrison a "fanatic," many leaders of the Society of Friends allied themselves with more respectable reformers and politicians who viewed the declaration of sentiments of the American Anti-Slavery Society as a document advocating race war and the dissolution of the union. By declaring slavery illegal, abolitionists demanded that churches speak out against the very constitution of the republic—churches were intended to become truly oppositional political entities. But powerful understandings of the constitutive role of religion in the young American republic would encourage Quaker caution and conservatism. In 1836, the relationship of Quakers to immediate abolitionists received comment by one no less significant than Vice President Martin Van Buren. When the North Carolina Yearly Meeting corresponded with the White House regarding abolition policy, Van Buren responded with the hope that Friends would "avoid the repetition of an error so unfortunate and mischievous as Abolition." The vice president was confident Quakers everywhere would rise to the challenge due to the "uniformity of [your] course upon this subject, the temperate manner in which it has been manifested, and the marked excellence" of the Society of Friends' "conduct and character." Known for their "industry, morality, intelligence, and republican habits," there is "no class of people in this country who have a deeper interest in the preservation of the Union and of the happy system of Government which it upholds." Van Buren hoped the Quakers would deal with the subject in a way that "shall repress instead of increase agitation" without "injustice to their principles."[33] For what would prove to be neither the first nor the last time, influential figures in antebellum America would desire Quakers to remain harmless exemplars of disinterested virtue, not rebellious radicals seeking a moral revolution.

To a great degree, yearly meetings of the Society of Friends more than met the challenge laid down by Van Buren. This was most apparent when Friends confronted the violence of "mobocracy" in the 1830s. As feared by many leading Quakers, the principled, uncompromising stance taken by members of the Anti-Slavery Society invariably opened up the frightening spectacle of urban chaos. Beginning in 1834 with the destruction of the interracial school of the Connecticut Quaker Prudence Crandall, continuing with the torching of a dozen houses in New York (including that of abolitionist Lewis Tappan), and culminating in a white terror in Philadelphia that left forty black families homeless and one person dead, anti-abolitionist violence plagued most cities in America on a yearly basis.

The danger of ushering in an orgy of violence with a simple act of self-defense seemed to become a reality when word spread among Quaker circles of the murder of Elijah Lovejoy in Alton, Illinois, in 1837. Objecting to the appellation "martyr" for a man who used a gun to defend himself, the *Friend* reminded Quakers that Lovejoy acted in "palpable violation of the positive precepts and benign principles of the gospel." The editor regretted that the "avowed pacific policy . . . of the anti-slavery associations had" been violated by this "Christian minister."[34] Lovejoy's murder even disturbed the vocal Quaker abolitionist Sarah Grimke: "How appalling the spectacle! A minister of Jesus Christ engaged in the work of killing his brother man . . ." Grimke doubted whether abolitionists' trust really was in God when they resorted to "physical force, to the weapons of death to defend the cause of God." Grimke ominously intoned, "the blood spilt at Alton will be the seed of future discord," and those engaged will simply "thirst for more."[35]

Just a year after this letter, both Grimke sisters would discover firsthand the destructive potential of anti-abolitionist mob violence with the infamous burning of Pennsylvania Hall. Built with the funding of many Friends and home to the Pennsylvania Anti-Slavery Society, Pennsylvania Hall had been called by John Greenleaf Whittier the "pantheon" of human freedom. But it would not remain standing for long. As Angelina Grimke called on the abolitionist assembly to ignite a "moral earthquake" second only to the martyr age of Christianity, an angry mob attempted to burst in on the congregation, throwing brickbats and shattering glass. Though the abolitionists were allowed to get away peacefully, the following evening, as the mayor looked on, a crowd razed the hall to the ground. Amid the onlookers an aged Benjamin Lundy, bulwark of Quaker gradualism, lamented that in the flames he could "read . . . the woeful destiny of this nation of oppressors."[36]

Many editorials in the Northeast railed against the radical initiatives laid out at Pennsylvania Hall and effectively blamed the victims for the violence meted out against them. Not only did the immediatists demand a quick end to slavery, intoned the critics, but they also allowed women speakers to preach to "promiscuous assemblies" and reportedly encouraged "whites and blacks" to throng "through the streets by scores."[37] Courageously advancing radical social experiments such as racial integration and women's rights, the abolitionists at Pennsylvania Hall would not back down from their high ground. If anything, they would interpret the violence perpetrated against them as a cue to push on in their struggle on behalf of Christian anarchism. The logical end of nonresistance would find many Garrisonian abolitionists in short order.

In contrast, yearly meetings of the Society of Friends remained on far more conventional footing when meeting the radical challenges of "party strife" and "mob violence." The way the Society tended to advertise its anti-slavery efforts as "mild" and "politic" has already been noted, but leading Friends also interpreted their history of opposing slavery in similar moderate fashion. Far from possessing the spirit of Garrison and the non-resistant wing of the Anti-Slavery Society, earlier reformers such as John Woolman and Anthony Benezet were nearly always portrayed by leading Friends as temperate and cautious. "The patient and persevering efforts of these ... men ... in whom the love of God was largely accompanied with its never-failing attendant, the love of man, were eminently blessed. . . ." The divinely ordained progress against slavery "gradually extended," and with the aid of "Gospel-love" advanced throughout all American Quaker meetings.[38] Almost never would one read of these Friends repeating the story of Benjamin Lay, who called his fellow Quakers apostates and splattered red pokeberry juice on elders during a meeting to show their iniquity as slaveholders. Nor did Friends care to remind their fellow Americans of the threats leveled at anti-slavery apostles in the South of being one step removed from the "black Jacobins" of Haiti. Instead, in "taking up a testimony against slavery, publicly and openly," the Baltimore Friends stated, we "did not desire to invade the privileges of [our] neighbors, nor in any way improperly interfere with them." With Friends it was "purely a religious concern, unconnected with any political or temporal consideration."[39]

By continuing to frame their sect's anti-slavery testimony in unobtrusive terms because of their sensitivity to being associated with religious ranterism and political treason, leaders of the Society of Friends encouraged personal attempts to discountenance slavery and cautioned against those (such as immediate abolitionism) viewed as overtly political and violent. Quakers believed it "their duty to lead peaceable and quiet lives toward all men." "In pursuing this noiseless path," members were to refrain from "intercourse with the parties and policies of this world," preferring "works of charity and benevolence" as their "share of the burden" to be borne for the sake of righteousness. Such "uprightness" would serve as an anchor "when commotions arise," when others "are in danger of being swept away by the various currents" of political activism.[40] One type of nonintrusive, benevolent act of charity came in the form of the "free produce" movement, a boycott of items known to have been produced by slave labor. This idea possessed a long lineage; John Woolman in the mid-eighteenth century advocated such a measure when opposing slavery. Elias Hicks also carried the mantel of free produce in the 1810s and 20s. As a correlative to inner purity, the free produce movement could function as the perfect apolitical demonstration of solidarity with the oppressed.

The Quaker "discipline," or list of potentially disownable offenses, had always included strictures against immoral economic transactions. Wealth garnered from lotteries, gambling, or other unseemly enterprises could bring a Friend under censure from his meeting. Not long after the sect's decision to outlaw slaveholding, official attempts were made to at least discourage the use of slave produce. These efforts continued throughout the 1830s and 40s in many American yearly meetings. In 1837, the Hicksite New York Yearly Meeting advised its members against "trading in slave labor produce," and two years later, Philadelphia Hicksites issued similar advice.[41] This declaration was eventually followed by an address to members of the orthodox New York Yearly Meeting supporting free produce in 1845.[42] While not advising its members for or against the movement, in 1840, the Hicksite Ohio Yearly Meeting asked its members regarding the "propriety of establishing a store to procure and vend free produce."[43] The strongest stance taken against the use of slave produce, however, came from the Hicksite Genesee Yearly Meeting in western New York, which raised the recommendation against using slave produce to a point of discipline in 1842.[44]

The hope had always remained among those Quakers committed to the movement that support for free produce would grow even stronger among Friends and that more yearly meetings would actually discipline members who did not boycott items produced by slave labor. After all, the anti-slavery organizations most successful at attracting and maintaining Quaker support were those predicated on the slave produce boycott, and such associations drew support from both immediatist and colonizationist Quakers. In Philadelphia for example, George Taylor, a man who believed "that the two colors [black and white] had better be as far asunder as the breadth of the earth will permit," joined with far more radical abolitionists such as Lucretia Mott in supporting the free produce movement.[45] In New York City, George Fox White, an ardent foe of the American Anti-Slavery Society, preached powerful sermons in support of free produce. If any organization hoped to bridge the gap between differing groups of anti-slavery Quakers, the free produce association was the one.

Beginning in the late 1820s with the Wilmington Society for the Encouragement of Free Labor and the Pennsylvania Free Produce Societies, an assortment of Quakers, free blacks, and abolitionists came together to advance the boycott of slave-manufactured merchandise. These groups also played a role in founding the American Free Produce Association in 1839. In time, many associations would form with some degree of official Quaker sponsorship, such as the Free Produce Association of Friends of Philadelphia Meeting, founded in 1845. This association sought to "procure correct information of the conditions of the countries" possessing free labor products, and it hoped to purchase such products "through the ordinary channels of commerce and manufacture."[46]

As time would show, however, countless challenges faced the free produce movement. While substitutes for rice, tobacco, sugar, and coffee could be found or grown outside of the slave states, in the slave states Quakers had to avail themselves of cotton grown by nonslaveholding whites. The problem was further complicated by the need to find individuals to gin the cotton. As a result, the American Free Produce Association rarely possessed more than five thousand dollars worth of "free cotton" in any given year, a sign of the movement's ineffectual character. The quality of the goods produced also left purchasers unsatisfied. As the abolitionist and women's rights activist Lucretia Mott wrote, "unfortunately, free sugar was not always free from other taints as that of slavery . . . free umbrellas were hideous to look upon; free candies an abomination."[47]

Furthermore, as the abolitionist movement developed its critique of a "pro-slavery" American nation, the demand that Quakers conspicuously opt out of any economic transaction that was related to slavery highlighted the unwillingness of the larger Society of Friends to collectively occupy an unpopular political and social stance vis-à-vis slavery. Supporters of the free produce movement among Friends repeatedly equated Quaker business interests and other commonplace economic transactions of their co-religionists with support for slaveholding. Samuel Rhoads, the publisher of a free produce paper, the *Non-Slaveholder*, linked all American Quakers with potential support for slavery: "The close connection, and intimate intercourse which is manifested between different sections of our common country, through the diversified and widely spread channels of business," stated Rhoads, may "blunt our sensibilities to the cruelties of slavery." He wished Friends would examine just how "far they are clear in these respects" and if deemed appropriate, they should "forego every prospect of gain, arising from the prosecution of business which is incompatible with the purity of our religious profession."[48] "It would be a lame objection to the labours of the friends of temperance," Rhoads argued, to attempt to end the consumption of liquor without a desire to cut off all connection with the "distillers and retailers of liquor." If the "markets of the world were instantly closed against the products of slave labour, they might be opened immediately by emancipating the slaves."[49]

The equation forwarded by Rhoads between Quaker participation in markets tainted by slavery and support for the institution of human bondage was seconded by Charles Osborn. After traveling around America in 1840, Osborn noted that "many Friends . . . have acquired much of their wealth by means of the cotton-trade, carried on with the slaveholders of the South." Friends have "taken a liberal share" of all the "improvements of the age," continued Osborn, and are living a life of "worldly grandeur and pompous show" financed by the "spoils of the poor."[50] "We have sinned," cried Osborn, by greatly polluting "our high and holy [anti-slavery] profession with BLOOD!" To Osborn, all members of the Society of Friends, but especially those in the cotton business, must "cease to covet the golden wedges, and Babylonish garments" purchased by the "gain of oppression."[51]

In his desire for Friends to extricate themselves from a society and an economy deeply intertwined with slaveholding, Osborn demanded a public and visible role for Quakers as a religious organization sufficiently set apart from the "people of the world." Osborn looked forward to the day when the "Free-Produce Associations" would receive "liberal support" and when Friends would "no longer be guilty of stealing, while we PREACH that a MAN SHOULD NOT STEAL." Quakers, in Osborn's opinion, needed to demonstrate a countervailing economic commitment to the Kingdom of God in a country that had rejected Christian simplicity: "Banking, manufacturing, slave-grown cotton, merchandizing, land speculations, oppressing the poor, fine houses, rich furniture, fine carriages and costly apparel . . . are but sorry proofs" of a life dedicated to "Him [Jesus] who had not where to lay his head."[52] The moral economics hinted at in Osborn's jeremiad was made even clearer by the New York Hicksite Lorenzo Mabbett. As editor of the *Champion of Freedom,* Mabbett linked the free produce boycott to the eventual elimination of all "non-producers" and to a society where "people would do for themselves."[53] Here was an attack on American "grabocratic" capitalism, much in the spirit of radical Quakers such as Cornelius Blatchly, attempting to be forwarded with the unobtrusive language of the free produce movement.

But the abolitionists, by blurring the boundaries between apolitical acts of benevolence and more robust political demonstrations of a counter-cultural anti-slavery identity, found that the Society of Friends could be a difficult institution to reform. The demand that Quakers wear their free produce and shun "polluted" economic interests as a badge of protest against the American slavepower was too difficult for most Friends to do in a nation that was in fact deeply involved in economic support for slavery. Throughout the 1840s and into the 1850s, more radical Quakers complained of the "deficiency reported in regard to the maintenance" of opposition to "slave labor produce."[54] Quakers had indeed taken part in the economic "improvements of the age," often finding themselves on the higher end of the "middling" economic stratum. No longer living in isolated farm communities, many Quakers lived near burgeoning northern towns and gladly benefited from the consumer culture of a market revolution.[55] Many northeastern Quakers had also directly benefited from a textile industry built with the "gains of oppression." The radical "comeouter" zeal expressed by free produce advocates such as Osborn was therefore bypassed as Quakers continued to ignore the admittedly strenuous demand that their opposition to slavery "without strife or commotion" include personal economic sacrifice.[56] That even such a supposedly apolitical form of protest failed to gain wide support from Friends did not bode well for the future of abolitionist efforts to convince leaders of the Society of Friends of the truth of immediate emancipation. Those who demanded more than an attention to Quaker purity against slavery and who tired of quietist understandings of moral suasion would continue unsuccessfully to insist that the institution of the Society of Friends publicly call on the U.S. government and its citizens to separate themselves from the "foul stain" of slavery. In the process, Quaker abolitionists would generate a provocative critique of the moral failure of American "pro-slavery" churches (including the Society of Friends) and argue for the need to reconstitute the Quaker community on a different moral, social, and political footing.

# 2

# Slavery, Religious Liberty, and the "Political" Abolitionism of the Indiana Anti-Slavery Friends

The steady escalation of disputes over slavery between Quaker abolitionists and their more conservative brethren soon led to divisions between the reformers and their coreligionists. The first open break within Quakerism caused by the abolitionist movement occurred in 1842 among the orthodox branch of Friends in Indiana. After being on a collision course with their leadership regarding support for immediatism for nearly a decade, a well-organized group of "orthodox" Quakers within the Indiana Yearly Meeting came to the conclusion that continued membership in the Society of Friends was inconsistent with support for the American Anti-Slavery Society. In 1843, these dissident Quakers founded the Anti-Slavery Friends, a group that applied the "orthodox" Quaker support for voluntary associations in a manner viewed as inappropriate by leaders of the church in Indiana.

The abolitionist controversy between the "orthodox" Indiana Quakers and the Anti-Slavery Friends demonstrated the limits of evangelical Quaker reform whether in the United States or Great Britain. Those Friends who had defended their involvement in voluntary associations out of a belief that the larger world was in desperate need of moral leadership from church communities often stopped short of attacking the American slaveocracy and racial prejudice in the years before the founding of the Republican Party. In the 1840s, most orthodox Friends belonged to, or displayed great sympathy toward, the Whig party of Henry Clay, and it is significant that the establishment of the Anti-Slavery Friends had followed a public confrontation between abolitionists and Clay when the presidential hopeful was visiting Richmond, Indiana, in 1842. As the voice of Whig moderation, Clay tied opposition to the abolitionists as necessary for the success of America's experiment in disestablished religion, as well as for the preservation of every other civil liberty enjoyed by white Americans.

Paralleling American Whig caution on the abolition question, the same British Quakers who had earlier called upon American Friends to support the immediatist movement changed their tune when confronting evangelical abolitionist "comeouterism." These former radicals seemed to agree with men like Clay, who claimed that abolition in the United States was a more difficult act than in Britain, in large part because of the country's supposed inability to assimilate African Americans as equal citizens. The marginalized status of abolitionists among orthodox Friends on both sides of the Atlantic reveals how Friends were willing to accommodate their oppositional theology to the public life of a slaveholding republic. Orthodox Friends understood the power of dissenting religiosity to damage American civil society, and they made clear their adherence to the private, unobtrusive nature of Quaker opposition to slavery and war.

The Indiana Quaker and abolitionist Benjamin Stanton repeated the widespread view within his church that Quaker involvement in a political movement to end slavery was dangerous and that "the Lord would abolish slavery in his own time." Stanton went on to state that the "view that the removal of moral evils and the promotion of virtue are religious concerns" not to be brought into politics "has done much to render the policies of this nation corrupt and wicked."[1] Yet this did not stop many Friends, such as the New York Hicksite Quaker David Geraeau, from continuing to accuse the Anti-Slavery Society of sowing "the seeds of discord and contention, and with unbridled zeal" promoting "the fierce spirit of party strife."[2] This fear of party strife destroying the republic, shared by other Quakers, had been expressed by many anti-slavery clerical leaders who also opposed American abolitionism. Catharine Beecher, for example, believed that those advancing immediatism needed to recognize the "liabilities to faction and party-spirit" existing in a nation that had legalized the "right of free discussion." Christians opposed to slavery, in her view, must eschew "party strife" and only support social movements that acted with Christian "charity and peace" toward other Americans.[3]

During the 1830s and 1840s, Christian ministers and politicians warned groups potentially sympathetic to the cause of immediate emancipation, such as the Society of Friends, that religious dissenters must not meddle in the affairs of state. The Anglican minister Calvin Colton reminded Friends that their church, in his opinion, had not previously supported efforts to "overthrow a fabric [of governance] which [you] cannot conscientiously support." Quakers, in Colton's opinion, were "good neighbors, good citizens, good, we presume, in domestic and private life . . . such is the legitimate action of Christianity."[4] The Society of Friends continued to define the meaning of their critiques of state power, embodied by their pacifist and anti-slavery stances, in ways that did not threaten the cohesion of the United States. At a meeting of leading Friends from around the country in Baltimore in 1841, members of the Society of Friends were warned that the abolitionists had "improperly . . . invade[ed] the privileges of their neighbors" and that Friends must "study to be quiet" in the face of a movement that could potentially "be the means of bringing destruction upon others."[5]

Often enough during the turbulent decade of the 1830s, Quaker ministers accused the abolitionists of fomenting a "war-like" spirit that would only threaten "the peace and harmony of the inhabitants of our country."[6] Evoking the image of abolitionists as seditious sectarians, other Quaker meetings characterized members of the Anti-Slavery Society as "disturbers of Israel" committed to "turning the world upside down."[7] Beginning in 1837, the orthodox yearly meeting in Philadelphia, as well as the New England Yearly Meeting of Friends, advised their members to keep free "from intimate association with persons whose opinions and principles [regarding abolition] are widely different from ours." Similar advice went out over the next five years to yearly meetings from upstate New York to Indiana.[8] With the apparent sanction of their yearly meetings, subordinate meetings threw up barriers in the paths of abolitionists attempting to use meetinghouses for anti-slavery lectures. In the New England Yearly Meeting, for example, William Bassett reported that after his meeting's pronouncement against mixing with others was pushed through, "prominent Friends talked of the consequences of our persisting in our course in the Anti-Slavery cause." Such consequences included disownment for those who refused to obey the meeting's advice and who continued to host abolitionist lectures, or who otherwise brought up the subject before meetings for worship. When Bassett received a personal letter from a leading Friend cautioning Bassett against further involvement with anti-slavery societies, the New England abolitionist published a response that was disseminated by several anti-slavery journals. In characteristic abolitionist style, Bassett compared leaders of his society who called for "quiet" to the "Priest and Levite" who lamely claimed that they had no "express command to relieve him who had fallen among thieves." To Bassett, all Christians, abolitionist or not, must "endure hardness as a good soldier; to be a co-worker with Christ in the renovation of a world lying in wickedness."

Refusing to be intimidated by hostile clerics, abolitionists met disapproval for the cause of immediatism with louder and more defiant protests against moderation. Abby Kelley, in concert with her future husband Stephen Foster, had begun by 1840 to take the drastic step of walking into churches, such as a Methodist congregation in New York, interrupting the service, beginning to speak against slavery, and, when told to desist, pronouncing the church "worse than any house of ill-fame or brothel in New York" in its promotion of popular sins such as human bondage.[9] Instead of meekly submitting to the censure of their church leaders when these leaders arrayed the social force of the meetinghouse against abolitionists, members of the Anti-Slavery Society pressed on in their attempts to "abolitionize" Quaker meetings. For members of the American Anti-Slavery Society, the desire to bring their beliefs about slavery into the meetinghouse represented nothing less than a religious duty. Their version of "vital religion," possessing as it did a defiant, principled stance against the sinful behavior of the world, connected Quaker abolitionists' meetinghouse activities with those of organizations such as the American Anti-Slavery Society, the Non-Resistance Society, or the Liberty Party. Abby Kelley, for example, believed that until she had discovered the anti-slavery movement she had been "without God . . . with no anchor for my soul." "Inspired by the doctrine that he who loves God will love his neighbor, *there* I saw Christianity and went to work in accordance with it."[10]

Abolitionist Quaker women were no less immune from censure than men, and this fact, over time, would only further divide meetings of the Society of Friends. After rising in a Quaker meeting to preach, Sarah Grimke felt moved to speak on both the subjugation of slaves and of women, and did so until she was interrupted by an elder with the comment that "perhaps the Friend may be satisfied now." Though Grimke acknowledged that lifting "the veil and expos[ing] the faults of those to whom I have been so bound is hard work," she believed it was a "duty" to speak out against Quaker complacency.[11] In New England, Elizabeth Buffum Chace confronted her meeting for worship regarding their policy against mixing with others in anti-slavery endeavors, declaring, in her own words, that "acceptable worship was impossible so long as members were living in indifference to the sufferings of our brethren and sisters in slavery."[12] Far from subsiding, then, abolitionist protests against Quaker moderation only increased in the late 1830s and early 1840s, representing a determination on the part of reformers to push on in their holy work even at the cost of "alienating almost every friend" around them.[13]

After being censured by the leaders of the New England Yearly Meeting, William Bassett soon came to believe that the Anti-Slavery Society's campaign for physical emancipation was evolving into a fight for the "mental enfranchisement" of thousands of Christians from a church "interposing its influence to prevent the free exercise of the power [of its members] . . . for the good of our race."[14] In agreement with Bassett, many abolitionists had come to the conclusion that institutional religion in the United States was using its power to destroy the rights of abolitionists to communicate the dictates of their consciences. "The right of speech—the liberty to utter our own convictions *freely,* at all times and in all places, at discretion, unawed by fear, unembarrassed by force—is the gift of God to every member of the family of man, and should be preserved inviolate."[15] By revoking this right, American churches were destroying the abolitionists' religious duty to use the forum of the church for the work of advancing human rights. Failing in their attempt to balance membership in antislavery societies with membership in the Society of Friends, many of Bassett's ideological compatriots began to quote the admonition of the Book of Revelation (18:4): "And I heard another voice from heaven, saying, Come out of her, my people, that ye may not be partakers of her sins, and that ye receive not of her plagues."

Typifying the growing gulf between abolitionist Friends and their clerical leadership, many noted Quakers left, or were thrown out of, their meetings between 1838 and 1845. Besides the disownment of Bassett, which occurred in 1840, Elizabeth Buffum Chace and Abby Kelley left the New England Yearly Meeting in the early 1840s, Charles Marriott and Isaac Hopper, both in New York City, were disowned in 1842 after publishing editorials in the *National Anti-Slavery Standard* critical of the Society of Friends, and Eliab Capron in upstate New York published his resignation from the Genesee Yearly Meeting in the *Liberator* in 1844. Not unlike the other disaffected Quakers, Capron charged his sect with standing "directly in the way of efforts now being made to liberate three millions of our brethren."[16] Among the Philadelphia Orthodox Friends, both Grimke sisters found themselves in danger of disownment for their abolitionist activities, and when Angelina married Theodore Weld, a non-Quaker, and Sarah attended the wedding, their estrangement from Quakerism was complete. Sarah's pronouncement on the Society of Friends in America was harsh: "the very constitution and doctrine of the society . . . crushes the freedom of the mind, and almost inevitably leads to a surrender of the conscience into the keeping of those to whom we are taught to look as the viceregents of God."[17]

But these were not the words of one who had totally given up on the power of American Christianity to potentially bolster the abolitionist cause. Even as abolitionists, Quaker and non-Quaker alike, had begun to develop a critique of "pro-slavery" American religion by the early 1840s, these same abolitionists also began to work for a redefinition of religious fellowship that would demonstrate the potential coexistence of social activism and spiritual worship. Because abolitionist Quakers understood the cultural and political power of institutional religion in the United States, they believed in the necessity of building communities of Christians that might lead a reformation of "pro-slavery" Christianity in the United States. Stephen Foster, husband of New England Quaker Abby Kelley, communicated the abolitionist belief that American churches could mold and "give character to public sentiment" in a fashion that was unrivaled; "the ear of the nation is open" to the dictates of the church. For this reason, the hostility manifested by all denominations of organized religion in the United States to the cause of immediate emancipation was not only inexcusable, but it served to protect the institution of slavery. Especially by supporting "one of the two great political parties," declared Foster, all churches in the United States had refused to reject the "infamous compact with Southern man-stealers [the Constitution]," which gave explicit legal sanction to slavery. Even the so-called "anti-slavery sects," such as the Society of Friends and Freewill Baptists "legalize[d]" slavery by their continued support for political parties as well as by their rejection of public efforts made by immediatists to advance human freedom.[18] But hope existed that if churches could be made to oppose this "system of evil," then slavery might "melt away like the snow beneath the warm rays of an April sun." "Judgement" regarding "national crimes," must "begin at the house of God."[19] What would come to be known as abolitionist "comeouterism," then, was not only a negative idea rooted in efforts at individual purity, but rather constituted a bold attempt to establish purer forms of religious community dedicated to the principles of immediate abolitionism.

At the same time, however, that this "comeouter" spirit was setting

Quaker abolitionists against their clerical leaders, it was also fracturing the American Anti-Slavery Society and eventually led to the establishment of two separate anti-slavery organizations. Taking their lead from William Lloyd Garrison, Angelina Grimke, and Henry Wright, the radicals in the Anti-Slavery Society turned their distaste with the coercion of slavery toward the inequities of gender relations, and of government itself, whether clerical or secular. The violent reaction these abolitionists had received only increased their alienation from American society, a society that was in their eyes so mired in sin that nothing less than a moral revolution against all sinful behavior was needed. Violence existed on every level of American society, argued the "Garrisonians," and therefore had to be destroyed root and branch. By advocating "no human government," the Garrisonians anticipated the government of God, a state of being where the coercion used by humans to maintain order would be unnecessary. This faith in Christian anarchism informed the agenda of the New England Non-Resistance Society, founded in 1838. As one supporter put it, "all Institutions [standing] in the way of Christ's kingdom must be done away with."[20]

This change within the Anti-Slavery Society hardly went unchallenged. The denunciation of ministers against "promiscuous assemblies," and the distaste of more conventional Christians for the "infidelity" of nonresistance and anti-sabbatarianism, fueled a backlash against Garrison and his supporters. Those who disagreed with Garrison formed the American and Foreign Anti-Slavery Society, as well as the Liberty Party, in 1839. The Garrisonians maintained control of the American Anti-Slavery Society. Though historians have often viewed men like the Liberty Party's founder James Birney as the counterrevolutionaries within the immediatist abolition movement, these evangelical or political abolitionists offered their share of innovative "comeouter" tactics. Viewing Garrison's insistence that it was "sin" for him to vote as negligently apolitical and escapist, Liberty Party men and women sought to infuse the highest government offices in the land with anti-slavery fervor. Offering an abolitionist alternative to voters in the 1840 election, James Birney, Henry Stanton, and Gerrit Smith urged anti-slavery Americans to "vote as you pray and pray as you vote."[21] Putting a "true" Christian politician on the ballot, James Birney, the Liberty Party advocated the abolition of slavery in the District of Columbia, the termination of the interstate slave trade, and a prohibition on the further admission of slave states into the union. They also officially endorsed the principle of immediate emancipation. In the aftermath of various failed attempts to influence the existing party system, Liberty abolitionists established a party of their own. In this way, they had adapted "comeouter" tactics to the American political process.

The vision of the Liberty Party founders linked the creation of an anti-slavery political party with the creation of anti-slavery churches. Although disagreeing with men such as Stephen Foster regarding the "no human government" ideal, political abolitionists like Birney agreed that American churches and the American state were pro-slavery institutions. "Slavery has corrupted the whole nation, so that it seems to me we are nearly at the point of dissolution. I must say—and I am sorry to believe it true—that our form of government will not do," wrote Birney in 1842.[22] "What we want is, a government not in any respect, opposed to the Divine government." Government inspired by divine precepts "is the only one which will stand."[23] Many Liberty Party abolitionists, therefore, in their effort to reconstruct human authority in accordance with the "government of God," sought to revamp existing structures of clerical authority to "introduce perfectionism into the social system," in the words of William Goodell.[24] After having lived under tyrannical clerical oppression that violated the rights of conscience of concerned church members who advanced immediatism, many political abolitionists began to seek a reconstitution of church authority that allowed for a forthright advancement of the cause of the "Heavenly Kingdom": "in spite of fraud and force, under any form and in any degree . . . in God's name [we] do whatever" the "welfare and improvement" of the human family demands, thundered Beriah Green in 1848.[25] All abolitionists must gather together to forward the "sublime ends" of God's kingdom. Not to do so would be an acknowledgment that God's children were in fact "orphans and outcasts," in league with the devil himself.[26]

Beginning in the 1840s, nearly all the Protestant denominations in the United States lost members to abolitionist "comeouter" groups. New sects, such as the Wesleyan Methodist Connection, the American Baptist Free Mission Society, and the Union Church, yearned for a fellowship that condemned "the prevailing sins of covetousness, slavery, war, intemperance, licentiousness, [and] secret societies" in favor of "free" churches liberated from a hypocritical clerisy.[27] Over the course of the 1840s, the Society of Friends would be rocked by comeouterism of both the Garrisonian variety and by that espoused by political abolitionists such as Birney. Their first confrontation with comeouterism, however, would come in Indiana from those more sympathetic with political abolition.

The leaders of the orthodox Indiana Yearly Meeting included several veteran abolitionists, among them Levi Coffin, Charles Osborn, and Benjamin Stanton. By 1840, the abolitionists would gain the fellowship of Arnold Buffum, a former colleague of William Lloyd Garrison from the New England Anti-Slavery Society. Through their leadership on the Committee on the Concerns of the People of Color, these Quakers had begun an attack on the fallacy of colonization societies in 1838. In that year, the committee published a minute stating that Friends "cannot say to [the slave] he must go to Haiti or Liberia ... to entitle him to the full enjoyment of his freedom." "Liberty," continued the minute, is "the right of all"; slavery must not be "prolonged for a single day." In the eyes of the abolitionists, the "pure and holy religion" of Quakerism demanded that such justice occur, regardless of the consequences.[28] Besides condemning colonization, abolitionists in Indiana launched newspapers advancing various aspects of their agenda. In 1841, Arnold Buffum began printing the *Protectionist,* dedicated to Liberty Party politics, and the same year Benjamin Stanton released copies of his *Free Labor Advocate and Anti-Slavery Chronicle.* Several local anti-slavery societies, both male and female, were also founded to agitate on behalf of immediatism.

As activists within Quaker meetings, the Indiana abolitionists desired that all Quakers support the free produce movement and the Liberty Party. In 1840, abolitionists such as Walter Edgerton attempted to modify the Quaker discipline to make the purchase of slave-produced merchandise a disownable offense. However, even members of the Committee of Concerns of the People of Color, let alone the executive Meeting for Sufferings, reacted to this attempt in a "state" of "great excitement," and rejected any abolitionist modifications of the discipline.[29] The rise of the Liberty Party also found many Quaker abolitionists working toward new understandings of Friends' political involvement. In 1840, the Quakers Levi Coffin, William Beard, and Arnold Buffum disrupted a Whig rally to nominate Liberty Party electors for president, and in 1841 held the state convention of the party in the Quaker-dominated community of Newport. Having held Liberty Party meetings, as well as anti-slavery lectures, in local meetinghouses, the abolitionists made clear their desire to enlist the Society of Friends in a revolutionary political movement.

In response to the agitation on behalf of the free produce movement and the Liberty Party, the Indiana Yearly Meeting began to warn against "anti-slavery" societies as "hurtful" to the unity of Friends' meetings, and therefore advised Friends to discontinue any involvement with the immediatist anti-slavery movement. The Indiana Yearly Meeting also disclaimed responsibility for the abolitionist newspapers published by Buffum and Stanton.[30] Two of the driving forces behind this move were Elijah Coffin, the clerk of the yearly meeting, as well as the "weighty" minister (and colonizationist) Jeremiah Hubbard. Hubbard's views have already been noted, but those of Coffin evinced significant distaste for immediatism as well. As a colonizationist, Coffin had actually advocated the forced expulsion of blacks to the American West, arguing that a "people who have been shut from the lights of science so long" would not be able to "understand their own interest." Approving of the "course" of migration used with Native Americans, Coffin wondered why it should not be used "in the case of Blacks?"[31]

The life of Elijah Coffin, a distant cousin to the more radical Levi, again demonstrates how many gradual abolitionists resisted the radicalization of the anti-slavery cause from the mid-1830s until well into the 1850s. Elijah had been a secretary of the North Carolina Manumission Society in the 1820s, but witnessed firsthand the virulent opposition to African American autonomy in the slave states. After moving to Indiana, Elijah defended African American rights when the legislature attempted to pass black laws in 1831.[32] But for Coffin, as for so many other Friends, there were limits to the possible when it came to transforming American race relations. The Liberty Party, for example, seemed reckless to Elijah Coffin; chaos would be the only result of such "political action" to end slavery immediately. The "free states" would "fill up with runaway Negroes" who would then "disturb the peace and harmony" of sister states. Since desperate blacks would have "free[d] themselves by force and arms," Coffin feared a scene of "blood and carnage more appalling than Slavery itself" if states declared slaves free once they had escaped to their soil. And, continued Coffin, poorer whites would never allow themselves to "compete with free Negro labour at a price greatly reduced from what it is at present." In short, the "unconditional abolitionists" supporting the Liberty Party "have no hope of accomplishing what they profess to be aiming at."[33] Coffin's views of the slavery issue fell in line with the leading politicians of his time; the dissenting social vision of Quakerism had been submerged beneath conventional white fears of slave revolt and of immediate emancipation's economic dislocation.

Like many orthodox Quakers, men such as Coffin and Hubbard gravitated toward the Whig Party because of its receptiveness to reforms such as temperance and sabbatarianism. In the early nineteenth century, increasing numbers of orthodox Quakers began to take an active interest in politics, and in Indiana, Quakers often served on state legislatures and in constitutional conventions.[34] Not since the days of William Penn's Pennsylvania had Friends so actively courted those with political power, and this trend paralleled orthodox Friends' growing acceptance of America's wider evangelical culture. At the same time, however, the association of orthodox Quakers with the Whig Party encouraged less conventional political allegiances among the Quaker radicals. Drumming up support for the Liberty Party, Arnold Buffum applauded attempts to join with any institution of "Christian philanthropists . . . for the improvement of the human race" and hoped other members of his meeting would not repeat the Hicksite error of viewing such Christian work as un-Quaker.[35]

A powerful irony of orthodox Quaker abolitionist support for the Liberty Party, then, was that men like Arnold Buffum or Charles Osborn used the evangelical rationale of godly leadership for society to advance the cause of immediate emancipation as a reform worthy of large-scale church support. Yet many orthodox Quakers could not accept the notion that abolitionists really were moderate, respectable, and peaceful "Christian philanthropists." The orthodox Quaker commitment to Whig political values of stability and moderation proved too powerful for Liberty Party enthusiasts to overcome. In upstate New York, Henry Williams reported that orthodox Quakers in Waterloo "*generally* love Whiggery better than Abolitionism." Williams also believed that "until [Quakers] go Old Tip [William Henry Harrison] they can have no voice in the cabinet."[36] After the passing of Harrison, orthodox Quakers threw their support behind Whig leader Henry Clay and continued to eschew third-party politics. Leaders of the Society of Friends cultivated a cordial relationship with Clay, particularly once it became clear that he was running for president. This often meant distancing the Society of Friends from the taint of abolitionism, apparently more than necessary in the Kentucky politician's eyes.

In 1839, Clay, on the floor of the House, had cautioned Quakers against anti-slavery radicalism during the gag rule furor by contrasting their moderate anti-slavery tactics with those of the fanatical "ultra-abolitionists." Not unlike President Van Buren and later President Tyler, Clay believed that to abolitionists "the rights of property are nothing" and that the "dissolution of the union, and the overthrow of the [American] government" had been actively sought by abolitionist leaders. Yet at the time, Clay had congratulated the Society of Friends for remaining "opposed to any disturbance of the peace and tranquility of the Union" by maintaining an "abhorrence of war in all its forms."[37] But in a meeting with the clerk of the orthodox New York Yearly Meeting, Mahlon Day, Clay privately worried that some Quakers had supported abolitionists who, in his opinion, produced abundant "mischief without any prospect of good." For his part, Day quickly put Clay right on the subject, declaring that Friends had been "disconnected with the wild modern abolitionists of the day." Clay was relieved by Day's comments and noted the moderation and consistency of the Society of Friends' anti-slavery views.[38]

Quaker abolitionists such as John Greenleaf Whittier were disheartened by the willingness of leading Friends to be influenced by the "pretended compliments" of powerful politicians such as the Speaker of the House. "Instead of ministering to their self-complacency and pride of reputation," Whittier believed that a slaveholder like Clay professing such respect for Quaker pacifism should lead members of the Society of Friends "to seriously inquire whether there has been no occasion given to the shrewd and crafty politician" to doubt the seriousness of the Quaker testimony against slavery.[39] This testimony, in Whittier's opinion, demanded that members of the sect turn away from a desire for worldly popularity to become latter-day prophets for a sinful nation. Though few Quakers took these words to heart, Whittier's abolitionist counterparts in Indiana could not have agreed more with the Massachusetts abolitionist's principled sentiments.

In 1842, Henry Clay planned a visit to the Midwest to drum up support for his presidential run, and he included a stop in Richmond, Indiana, the seat of the Indiana Yearly Meeting. Elijah Coffin, the meeting's clerk, acted as Clay's host, seated him near the head of the yearly meeting, and gave the presidential hopeful a tour of the meetinghouse grounds. Quaker abolitionists had also looked forward to meeting Clay, but hardly out of a desire to fawn over a powerful politician. Rather, they looked upon his visit as an opportunity to protest Clay's continued possession of human chattel. As Liberty Party supporters, abolitionist Quakers wanted politicians like Clay to be openly challenged and, if need be, threatened with party defection if they backed away from a principled stance against slavery. (In the coming election, the Liberty Party would in fact cost Clay the presidency.) Throughout the fall of 1842, local Quakers gathered several hundred signatures for a petition to demand the manumission of Clay's slaves. At the end of a Whig rally estimated to have had more than ten thousand people present, Hiram Mendenhall read the Whig leader the abolitionists' request to "unloose the heavy burden" of the "oppressed under your control" and "give liberty to whom liberty is due." The petition went on to say that Clay had "deprived" his slaves of the "sacred boon of freedom" and told him to "set an example" for slaveholding Americans through manumission.[40] Although the petition referred to Clay as a "great and good" man, it provided a visible demonstration of the abolitionist desire to confront the sinful behavior of America's secular leaders.

After the crowd took a collective gasp, Clay told Mendenhall that his slaves had to be "prepared for freedom" and that he would have to be compensated fifteen thousand dollars for the loss of his slaves. Clay went on to tell Mendenhall that "slavery is our misfortune, not our fault, but whether our misfortune or our fault it is none of your business."[41] Continuing to scold the abolitionists and their petition, Clay denounced the literal interpretation of the Declaration of Independence's promulgation that "all men are created equal": "in no society that ever did exist, or ever shall be formed, was or can that equality asserted among the members of the human race be practically enforced or carried out." And, Clay stated, "if the doctrines of the modern ultra political abolitionists had been seriously promulgated at the epoch of our revolution, our glorious Independence would never have been achieved—never—never!" (This last remark found several members of the audience applauding and echoing "never.") Finally, Clay feared the great "evil" of "amalgamation—that revolting admixture, alike offensive to God and man" as the ultimate consequence of the misguided sentiments of "ultra-abolitionists."[42]

By accepting the American republic's legal sanction for slavery, and by affirming the social and racial inequality written into founding documents such as the Declaration of Independence, Clay exposed the wide gulf that separated political abolitionists from the two major political parties. Seen as reckless visionaries attempting to destroy private property and upend the American racial order, Liberty Party abolitionists among the Quakers advanced their cause at great cost. In his speech, Clay went out of his way yet again to contrast the abolitionist flirtation with "blood, revolution, and disunion" against the Society of Friends' "genuine spirit of our benign religion." Unlike the abolitionists, argued Clay, Friends do not use "instruments of war, but of peace." "Unambitious they have no political objects or purposes to subserve." He admonished the abolitionists—Quaker and non-Quaker alike—to "limit your benevolent exertions to your own neighborhood. Within that circle you will find ample scope for the exercise of all your charities."[43] This was a bizarre statement given the involvement with the Whig Party by Quaker leaders such as Coffin. Yet by defining the Friends as anti-political, Clay reinforced the contemporary fear of religious sectarianism fostering political and social upheaval. This public statement separating Friends from the "revolutionary" elements of the abolitionists allowed leading Indiana Friends an open opportunity to ally themselves either for or against the slavepower. Perhaps not surprisingly, most Indiana Quakers passed up the opportunity to publicly support abolitionism.

Deeply embarrassed and insulted by the abolitionists' treatment of Clay, Elijah Coffin informed Clay that the yearly meeting had "nothing to do with the [abolitionists'] petition."[44] In speaking for other Whigs in the Quaker community, the *Palladium* declared its "utter contempt for the ... demagogue who would offer such treatment" to a leading national politician.[45] Many Quaker leaders felt the same way. The Indiana Yearly Meeting stated that although the petitioners "appeared to be Friends," they "were not actuated with a sincere love of the Gospel," and it lamented how the "place and influence" which the Society of Friends enjoyed with the "rulers of the land" had been jeopardized.[46] A later pamphlet published by the Meeting for Sufferings said that Henry Clay was "an eminent politician and statesman" who should not have been "mobbed" during his own rally by abolitionists demanding the manumission of his slaves.[47] Stemming from such deep conflicts over anti-slavery tactics, the 1842 Indiana Yearly Meeting removed eight abolitionist members from its executive committee (the Meeting for Sufferings), warned subordinate meetings to "be careful" not to appoint abolitionists to positions of power, and continued to caution against the "excitement and overactive zeal" of the anti-slavery movement.[48]

In reaction to their proscription, the censured abolitionists attempted to discuss their future course of action after the 1842 yearly meeting had ended, but a representative of the meeting told the radicals to vacate the meetinghouse premises or else be locked inside.[49] Taking their cue, they did indeed vacate the building; by the winter of 1843 they had formed a new group of Friends dedicated to the principles of abolitionism. Deciding to hold their yearly meeting in Newport, Indiana, home of the Underground Railroad president and ubiquitous radical Levi Coffin, the Indiana Yearly Meeting of Anti-Slavery Friends was born. Ultimately, about 2,500 out of the 25,000 orthodox Quakers in the Indiana Yearly Meeting left their parent "Body" and joined the new abolitionist sect.[50]

Denouncing the decision of the "Body" of Indiana Quakers to crack down on abolitionism, Whittier counted the meeting's leaders as among the "timid, the self-indulgent, [and] the conservative" of every age who possess ears "too delicate for the severity of truth." "Querulously" exclaiming, "Let us have peace in our day," continued Whittier, these men always dread "agitation," sigh for "peace in sin," and lament that leaders are being "tormented before their time." "When George Fox thundered in the ears of Priest and Ruler the great truths of spiritual liberty," asserted Whittier, he did not manifest an outward "show of peace," because he wanted his nation to "be purified" in advance of a state of calm. Because Americans were oppressing other human beings as chattel slaves, believed Whittier, the nation by definition "cannot be at peace." Hidden beneath its "exterior appearance of quiet" existed the "jarring and discordant elements of [America's] future destruction." In similar fashion to the "jewish nation when it was troubled by the warnings of the prophets," Whittier believed the peace called for by men such as Clay was "but the . . . deceptive calm which preceded the thunderbolt of Babylonian invasion."[51] Quaker abolitionists, such as Whittier, mobilized a dissenting, prophetic tradition of Christianity possessing a critical view of the American state as well as of God's purposes for that state. The Indiana comeouters had weighed the consequences of their agitation and found them to be far less dire than the destructive national outcome of continued moderation and compromise over the slavery issue.

Abolitionist reformers viewed Quaker defenses of sectarian exceptionalism as nothing less than a fraudulent cover for pro-colonizationist sentiment. To Charles Osborn, the pull of colonizationist support among leading Quakers produced a "pro-slavery influence" within the Indiana Yearly Meeting. This influence alone, declared Osborn, brought about "proscription and separation."[52] At the time of his censure, Osborn's name was "cast out as evil," and the days surrounding his decision to establish a new Quaker sect were those of "inexpressible weight and deep exercises of mind." This veteran minister had believed that the "Society of Friends was an Anti-Slavery Society" but when he realized that a Quaker could be disciplined for agitation on behalf of oppressed humanity, it was "one of the bitterest draughts" Osborn had "ever had to drink." Quoting the prophet Isaiah, Osborn wrote, "I did mourn as a dove; mine eyes fail[ed] with looking upward; O Lord, I am oppressed: undertake for me."[53] Whether or not the Lord would undertake for abolitionists such as Osborn, the Anti-Slavery Friends formed their own church and garnered the support of twelve monthly meetings of Friends from Michigan to Iowa to aid in the task. Having given up on the established mechanisms for reform, the Indiana radicals pursued other means toward establishing a purer, more committed abolitionist fellowship. The Indiana Yearly Meeting of Anti-Slavery Friends, as a new sect founded on abolitionist principles, sought to redefine the Society of Friends' social and political witness against sin.

The Anti-Slavery Friends maintained that they wanted to be able to enjoy "the privileges of religious society" and did not intend to modify the basic tenets of Quakerism. In most respects, the organizational setup and procedural "order" laid down by the Anti-Slavery Friends resembled those of other orthodox Quakers in antebellum America. However, the Anti-Slavery Friends' discipline differed in two very important ways from the "Body" of Indiana Quakers: they demanded that members of their sect support both the free produce movement and the Liberty Party. The Anti-Slavery Friends later announced that only their body of Quakers occupied such "firm, radical, though Christian ground" on these two subjects.[54] Elevating abolitionist practice to the status of enforceable doctrine, the Indiana radicals had finally succeeded in "abolitionizing" the Quaker meetinghouse.

Freed from the restraints of hostile Quaker authority, the Anti-Slavery Friends found the ability to agitate as loudly as they chose on behalf of slaves and freed blacks. The Anti-Slavery Friends' first published pamphlet warned all slaveholders in America of the "necessity . . . of an immediate abandonment of th[e] crying evil" of slavery and declared how the "corrupt state of public opinion" in their nation demanded an urgent reformation. As a new sect, the Anti-Slavery Friends had particularly harsh words for American churches, calling them bulwarks of slavery and racial prejudice. The anti-slavery radicals asked "the professors of Christianity everywhere" not to forget the "declaration of the Holy Redeemer: 'Ye are the light of the world.'" No longer should this light remain hidden away; the church must desist from supporting "the world in opposing the progress of the Anti-Slavery enterprise, which we have no doubt is an offer of mercy to a guilty world of oppressors." The Anti-Slavery Friends wondered aloud if slavery could exist "had the church in reality continued to retain the character of the light" and to "shed that light in its unabated lustre on all who come within" the churches' influence.[55]

The Anti-Slavery Friends exhibited a desire to publicly demand racial equality in ways that surpassed the main "Body" of Indiana Orthodox Friends. A report from one of their governing committees declared that all Anti-Slavery Friends were "trying to live down that unrighteous prejudice which is entertained against them [blacks] on account of their color," and the committee encouraged Friends to take part in "social intercourse" with the free African Americans in their area.[56] Since many of the radical Friends such as Levi Coffin had long attracted free black refugees from the South and elsewhere to the area near the Quaker community of Newport, Indiana, this request demonstrates how abolitionist Quakers sought out an alternative to the racial order of conventional American society. The village of Spartanburg, near Newport in Randolph County, Indiana, was home to well over a thousand free people of color.

Quaker comeouter involvement in efforts to educate free blacks in this area largely surpassed that of their brethren as well. The Union Literary Institute, established in Spartanburg, claimed to go beyond the usual practical training often afforded people of color by teaching them geometry, algebra, natural philosophy, and chemistry. According to the Anti-Slavery Friends, the institute was devised to make an "education in the higher branches of science within the reach of all who have not the means and facilities for the acquisition of scientific knowledge."[57] Demonstrating their personal commitment to the uplift of African Americans, the Anti-Slavery Friends even told members of their church to spend at least three months of each of their lives as teachers to African Americans.[58] Because of their proximity to Spartanburg, the Anti-Slavery Friends counted 2,312 people of color to whom they extended some form of "care" in 1845. This number represented nearly the same number of white members of the Anti-Slavery Friends.[59]

In addition to their involvement with African American "uplift," the Anti-Slavery Friends continued to participate in ecumenical endeavors with other abolitionists to purge America's churches, as well as the nation's benevolent institutions, of the taint of slavery. Levi Coffin attended the Cincinnati Convention of the Church Anti-Slavery Society in 1850 and signed the meeting's document sanctioning secession "from all churches, ecclesiastical bodies, and missionary organizations, that are not fully divorced from the sin of slaveholding."[60] The Christian anti-slavery conventions of the 1840s and 50s were largely ignored by the Society of Friends in the United States, however. The call for secession, furthermore, may have hampered reform within existing institutions, though as the Anti-Slavery Friends saw it, their communion was a final attempt to demonstrate that abolitionist Christianity could in fact exist within a slaveholding nation. Their promotion of the "anti-slavery enterprise" was an "offer of God's mercy to our guilty nation . . . to undo the heavy burdens and let the oppressed go free."[61]

Viewing America's churches as a springboard for moral revolution, the Christian comeouters sought to redirect the social force and organizational power of religious institutions to combat a sin that, in their eyes, was unparalleled in brutality and injustice. Because millions of Americans belonged to and participated in church life, the comeouters understood the potential of a united moral army of American Christians committed to abolitionism. To them, true worship consisted of involvement in social activism. This activism, however, was not totally divorced from the sacerdotal power of sectarian, reformed Protestantism; rather, it looked to infuse the godly example of sanctified Christianity into a society desperately needing moral leadership. Comeouters saw their churches as the epitome of Christ's injunction to "be a city set upon a hill."

Enlisting in the battle against churches that worried over the mixing of politics and religion, the Anti-Slavery Friends anticipated the message of social Christianity: all Christians must "labor, and pray, and give until the whole moral and political power in the country, so far as it is lawful, is brought to bear with united and concentrated energy upon this unearthly crime."[62] Quakers must "enlighten the public mind on the subject [of slavery]" so that by evoking the "Lord God of Elijah" the work of immediate emancipation might be accomplished.[63] The active engagement of a religious institution with a social movement, indeed the realization that politics and religion were one and the same, collided with the views of Quaker leaders who sought to insulate their flock from exogenous movements and organizations that would continue to "divide and scatter" meetings of the Society of Friends. Fighting against sectarian customs or against any interpretation of theology that rejected the possibility of human effort to bring about God's kingdom, the Anti-Slavery Friends believed there were "none who do not possess some reformatory influence in this matter [of abolishing slavery]" because "whatever concerns humanity, concerns" Christians. To Anti-Slavery Friends there was hope that all devoted Christians could bring about the "speedy termination of all tyranny and oppression, hasten the day when righteousness shall cover the earth as the waters do the sea."[64]

But as the years ahead would show, the vision of groups like the Anti-Slavery Friends was generally relegated by other believers to the margins of respectable Christianity. The "false" and "slanderous" course of the antislavery comeouter movement, a movement that denounced churches as un-Christian for opposing "the amelioration of the condition of the poor slave," should be rejected by all good Christians, according to a group of ministers in correspondence with James Birney. These Christian ministers linked the Christian comeouters with William Lloyd Garrison and his wish to "blot out the christian Sabbath, the church, the ministry and the constitution of the country in order to get rid of Slavery." To the reply that abolitionists possessed virtuous motives, the Ohio ministers insisted that "the French revolutionists may have had good motives," but they still sanctioned "Loire marriages" and the "work of the Guillotine." By undermining clerical power in their condemnation of pro-slavery religion, abolitionists were in danger of fostering "either a shameful infidelity on the one hand or a reckless spirit of disorganization on the other." Furthermore, Christian comeouters were a "political party" determined to "elevate [their] party without let or hindrance" and therefore injected a spirit of "strife" into Christian churches.[65] Because of the influence of these beliefs central to antebellum understandings of the meaning of religious freedom, the agenda of the Anti-Slavery Friends represented a marginal and unpopular interpretation of the Quaker social message. The Anti-Slavery Friends never received widespread support from American Quakers, and in fact their membership began to decline by the late 1840s.

Seconding the view of American Christians that Christian comeouters were working for the destruction of Christian institutions, the Society of Friends in Britain also rejected anti-slavery comeouterism. This development, however, came as a surprise to many American abolitionists and underscores the complex relationship of American and British abolitionism. Because the British had come out in favor of immediatism in the early 1830s, the Anti-Slavery Friends thought they could enlist the support of their "orthodox" Quaker counterparts across the Atlantic in their cause. The efforts of Joseph Sturge had further buoyed the hopes of the Anti-Slavery Friends regarding the popularity of their comeouter movement in Britain. Sturge had visited American Quaker meetings in the United States in 1842 and criticized his foreign brethren for closing meetinghouses to abolitionist lectures. Noting that Gracechurch Street meeting in London welcomed the British and Foreign Anti-Slavery Convention in 1840, Sturge commented that Friends in England "think it their duty to render every aid in their power to the anti-slavery cause." Sturge was disappointed to learn that the "whole weight and influence of the Society" in America had been thrown "against a movement which, although doubtless partaking of the imperfections attendant upon all human instrumentality, had already aroused the whole country to a sense of the wrongs of the slave." The objection raised by leading American Quakers that the Society of Friends had not been favored with the "immediate guidance of the Holy Spirit" to support the American Anti-Slavery Society was simply a "neglect of duty" on the part of the majority of American Quakers. Sturge believed the "total and immediate" abolition of slavery deserved the full attention of Friends in the United States; his "prayer" was that Quakers would be "made instrumental, [by] the divine hand" for the destruction of such inhuman oppression.[66]

Responding to the complaints of Quakers such as Sturge, the *Friend* ran a series titled "Defence of American Friends" in 1844. Repeating the long-held view of many American Quakers that abolishing slavery in Britain was a fundamentally easier act than in the United States, the *Friend* demanded critical British Quakers "regard ... the magnitude of the obstacles" facing American Quakers when "slaves are a source of political power." The editors also believed that British Quakers should think twice about criticizing the conservatism of American Friends when British Friends remained inactive regarding the "peculiar institutions of Great Britain." The "unjust exactions and artificial state of society" that had caused "thousands" to lack "the necessary means of sustenance" could have led to British Friends' support for radical politics, but such was not the case. American Friends could have asked "why is there so much apathy and inaction among [British] Friends?" but they had not. The Americans continued: "If we should inquire why Friends in Great Britain do not unite with the Chartists and Irish Repealers in bringing about a salutary reform, would not the answer be that Friends cannot unite in the measures of those parties ... without violating their sense of propriety, and compromising" their principles? The answer would be yes, and "in that answer may be found our reasons for not joining the abolitionists in America."[67]

This revealing comparison between revolutionary movements in Britain and the abolitionist movement in the United States demonstrates the differing views among Friends of the meaning of abolitionism in the United States versus its meaning in Britain. Again, in this comparison, American Quakers fell in line with the sentiments of many Whig leaders concerning the impracticality of British immediatism being planted onto American soil. Henry Clay, for example, hoped that few would forget that the slaves emancipated by the British were not "in the bosom of the kingdom" (as they were in the United States) and that the British did not have to deal with the "disasterous" [*sic*] effects of emancipation within the borders of Great Britain.[68]

Several British abolitionists among the Society of Friends, while privately agreeing with Sturge that American Friends ought to throw their support behind immediatism, still acknowledged the unique difficulties facing Americans and publicly supported the decision of yearly meetings in the United States to distance Quakers from abolitionism. As early as 1838, William Lloyd Garrison noted that when Joseph John Gurney visited Philadelphia, he "scarcely opened his lips on the subject of slavery" even though he had been a "flaming abolitionist in England."[69] In 1839, Arnold Buffum expressed displeasure that Jacob Green and Daniel Wheeler, both abolitionists from Britain, threw "their influence into the pro-slavery scale" when the Ohio Yearly Meeting decided to advise against anti-slavery lectures.[70]

Perhaps most alarming to the abolitionist-supported Anti-Slavery Friends was the decision of the London Yearly Meeting to back the "Body" of Indiana Quakers against the separatists. Again, even as many British Quakers openly declared their support for immediatism, they nonetheless disliked the destructive turn toward "comeouterism" taken by many abolitionists in the United States. A delegation of London leaders visited the fractured Indiana Yearly Meeting in 1845, and though they never specifically addressed the issue of slavery, they spoke of the "preciousness and the safety of true gospel unity" and asked "those who have recently separated" to return to the Indiana Yearly Meeting.[71] The London Yearly Meeting evidently did not feel that arguments over the proper way to oppose slavery should be allowed to hinder the all-important Quaker "unity in the spirit." The fact that the London Yearly Meeting essentially turned its back on the Quaker abolitionists in Indiana ostracized the Anti-Slavery Friends from the rest of the church worldwide.

This was not the first time, however, that British abolitionists had distanced themselves from the disruptive tendencies of comeouterism. It may be that they associated all comeouters with Garrison (something that, as earlier noted, was erroneous). It was the opinion of William Howitt that the World Anti-Slavery Convention in London had become "the fag-end" of the London Yearly Meeting of the Society of Friends and its interest in persecuting Hicksite separatism when it rejected the demands for women's involvement in the proceedings of the convention.[72] Even Joseph Sturge, when criticizing the Society of Friends in the United States for its lack of support for immediatism, nonetheless cautioned against the proclivity of American abolitionists to "connect other topics" to that of abolition that therefore damaged this "simple and momentous object." Sturge also made an oblique reference to Garrisonianism when he admonished Quaker abolitionists not to "compromise Christian principle" when joining with others to agitate the slavery question.[73] Skepticism toward comeouterism may have been an acknowledgment of the legitimacy of leading American Friends' fears regarding the social and political dislocation caused by many abolitionists in the United States. No yearly meeting outside the United States would even receive correspondence from the Anti-Slavery Friends, let alone sympathize with their plight.[74] The comeouters' attempt to reconstitute the Society of Friends upon abolitionist principles had failed; in 1857 the Anti-Slavery Friends finally disbanded.

Many contemporary ministers and politicians tended to deliver a negative verdict regarding the meaning of abolitionist comeouterism. Seen as irresponsible agitators ripping apart the cords of union, the abolitionists involved in dividing America's churches over anti-slavery reform were, in the eyes of their numerous critics, enacting a prelude to civil war. With the comeouters, asserted James Porter, "every man is a bible to himself, and we [will] have as many scriptures as there are different convictions." Following in the footsteps of these deluded abolitionists would lead to one thing: the "break down . . . [of] the state."[75] This viewpoint, however, purposefully ignored the rationale of abolitionist comeouterism, however utopian such a rationale had been viewed by the abolitionists' opponents. The abolitionist churches, believed the Anti-Slavery Friends, should have been the vehicles of slavery's abolition and of the union's just preservation. As Walter Edgerton, the clerk of the Anti-Slavery Friends Yearly Meeting, wrote in 1855: "Had Friends in the United States, together with all others professing the Christian name, but seconded the efforts of the Anti-Slavery Societies, the annexation of Texas, the Mexican War . . . the infamous Fugitive Slave Act" as well as the expansion of the slavepower "would never have taken place." An "appalling amount of crime and suffering might have been prevented by Christians," lamented Edgerton, "had they united in this great work of benevolence."[76] Instead, concluded Edgerton, members of the Anti-Slavery Friends would have to settle for the consolation of having acted in accordance with the dictates of their conscience. By successfully resisting worldly calls for compromise regarding abolitionism, the Anti-Slavery Friends had remained true to the gospel of Jesus Christ. A dramatic expression of this feeling came from the dying lips of an Anti-Slavery Friend, Newton Stubbs, in 1844: "Although the course I have pursued with reference to the anti-slavery cause may not do to live by, it will do to die by. I am now prepared to meet my final judge in peace."[77]

Figure 1. Executive Committee, Pennsylvania Anti-Slavery Society, circa 1860. Seated bottom left is Oliver Johnson, supporter of the Progressive Friends. Abby Kimber and Sarah Pugh, standing fourth and sixth from the left, were Quakers, as were the better-known James and Lucretia Mott, seated at the far right. Frederick Gutekunst, Civilian Groups, Society Print Collection, Historical Society of Pennsylvania.

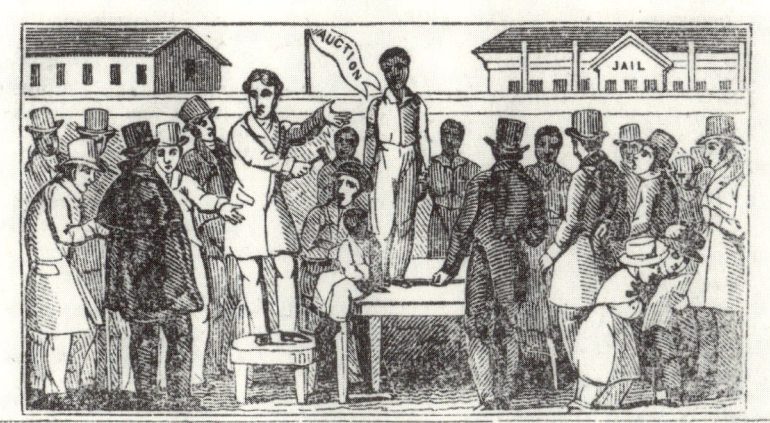

Figure 2. "The Nation's Act. Man Auction at the Capital," from the Anti-Slavery Almanac . . . for 1839. The American Anti-Slavery Society's petition campaign of 1835–36 included an attack on slavery in the nation's capital.
Courtesy, The Library Company of Philadelphia.

Figure 3. "Colored Schools Broken up, in the Free States," from the Anti-Slavery Almanac . . . for 1839. Quaker abolitionist Prudence Crandall learned firsthand from a mob the unpopularity of interracial education when her school for colored girls was attacked in Canterbury, Connecticut, in 1834.
Courtesy, The Library Company of Philadelphia.

Figure 4. J. T. Bowen, Destruction by Fire of Pennsylvania Hall on the night of May 17, 1838. The destruction of this abolitionist meetinghouse by a mob of all classes in Philadelphia signaled to many Quakers the dangers of supporting the American Anti-Slavery Society in the 1830s.
Courtesy, The Library Company of Philadelphia.

Figure 5. Indiana Yearly Meeting of Friends, 1844, by Marcus Mote.
Courtesy, Friends Collection, Earlham College, Richmond, Ind.

Figure 6. Arch Street Meetinghouse in Philadelphia, 1868; photo by John Moran. This meetinghouse was the site of some controversy over its use of the Negro pew in the 1840s and 1850s.
Courtesy, The Library Company of Philadelphia.

Figure 7. Longwood Progressive Friends Yearly Meeting, 1865. William Lloyd Garrison (standing in front bareheaded and holding flowers) had rejected formal religion by this time but was still a frequent attendee at meetings of Progressive Friends.
Courtesy, Chester County Historical Society, West Chester, Pennsylvania.

Figure 8. Thomas Garrett, noted Underground Railroad operator, ca. 1860.
Courtesy, Chester County Historical Society, West Chester, Pennsylvania.

# 3

# Friends and the "Children of Africa": Quaker Abolitionists Confront the Negro Pew

Throughout the antebellum era, radical anti-slavery Quakers sought to redefine the meaning and organization of church membership by demanding church leaders end worldly hierarchies that impeded the realization of God's kingdom in this world. Like their activist counterparts in other Protestant denominations, Quaker abolitionists believed that their church should speak out against or work to eliminate racial prejudice occurring within the walls of Northern churches. For the abolitionists, the so-called "Negro pew" set aside for African American worshippers was an unacceptable nod to the power of slaveholders in the antebellum United States. In common with other antebellum churches, certain Quaker meetings utilized Negro pews to separate white from nonwhite worshippers. The argument over ending the Negro pew among Friends in the early 1840s—an argument that the abolitionists oftentimes lost—serves as an example of how the Society of Friends chose to frame efforts at racial equality as a dangerous and public politicization of the Quakers' private anti-slavery testimony.

Although Quakers had long been associated with efforts to assist African Americans in the free states and did belong to the vanguard of the white conscience when it came to race relations, the Society of Friends still possessed something of a mixed record when it came to racial prejudice, at least in the eyes of the abolitionists.[1] Quaker philanthropy in terms of education and legal assistance to freed blacks had been unparalleled for a church of comparable size, yet the church had not extricated itself completely from the racism of the antebellum American republic. Although the segregation of Quaker meetinghouses clearly varied by locale and was not universal, there is no question that several communities of Friends assented to the customary separation of white and black worshippers within churches. For their part, abolitionist reformers had little patience for compromise with popular conceptions of the status of free blacks in the North, and they demanded an end to any vestige of prejudice within institutional Christianity.

Abolitionists recognized how public racial segregation, such as separate "Negro" pews or benches for worship in churches, helped legitimate the existence of slavery in the United States. Segregation further supported the notion that freedom for blacks was anomalous or, worse yet, that slaves were better off than Northern free blacks. According to Frederick Douglass, this last opinion, that slaves in the South were in fact "better off than the [free] colored people of the North," was exactly what the leading Hicksite Quaker minister, Nicholas Brown, had told Douglass in 1849. For the leading African American abolitionist, such sentiments were reputedly "among many" made by ministers in the Society of Friends that "exerted an injurious influence" on the cause of emancipation.[2] For white abolitionist Arnold Buffum, the failure of the avowedly anti-slavery Friends to overcome racial prejudice stood as a glaring example of how a "great evil" [slavery] had "diffus[ed] a baneful demoralizing influence throughout the whole land" so that the "public sentiment of a nation" regarded African Americans as fit for little else than legalized bondage.[3]

Arguing that the organization of church spaces lent powerful support to slavery and racial prejudice, the Nantucket Quaker Nathaniel Barney feared that the segregation of houses of worship had made Christian institutions "foremost in proscribing color" by "encourag[ing] a lawless violation of the rights of humanity." Barney recounted the response of a member of a school board in Massachusetts when asked why schools in New England were segregated: schools, according the board members, "cannot be governed by a more tolerant spirit than our churches." Due to the social power possessed by churches, continued Barney, reformers within American churches must work to abolish segregation within churches in order to "give light to the people" on the evils of racial prejudice and slavery.[4]

As historian Nancy Isenberg has shown, nineteenth-century Americans' view of the Christian "ecclesia" was linked to their conception of who did and did not belong in the public sphere. All except white males possessed a less than equal station in the eyes of both church leaders and political authorities.[5] The interdependence of social arrangements within the church and within the civil society was understood by abolitionist reformers in the nineteenth century; because the "public ear is chained to the pulpit," asserted Frederick Douglass, the social customs and political views allowed in church spaces possess "the power of life and death" over the African American people in the free states.[6] The slaveholding Christianity of *all* regions of the United States, in Douglass's opinion, backed up the doctrine of the "divine right of complexion" that defined the "African race ... [as] a distinct and inferior people" in the minds of whites.[7] The efforts made by abolitionists—black and white—to carve out a space of social equality within institutional Protestantism represented an attempt to push against the deeply ingrained stereotypes, legal conventions, and political arrangements buttressing the American racial order.[8]

In their struggle to create more egalitarian places for worship, white and black reformers worked together in what for the time was a rare cooperative effort. The search for greater social equality represented by the movement against the Negro pew again represented how abolitionists dissented from prevailing white cultural norms, especially when considering how most Quaker meetings refused to acknowledge the legitimacy of abolitionist complaints regarding the Negro pew. The disappointing irony of this development was noted by several abolitionists at the General Anti-Slavery Convention in London in 1843. Describing the Negro pew as a demonstration of how American churches were "bulwarks of slavery," Arnold Buffum believed that Quaker unwillingness to "take them [African Americans] by the hand" and "treat them as brethren as Christ Jesus" was particularly troubling given that Quakers were "the first to become . . . friends" of the African American people. An African American abolitionist at the convention, identified only as "Mr. Howells," agreed with Buffum's comments on the special responsibility of the Society of Friends to fight racial prejudice, repeating the sentiments "of the late governor of New York," who remarked that Friends "had a lever by which they could uplift the world, and they would not raise it; they had a trumpet by which they could have given a blast that would awake the world and they would not blow it."[9]

For many scholars of the antebellum United States, the efforts of white abolitionists to advance some degree of social equality for African Americans has not been nearly as significant as the fact that most early Victorians possessed a "common set of assumptions about their [African American] incapacity, dependency, and need for external control."[10] Without denying the evidence that a belief in white racial superiority existed throughout the antebellum free states, it is important for historians to position the efforts of those whites who attempted to erase accepted racial boundaries against those who opposed them. In the end, efforts at racial equality often proved fleeting and unsuccessful—thereby confirming the view held by many historians that white racism in the antebellum period was pervasive and all-encompassing. But to imply that abolitionists had more in common than not with their broader white culture is to elide the subtleties and complexities of race relations in the antebellum period as well as to misrepresent the meaning of abolitionism for the culture and society in which abolitionists lived.

In an era in which racial violence had escalated to the point that the African American Robert Purvis described the "public estimation" of people of color in the minds of whites as "utter and complete nothingness," and at a time when state legislatures were enacting "black code" legislation to disenfranchise blacks and forbid their emigration into free states, the desire of abolitionists to fight against racial discrimination was an extremely unpopular and dangerous endeavor.[11] The Connecticut Friend Prudence Crandall, after unsuccessful efforts to integrate one school, decided to open a "High School" for "young colored Ladies and Misses," only to find her life threatened and the state legislature provoked to pass a law against the legality of her school. Ultimately, Crandall was forced to close her high school, not long after a state supreme court judge ruled that it was his "duty, to say, [that] they [free blacks] are not citizens" and therefore were not protected by the privileges and immunities clause of the U.S. Constitution.[12] Fourteen years later in Massachusetts, fellow Quaker Samuel Rodman took part in a public protest against the New Bedford Lyceum after it had denied membership to a "colored man," demanding that it sell tickets "without regard to sect or party, color or complexion." The proposal got nowhere, and the Lyceum's constitution was rewritten to grant "liberty to colored people to occupy the gallery" of the building "gratis." Rodman was shocked at the "inveterate prejudices" of his fellow New Englanders and found the Lyceum's declaration of "liberality" when establishing a separate section for one colored member insulting. Ironically, the title of the lecture to which the unnamed "colored man" had applied was "The Good in the World."[13]

The challenge facing white Quaker reformers attempting to dismantle racial distinctions that stood in the way of the egalitarian promise of Christianity possessed a history that in many ways dated to the founding of the Society of Friends. The founder of Quakerism, George Fox, believed that Friends bore responsibility for ensuring that slaves receive some spiritual instruction and that slaves should be able "to meet together, to wait upon the Lord."[14] These meetings, however, fell short of representing genuine spiritual equality, as they often amounted to white Quakers' instructing blacks regarding morality and religion. Referring to free slaves as being "under care," many Quaker ministers viewed blacks as in need of supervision; indeed these meetings often went hand in hand with the efforts of Friends to ensure that their former slaves did not become a burden to the larger white community. Sometimes, condescension crept into Friends' comments regarding these efforts. After one religious meeting for freed slaves near Princeton, New Jersey, members of that monthly meeting reported how the local blacks had "but little savor of true Religion."[15]

The segregation of public spaces in the free states had included churches since at least the late eighteenth century. In the aftermath of slavery's abolition in Pennsylvania, white Philadelphians attempted to reinforce spatially the legal restraints on blacks lost in the process of emancipation. The forcible ejection of two prominent African American leaders, Richard Allen and Absalom Jones, to the gallery of St. George's Methodist Episcopal Church while the two were kneeling during a service in 1787, besides giving impetus for the establishment of separate black churches, also made clear how whites envisioned their places for worship as expressions of racial separatism. Determined to establish a house of worship where free blacks could worship with dignity, Allen and Jones took the lead in founding the Free African Society, and often invited Quaker ministers to preside over their meetings. Yet it is notable that there was no larger effort made by Philadelphia Quakers regarding interracial worship during this period with this or any other African American group.[16] Although many yearly meetings of Friends had supposedly lifted barriers to African American membership during the late 1700s, the concern could still be heard from skeptical white Quakers that African American membership in the Society of Friends would lead to the "privilege of intermarriage with the whites," something viewed by many Friends as "objectionable."[17] The reality of Quaker aversion to African American social equality would be heard for the next several decades; in 1834 Jeremiah Hubbard noted that members of the "Society of Friends have no intention of giving [people of color] our sons or our daughters in marriage" and believed that few blacks would ever truly be welcome in any social setting among Friends.[18]

The existence of the so-called "Negro pew" within many Quaker meetinghouses revealed the continued inability of large numbers within the Society of Friends to imagine African Americans as equals within their spiritual fellowship. The number of African Americans who attended Quaker meetings was never great, though some, such as Grace Bustill Douglass, claimed that many people of color in the Philadelphia area were "inclined to attend" Quaker meetings. But few, if any, African Americans were offered membership in the Society of Friends in the years before the Civil War.[19] Yet in many ways, the paucity of African American membership makes the existence of the segregated seating in Quaker meetinghouses all the more surprising. That "worldly" caste hierarchies should have intruded upon the sacred space of the meetinghouse represented an important qualification regarding the commitment of the Society of Friends to dissent from pervasive, "worldly" social inequities. Those few white Quakers who gave descriptions of the Negro pew left behind a rare view of the commonplace assumptions possessed by Friends regarding the proper relationship between white and black worshippers. In general, it appears that the location of the colored seating was toward the back of the meetinghouse. However, the specific arrangement of the segregated seating was perhaps not as significant as the fact that the two races were meant to remain separate, and that white Quakers controlled where African Americans sat. For example, William Bassett reported that a white Quaker in Philadelphia was "severely reprimanded" by a minister of the meeting for choosing to sit on the "Colored" bench.[20] Similarly, the African American Quaker Sarah Mapps Douglass (no relation to Frederick) reported that the colored bench on which she normally sat was bookended, as it were, by two white members to ensure that white Quakers would not accidentally sit there.[21] In other locations, according to Susan B. Anthony, monthly meetings simply refused to seat black Quakers anywhere and practically ejected them from the meetings.[22] It apparently mattered little to white Friends where African American Quakers went as long as it was clear that those with darker complexions were not to mix with whites.

The resistance to African American membership in the Society of Friends reported by many Quaker abolitionists demonstrated how, in the eyes of many other Quakers, African Americans stood outside any normal definition of social respectability. According to Sarah Grimke, many members of the Society of Friends were wary of allowing African American membership because it would lead to interracial marriage.[23] Grimke also reported that many Quakers had a real fear of physical proximity to African Americans; one woman insisted on giving her black hired help separate dishes for meals. This Friend and her family "would no more [think] of using" the same dishes as blacks "than if a cat or dog had eaten on them." Grimke relayed the unnamed woman's confession that "such are the prejudices I was educated in, I have found it hard to overcome them."[24] One of the more frank expressions of the difficulty facing white Quakers attempting to transcend the dominant racial stereotypes of their society came from the Philadelphia Quaker Emma Kimber. Writing her mother during the Amistad case, Kimber found her own "enthusiasm for heroism wonderfully excited" by the liberated blacks' leader, but she had "to keep down the recollection of his wooly head, thick lips, and flat nose." "I am sorry for my prejudice—but there it is." Unfortunately for Kimber, she could no more imagine a "black hero or patriot" than she could imagine "a black Venus." "What does thee do?" she queried.[25]

For many Quakers, who often belonged to the upper middle economic class and who were of "old" English stock, groups that existed outside of their caste and class were viewed as naturally inferior. Significantly, this not only held true for African Americans, but it also extended to the Irish servants often brought into the homes of the many affluent Friends in Baltimore, Philadelphia, New York, or Newport. Martha Schofield would later relay the opinion of her sister Eliza, who accused free black servants as being "as bad as the Irish" and believed that both Irish and blacks were only fit to "wait on us the superior race and aristocrats!"[26] The racialized nature of class difference among white Quakers had also been experienced by the African American abolitionist Sarah Mapps Douglass, who recalled the first comments to her from a white female Friend from New York: "Doest thee go out a house cleaning?" The implications for Douglass were that the normal place for African Americans in the Quaker meetinghouse was naturally as a dependent servant and not as a social equal.[27] Even when Quakers attempted to act with charity toward those not of their caste, according to Angelina Grimke, their actions betrayed a belief that those being assisted were "unfortunate inferiors, not . . . suffering equals."[28]

When challenged regarding complaints from white and black abolitionists regarding the existence of a separate seating area for African Americans in Philadelphia meetinghouses, the editor of the *Friend* simply termed the charges "unfounded" and insisted that "there is no seat in any of our meetings appropriated to coloured persons . . . they sit on the same benches that the whites occupy." Moreover, the real reason African Americans felt unwelcome in Quaker meetings for worship was that Friends' "mode of worship does not suit their dispositions: they are fond of music and excitement" and therefore "prefer their own meetings."[29] This insistence that African Americans were by nature unwilling to join with Quaker worship demonstrated just what the abolitionists were up against in their fight against racial prejudice. The comments of the *Friend* hinting at the racialization of Quaker mysticism were made clearer by the anonymous American Friends' comments reported to the English Quaker William Tallack: black "minds are unable to appreciate the abstractions and refinements of our spiritual views" and therefore must worship with "singing and colloquial expressions."[30] These comments approached conventional characterizations of African Americans as childlike and inherently lacking the ability to comprehend abstract thinking, and they effectively blamed the marginalized position of African American Quakers on the African Americans themselves.

For many leaders of the Society of Friends in the United States, the abolition question had no business being "mixed up with the warfare against . . . prejudices in regard to the colored race."[31] Discussion of the slavery issue was to remain separate from more radical efforts at reordering race relations in all sections of antebellum America. Put more bluntly, Susan B. Anthony reported how an unnamed relative warned her not to attempt to "niggarize" the "good old Quakers" in upstate New York by forcing discussion within her meeting regarding racial segregation.[32] John Candler, a Friend from Britain visiting the United States in the early 1840s, accused American Friends of treating free blacks "as aliens—as a people who have no right to a possession in the land that gave them birth." When Candler confronted a Quaker elder regarding the issue, the man believed it was easier for a foreigner to "overcome this feeling [of racial prejudice] but we cannot."[33]

In their attempt to bring lecture campaigns into Quaker meetinghouses (before they were barred from so doing), abolitionists had desired that white audiences confront the human reality of slavery. By creating a space for the black body and mind within the imagination of white audiences, abolitionists furthered their subversive effort to alter race relations within white churches. During one lecture to a Quaker audience, Arnold Buffum told his audience that "we are too apt to look upon their [slaves'] sufferings as we do upon the abuse of the beasts that perish, rather than of our brethren by creation and redemption." Not unlike many of his fellow abolitionists, Buffum then proceeded to paint for his audience a vivid word picture of the daily suffering of black humanity: "imagine the piercing cries of yonder delicate female tied to a tree and writhing under a lash . . . her bare flesh mangled with the knotted scourge." Would not her cries "penetrate the inmost recesses of your hearts?" asked Buffum.[34] For

Angelina Grimke, along with her husband Theodore Weld, the publishing of eyewitness accounts of slavery represented "the troops, [the] weapons, and [the] victory" in the movement to stir the Northern anti-slavery conscience to action.[35] Abolitionist involvement in the creation of the slave narrative genre furthered these efforts to give slaves a platform to convey the horrors of enslavement. The narrative of the former slave Harriet Jacobs, produced in part with the financial assistance of Rochester Quakers Amy and Isaac Post, demonstrated the racial cooperation and understanding practiced by activist whites working to give people of color a voice in the American print media. In response to the support she had received from the Posts, Jacobs assessed their behavior in this fashion: "they measured a man's worth by his character, not by his complexion. The memory of those beloved and honorable friends will remain with me to my latest hour."[36]

From the start of their efforts to advance the principles of immediate emancipation, white abolitionists often (though not always) recognized the need to bring African Americans into their organizations as members. This recognition that blacks could occupy public space within a political organization was no small development. In the earlier anti-slavery and manumission societies, for example, African Americans had been excluded from membership. Edwin Needles complained about the racial segregation of older, gradualist anti-slavery societies, stating that many Quakers "suffered themselves to act incoherently towards their colored brethren, as through they really were an inferior race of beings, and not entitled to notice, further than was necessary to relieve them from the cruel bonds of slavery."[37] A connection existed in the minds of abolitionists between the creation of a public space for African Americans and the wider efforts to "revolutionize public opinion" in the cause of immediate emancipation. "How can we have the effrontery to expect the white slaveholders of the South to live on terms of civil equality with the colored slave," asked a report of the Massachusetts Anti-Slavery Society, "if we, the white abolitionists of the North, will not admit colored freemen as members of our Anti-Slavery Societies?"[38] Angelina Grimke demanded that all white abolitionists "mingle with our oppressed brethren and sisters" so as to become "convinced of the sinfulness of that anti-christian prejudice which is crushing" free blacks and slaves alike.[39] In an effort to combat the prejudices of whites who denied African Americans a public role in the life of the republic, in 1841 at an anti-slavery convention in New England, William C. Coffin requested that Frederick Douglass address a crowd of whites for the first time in his life. As Douglass later recounted, "it was with the utmost difficulty that I could stand erect, or that I could command and articulate two words without hesitation and stammering." But he was heard with great "enthusiasm" and was soon enlisted as an anti-slavery lecturing agent by the Massachusetts Anti-Slavery Society. "For a time," recalled Douglass, "I was made to forget that my skin was dark and my hair crisped."[40] The conventional assumption that black skin and exclusion from public life were natural, perhaps even necessary for the preservation of a slaveholding republic, was being slowly and fitfully overturned by abolitionists.

The galvanization of African American activists by the immediatist movement brought attention to many accepted forms of prejudice and created to some degree a biracial solidarity among activists. Through contact with those who experienced racial discrimination daily, white abolitionists increased their awareness of forms of discrimination and began efforts to eliminate them. The experience of Sarah Mapps Douglass demonstrated how the inclusion of African Americans in the work of anti-slavery societies enabled white reformers to broadcast the debilitating challenges posed by American racism to those working for an end to slavery. As a member of the Philadelphia Female Anti-Slavery Society and as the daughter of Grace Douglass, a woman who helped to found the organization, Sarah came into contact with many Quaker abolitionists, such as Sarah and Angelina Grimke, William Bassett, and Abby Kelley. Within the context of this social movement, it appears that Douglass received her first opportunity to communicate her experience to whites concerning the Negro pew in Friends' meetinghouses. Beginning in 1837, after having been asked by William Bassett about racial discrimination in Friends' meetinghouses, Douglass wrote the first of merely a handful of letters about the Quaker Negro pew. These letters are the only examples of their kind documenting an African American Quaker's view of the public segregation practiced in Friends' meetinghouses.

Writing to William Bassett, Douglass asserted that if Friends "only knew the anguish this one common expression of theirs, 'this bench is for the black people—This bench is for the People of Color' inflicts on the sensitive and tender amongst us: if they knew how it shuts up the springs of life, and causes us to turn away from their Meetings weary and unrefreshed" spiritually, Friends "could not use it so often." Douglass hoped that the "darkness" that had "enveloped their [white Friends] minds on this point" might be lifted by drawing Quaker attention to the feelings of people who had been otherwise pushed to the margins of the Friends' community. Douglass then recounted how as a child during

Quaker meetings her "soul was made sad by hearing five or six times during the course of one meeting" a "language of remonstrance to those [whites] who were willing to sit by us." After such encounters, Sarah "often ... wept" and "at other times ... felt indignant, and queried in [her] own mind, are these people Christians?"[41]

As relayed by Douglass, the temporal social customs and arrangements—such as the Negro pew—hindered the spiritual equality and justice promised by the Christian message. Douglass was particularly eloquent in her depiction of the effects of racial prejudice on her late brother Charles. For Charles Douglass, the inconsistent conduct of "professing Christians was a stumbling-block" to his Christian faith. The racial prejudice and "contempt" of Friends, that "stung [him] almost to madness," also nearly "drove [Charles] to the very verge of Infidelity," in Sarah's recollection. As an adolescent who had apparently suffered from a terminal disease for some time, Charles's struggle with his faith was all the more poignant for his family, as there was concern that he would die an unbeliever.[42]

However, largely under the guidance of Grace Douglass, Sarah and Charles's mother, Charles came to understand that, in the words of the New Testament, "neither heights nor depths, principalities nor powers, things present nor things to come, shall ever be able to separate us from the love of God in Christ Jesus." This promise of Christianity that transcended the ways in which human beings distorted the message of its founder eventually attracted Charles back to the Christian fold. Nearing death, Charles renounced his earlier disbelief and professed, "glory to God, all is clear now." Charles then called out, "Oh Lord Jesus, take me to thine everlasting arms of love" shortly before dying. For Sarah Mapps Douglass, the debilitating impact of Quaker racial prejudice on her young brother provided a poignant example of the unnecessary constraints affecting African Americans who sought to be a part of the white-dominated Society of Friends. Charles Douglass, by recovering his faith at the end of his life, had, at least in part, "escaped from the suffering inflicted by scorn and prejudice" that many other African Americans confronted constantly from many Quakers.[43]

Nonetheless, the reaction among many Quakers to the efforts of Sarah Mapps Douglass and her white counterparts to expose the racial prejudice of the Society of Friends was apparently a mixture of silence and denial. As noted above, the *Friend* came out with a forthright denial in 1843 regarding the Negro pew, and the issue was never addressed again by this leading organ of orthodox Quakerism. In response to this denial, however, Sarah Mapps Douglass published an editorial in the *National Anti-Slavery*

*Standard* in which she debunked the myth that it was African American culture or society that explained the paucity of African American attendance at Quaker meetings. Sarah insisted that she had been told by many people of color in Philadelphia that they were attracted to the "still small voice" and "quiet" of Quaker meetinghouses but that they could not "bear the cross of sitting on the 'black bench.'" Sarah made a reference to her mother, Grace Bustill Douglass, who had attended Quaker meetings for decades while having to suffer the double insult of never being offered membership as well as of being seated on the Negro pew. Bustill Douglass told her daughter that she knew of many fellow people of color who would attend Quaker meetings but for the prejudice found there. Indeed, the Friends' maintenance of the color line must have been shocking to other free persons of color who observed the case of Grace Bustill Douglass. Grace was half European American, with only one grandmother who had actually been a slave. She was also financially independent and a social equal to the prominent Forten family. Yet for all her claims to respectability, she could not find decent treatment during worship from the Society of Friends in Philadelphia, and it remained that way until she died in 1842.[44] Grace Bustill Douglass's phenotypic identity trumped any effort to attain social equality with people who, under other circumstances, would have been her equals. It was this kind of racial prejudice that led Sarah to write bluntly of Friends that the "Lord has a controversy with Friends on this account. Let them see to it."[45]

Apparently few did. Complaints regarding the continued existence of the racial segregation within Friends' meetinghouses continued in the years ahead. The editor of the *Non-Slaveholder* mentioned the practice as one that has a "strong tendency to prevent the attendance" of African Americans to Quaker worship.[46] Sarah Mapps Douglass herself mentioned that she attended a Philadelphia meeting that sat her in the back as late as 1854 (it appears that changed at some point around the beginning of the Civil War).[47] In 1851, the African American abolitionist Samuel Ringgold Ward wrote that even as Friends "will aid in giving us a partial education," it would never happen "in a Quaker school, beside their own children."[48] Ward also found many Friends in the Philadelphia area to be "bitter and relentless negro despisers" who often "ridicule niggers."[49] Even though no known complaints of racial segregation came from the Midwest, it is still significant that the clerk of the Indiana Anti-Slavery Friends, Walter Edgerton, continued to write of Friends' racial prejudice in that supposedly more egalitarian setting. Without naming names, Edgerton recorded how when Indiana Friends faced the prospect of African

American emigration into their neighborhoods, they exhibited "as much prejudice . . . as in other people." "The say that [blacks] ought to be free but they do not want them in Indiana."[50]

On the other hand, for at least some abolitionists, the charges leveled at the Society of Friends from black abolitionists such as Douglass did have the effect of encouraging individual investigations on the part of whites regarding the status of African Americans within their church community. For example, Isaac Collins, after hearing Arnold Buffum's complaints at the World Anti-Slavery Convention in London in 1843 regarding the racial prejudice of Friends, decided to actually speak with those African Americans in his church who, "from their plain dress and address, and regular attendance at meetings, were generally supposed to be members" of the church. Yet after taking the trouble to meet with these potential Quakers, Collins discovered that they had in fact never been allowed membership in the Society of Friends. Though this episode demonstrates how the abolitionist movement fostered a greater understanding between white and black Americans on some level, the inability of white reformers to dismantle pervasive social prejudices testifies to the difficulties faced by abolitionists even from an anti-slavery religious community. Again, it appears that little came from Collins's encounter with Quaker racial prejudice in his meeting in terms of the extension of Quaker membership to persons of color.[51]

The challenges faced by white abolitionists attempting to revolutionize the Quaker meetinghouse would only further the interests of those reformers in the creation of new church communities where distinctions of race, class, or gender would be erased. If Quaker abolitionists could not accomplish such a transformation from within the Society of Friends, they would have to continue the "comeouter" process of establishing newer church institutions that would remain true to the Quaker promise of egalitarian fellowship. Yet the inspiration for new church communities grew out of the Quaker tradition; Sarah Mapps Douglass, like other reformers, saw her fight against racial prejudice through the lens of dissenting Protestantism. At least from Douglass's few extant writings, it appears that her identity as a Christian was more significant than the phenotypic identity imposed upon her by discriminatory whites. Appealing to an egalitarian strain of Christian tradition, abolitionists of whatever appearance sought to overturn temporal qualifications made by some on the promise of God's kingdom.

When reading Sewell's *History of the People Called Quakers,* Sarah Mapps Douglass's mind was drawn to the story of Barbara Blaugdon, who, while being mercilessly whipped for her beliefs, sang out to the Lord. Douglass appropriated the struggle of this white seventeenth-century Quaker as her own, and she prayed that "a double portion of [Blaugdon's] humility and fortitude" would descend upon African Americans facing white prejudice. White cultural symbols deriving from the persecution of English dissenters—so integral to the identity of many Anglo-Saxon Protestants—had crossed the racial divide in Douglass's mind; she too was standing up for the message of God's kingdom in a corrupt world. The promise of the peaceable kingdom remained greater for Douglass than all the economic, legal, and cultural inequality so often faced by African American Christians. Douglass saw the day when "black and white [will] mingle together in social intercourse, without a shadow of disgust appearing on the countenance of either." This great revolution, continued Douglass, would be brought about because of the pure Christianity preached by Quakers such as Blaugdon in every age; it would be the "religion of the meek and lowly Jesus" that would one day transform American race relations. "Could I not thus look forward," concluded Douglass, "I should indeed despair."[52]

# 4

## "Progressive" Friends and the Government of God

By the end of the 1840s, Hicksite Friends confronted efforts by abolitionists to align their meetings with the political agenda of the American Anti-Slavery Society. The evolving and ultimately opposing positions of members of the American Anti-Slavery Society and Hicksite leaders vis-à-vis anti-slavery demonstrated the extremely contested legacy of the Hicksite "reformation" of the Society of Friends. As a type of Quakerism that prided itself on a rejection of "worldly" endeavors such as the organs of organized evangelical benevolence, many Hicksite Friends proved especially wary of organizations that drew Quaker spirits away from their proper focus on God. This reaffirmation of a kind of mystical "quietism," or retreat from the contamination of conventional society, prevented many abolitionists from gaining much support in their attempts to bring political discussion of slavery into Hicksite meetings for worship. Eventually, the ongoing battles with clerical authorities over the responsibilities of their church to support different types of social activism led the abolitionist heirs of Elias Hicks to retreat from their churches and create new "comeouter" religious communities dedicated to a wide-ranging "universal reform" of race, gender, and class relations.

Reformers such as Lucretia Mott believed that the Hicksite reformation had involved more than a reassertion of traditional Quaker tenets in opposition to Protestant evangelical efforts to create a "united front" against Christian unorthodoxy and skepticism. Radical Hicksites such as Mott or the McClintock family interpreted the reformation as a battle of religious liberty against creeds or other creaturely activity hindering the free expression of Quakers in their meetings for worship. Quakers such as Mott believed that religious liberty often included efforts to infuse religious worship with "political" or even potentially seditious discussion concerning movements like abolitionism or, later, women's rights. Yet many Hicksites did not intend to go this far in their search for religious liberty, and in the context of an expanding abolitionist movement, the radicalism of Quakers such as Lucretia Mott or of Amy and Isaac Post quickly became controversial and divisive.

By 1846, Mott announced that she had "grown disgusted" with the "intolerant, proscriptive course of those in power [in Hicksite Quakerism]" regarding the rights of free religious expression. Mott's distaste for the "select meetings" of Quaker elders who conducted the business of the society, devised the disciplinary code, and played a large role in determining who would be "recommended" as a Quaker minister demonstrated lingering dissatisfaction with the outcome of the reformation of 1828.[1] During the 1820s, Mott's disappointment had been anticipated by the controversial women's rights activist and communitarian socialist Frances Wright. In an open letter to the Hicksite members of the Society of Friends in Wilmington, Delaware, in 1830, Wright lamented how "even in your reformed society, spiritual authority still coerces the mind, padlocks the lips and stops the ears against the words of truth." Wright continued: "the present habits of [your] society . . . place in the way of the young enquirer" many "hindrances" that "are truly . . . forcible and numerous."[2] The "young enquirers" referred to by Wright represented those Friends sympathetic with Frances Wright's and Robert Dale Owen's unconventional views regarding "orthodox" religion, the educational system, and wage labor.

A desire for "free enquiry" and for experimentation with different social and theological theories existed at the edges of the Hicksite reformation in the 1820s and early 30s. "Orthodoxy," whether political, social, or religious, had been attacked by these dissident Friends as an enemy to mankind. "Instead of listening to the voice of God in their consciences," asserted a Methodist minister sympathetic to the Hicksite reformation, conventional Christians "only listen to the eloquent voices of their sinister preachers and politicians."[3] The principles of "pristine purity" advanced by Hicksite Friends against the "orthodox" condemned attempts by the clergy in the United States to "deprive [people] of their civil, religious, and independent liberties."[4] Therefore, radical Hicksites placed great importance on the elimination of sectarian customs and "cursed aristocracies which are crushing the multitudes of the people."[5]

However, largely because of the extreme unpopularity of Frances Wright's and Robert Owen's deism and radical political views, these two leaders could not mobilize unorthodox Quakers in a similar fashion as would the abolitionist movement of the late 1830s and early 1840s. Within the context of abolitionism, however, the radical Hicksite concern with the dangers of coercion within American society would gain a greater sense of urgency when clerical authorities roundly condemned the agenda of the Anti-Slavery Society and shut the doors of their churches to abolitionists. In response, concrete attempts to reconstitute the Quaker community on radically different footing would be advanced by 1850, and meetings of "Progressive Friends," "Congregational Friends," and "Friends of Human Progress" came into being to advance numerous reform causes in the hope of ushering in the millennium.

Included among the Hicksite Quakers attempting to create new forms of religious community were many women who fused older protests against female inequity within Friends' meetinghouses to newer, broader demands for spiritual communion free from any man-made restraints on religious expression. Yet the previous experiences of many Quaker women within the Hicksite reformation probably eased their transition to support abolitionist efforts at comeouterism. For some time, an important demonstration of overbearing authority within the Society of Friends had been the fact that female Friends did not possess any power over the proceedings of the Meeting for Sufferings, the most powerful arm of the yearly meeting. The specific concern regarding women's equal status in Quaker meetings dated from at least the 1820s among some supporters of Elias Hicks. James Mott, for example, in 1820 wrote to his parents how the "distinction . . . made in the power of the men's and women's meetings for discipline" was to him impossible to justify. Mott hoped that as "we become more enlightened and civilized, this difference will be done away and the women will have an equal voice in the administration of the discipline."[6] The Philadelphia minister Jesse Kersey noted around 1830 that the "great change" having taken place regarding female education "in the last thirty years" has had the "important effect in bringing them out into greater degrees of independence." Kersey anticipated the day when female clerks would preside over Quaker meetings and when women's meetings would have greater power regarding the disciplinary proceedings of Friends.[7]

The fight against "orthodoxy," as outlined in the introduction, led many Hicksites to support the workingman's movement, and in particular the fight for universal public education. It is also clear that some Quakers—usually though not always Hicksite—had been receptive to the ideas of women's rights activists such as Mary Wollstonecraft, Harriet Martineau, and even the "notorious" Frances Wright, who received support from individual Quakers in her lecturing tours in the United States in the late 1820s. The *Delaware Free Press* reprinted an essay on the "Education of Women" that questioned why the "education of women should differ in its essentials from that of men." The essay further stated that the lack of a real education for women caused men to act in a manner of "selfishness and insolence" toward women for whom they had no "respect" since "a large class [of women] are taught less to think than to shine."[8] The *Free Press* later published the opinions of Robert Dale Owen on marriage in which he advocated altering marriage law in order for "married women to hold property."[9]

In a statement of her own early support for women's rights, Lucretia Mott, beginning in the late 1810s, lent her copy of Mary Wollstonecraft's *Vindication of the Rights of Woman* "when[ever] she could find readers."[10] The young Quaker poet Elizabeth Chandler had been sending her writing on women's rights and abolitionism to Benjamin Lundy's *Genius of Universal Emancipation* since 1826; in one essay Chandler wrote to a critic who disliked seeing a woman speak out on political subjects: "It is a restitution of *our own* rights for which we ask—their cause [that of the slave] is our cause—they are one with us in sex and nature."[11]

Emboldened by the abolitionist movement's head-on collision with hostile church leaders, many female Quakers joined their male counterparts in demands that meetings become more democratic and that the Society of Friends openly support the reforms such as immediatism. In this struggle, Quaker women redefined the boundaries of the traditional limits of Quaker womanhood, even though in their own minds they were simply carrying the rationale of female preaching to its logical conclusion. After all, women such as Lucretia Mott, Amy Post, Susan B. Anthony, or Martha Coffin Wright (as well as Unitarians such as Lydia Maria Child and Maria Weston Chapman) had been heirs to a dissenting Protestant culture that was far from hostile to aspects of women's social equality.

As so-called "mothers in Israel," Quaker women had always possessed certain privileges within the Quaker community not found in the larger Anglo-American world. Retaining supervisory authority regarding marriage as well as other aspects of sectarian morality, female Quakers were given an authority that few other Americans would have found agreeable. Quaker women were able to travel around the Western world—and sometimes beyond—to nurture the faithful, and, especially in the earlier days of the sect, to gain converts for "the children of light." Notably, nearly equal numbers of men and women brought the Quaker faith to the American colonies in the seventeenth century. Such visible roles for women, even when restricted to an exclusive religious community, nonetheless struck fear in the hearts of male observers who resisted any diminution of patriarchal authority.[12] But subtle changes in gender relations could not be halted by more traditional critics. Particularly after 1750, through various female "academies," Quaker women received opportunities for education that eclipsed those of their female counterparts. After the American Revolution and continuing into the early nineteenth century, Northern, upper-class women—including many Quakers—benefited intellectually from the rise of female seminaries. Such institutions paved the way for the entrance of women into the teaching profession, a previously male-only occupation.

Women also began to take an interest in public philanthropy after the republic's founding, fighting prostitution, aiding orphans, or supporting education projects. Historian Margaret Morris Haviland has argued that among female Philadelphia Quakers, the involvement of "enterprising young women" in charity work demonstrated how women could adopt "tasks commonly performed by men" such as "raising money, working with government officials, and managing complex business operations" to their benevolent endeavors.[13] This larger presence for women in the life of the young nation, though by no means an indication of gender equality, represented a growing belief in the necessity of female involvement in a republican society.

Catharine Beecher, the founder of a teaching academy in Connecticut, took seriously the view that women could greatly influence the moral character of the American nation, and she would have a profound influence on the life and thinking of many American women, including the Quaker Angelina Grimke. Beecher articulated the view that women were ideally suited to be moral leaders within their society because they possessed traits of self-sacrifice and submissiveness.[14] Though hardly a women's rights radical, Beecher's view regarding the female role in society nonetheless represented progress: women's education would improve the moral, social, and economic condition of all Americans. (Lucretia Mott later applauded the early efforts of Beecher that advocated "an improved condition of woman."[15]) While many historians have noted the confining nature of the Victorian idea of a "woman's sphere," the view that women were repositories of virtue would eventually fuel the demand for greater political rights. Furthermore, in the antebellum period, the ideology of the female sphere had also led to the growing influence of women in the life of America's churches. The feminization of church membership in the early nineteenth century has been noted by students of antebellum America, and many contemporaries would have agreed with the opinion of William Ware that true Christianity was in its perfection a "feminine" entity.[16]

Yet at the same time, and as more than one female abolitionist could attest, significant opposition existed in the antebellum republic to women's occupying roles that were seen as public, political, and "promiscuous." Such opposition became particularly evident during the early years of the American Anti-Slavery Society's campaign for immediatism. By galvanizing thousands of Northern Protestants—regardless of gender—to take up a moral crusade against slavery, the Anti-Slavery Society encouraged public female speech. But clerical authority tended to have different ideas about the gendered nature of social activism. One of the first skirmishes over the proper role of women relative to the discussion of political topics (such as slavery) occurred in 1837 in the aftermath of the Pastoral Letter sent out by leading Congregationalist ministers from Massachusetts declaring the duties for women "stated clearly in the New Testament" were strictly "unobtrusive and private." "Degeneracy and ruin" both for the church and the nation, continued the letter, were the inevitable outcome of women assuming rights and responsibilities reserved for men.[17]

In response to this rejection of female abolitionism, Sarah Grimke issued her "Letters on the Equality of the Sexes and the Condition of Women," in which she took on the gender inequality within the ministry; the "present organized system of spiritual power and ecclesiastical authority . . . is now vested solely in the hands of men" and represented the "fallacy . . . which forbids women to exercise some of her noblest faculties. . . ."[18] Angelina Grimke included the Society of Friends as an example of a religious institution that while recognizing women's spiritual equality, did not recognize their equality as "human beings" because women had "no voice in framing the discipline by which she is to be governed."[19] To Grimke, "[m]en and women were CREATED EQUAL; they are both moral and accountable beings, and whatever is *right* for man to do, is *right* for woman."[20]

Unfortunately, even many male abolitionists (though hardly all) feared the implications of women speaking publicly with men. At the World Anti-Slavery Convention of 1840, for example, British Quakers William

Allen and George Stacey put forth a resolution to exclude female delegates from the proceedings because of the customary arrangement that "in all matters of mere business" women were "not . . . a part of the working committee" to determine laws or resolutions. This view was challenged by several male abolitionists, most notably Wendell Phillips and George Thompson, but the prevailing opinion of the meeting was that the question of women's rights was a distraction from the proceedings and would "prove an apple of discord" to a movement already suffering from a lack of public credibility in places like the United States.[21] Yet the exclusion of female delegates would later be recalled by Elizabeth Cady Stanton as an occurrence that "roused" women to "distrust . . . all men's opinions on the character and sphere of women."[22]

The unequal status afforded women within the Anti-Slavery Societies, as well as the dislike of many male abolitionists toward female public speaking, only provided further motivation for female abolitionists to demand new rights. Angelina Grimke referred to her experiences fighting for the rights of slaves as the "high school" of all human rights, and it caused her to conclude that as long as women were not respected as "moral agents," no genuine reform movement in the world could possibly succeed.[23] Abby Kelley, who had never before addressed a "promiscuous assembly" when she rose to speak at Pennsylvania Hall in 1838, counted the experience as one propelling her to "plead the cause of God's perishing poor," regardless of clerical opposition to women's activism.[24]

However, women's equality was only one of many reasons for the estrangement of Quaker abolitionists from their meeting's authority figures, and the women's cause would exist beside other forms of un-Christian coercion identified by members of the American Anti-Slavery Society in the 1830s and 40s. Public confrontations over the uses of religious authority relative to social activism seemed to multiply wherever abolitionists organized petition campaigns or sought the use of churches for anti-slavery lectures. Amy Post wrote in 1844 how the "dead formality of attending meeting under the pretence of worship" when leaders censured individuals both male and female for involvement in abolitionism was creating much "suffering" among Quakers in New York.[25] Joseph Post, writing from Long Island, deplored the closing of meetinghouses to abolitionist lectures by Frederick Douglass and Abby Foster and chided Friends who were "compromising with evil" by supporting the crackdown on such lectures.[26] Post also criticized the sermons of several Quaker preachers, such as those given by Daniel Quimby, that "seemed to lack the life for these reform times" by making "no allusion to the present subjects that agitate the community."[27] Similar complaints were heard elsewhere. Isaac Hopper believed that the Society of Friends in New York City had "sank faster and deeper" than any "society of professing Christians" regarding social activism and was therefore becoming a "dead weight upon the reforms of the present day."[28]

Leading the charge against religious institutions retarding the liberating potential of Christianity, radical Hicksites from Indiana to New York began to demand clerical reform. However, the efforts met with mixed success. In 1837, Hicksite Quakers in Rochester, New York, sent up a petition to the Genesee Yearly Meeting asking that "the discipline be so alter'd that men and women shall stand on the same footing in all matters internal in which they are equally interested."[29] The meeting tabled the request, though it eventually conceded some disciplinary power to the women. At the Philadelphia Yearly Meeting of 1840, members of the Caln Quarter presented a petition requesting gender equality in spiritual matters, but the request was sent back and no change was made.[30] Beginning in 1843 within the New York Yearly Meeting, the Cornwall Quarterly Meeting desired that the yearly meeting discontinue the requirement that overseers visit with Quakers regarding infractions of the discipline, but the response was negative.[31] However, the New York Yearly Meeting did place men and women on equal footing in terms of the discipline. Some orthodox meetings in New England that had long been sympathetic to "new light" Quakerism were also being reprimanded in the 1840s on account of their support for "non-resistance" radicalism, and in the years ahead they faced the prospect of being collectively disowned.[32]

But it was in the Midwest where the seeds of discord first began to bear separatist fruit among Hicksite Quakers. In Ohio and Indiana, Joseph Dugdale directed protests against ministerial authority from the Green Plain Quarterly Meeting (that straddled both the Ohio and Indiana Yearly Meetings). Frustrated by the attempts of the anti-abolitionist Hicksite minister George White to crack down on members of his meeting, Dugdale and fifty-one other members of the Green Plain Quarterly Meeting published a minute in 1841 demanding that White "repent." "We feel bound as Friends . . . to utter publicly our solemn protest," continued the minute, against White's anti-abolitionist smear campaign. At about the same time, Green Plain desired that ministerial distinctions be done away with in an effort to promote a more egalitarian religious community as well as to guard against the abuses of power in the hands of men like White.[33] Instead of addressing their complaints, however, both the Ohio and Indiana Yearly Meetings issued declarations against certain "expressions" made by the Green Plain Quarter. One of the warnings from this period, issued by the Indiana Yearly Meeting, expressed a growing sense of alarm that "young Friends" were shirking their responsibility to maintain the "precious testimonies" of Quakerism. In an epistle signed by William McKimmey, leading Indiana Hicksites condemned the "neglect of the attendance of our religious meetings . . . a departure from primitive plainness in dress and address, and a disposition to unite and mingle with political parties, and those who are engaged in promoting the popular movements of the day." In their opinion, "all of [these tendencies] . . . draw away the mind from its proper dependence upon the inward Teacher, who never fails to direct aright, all those whose minds are staid on Him."[34]

Few records exist to detail the collapse of quietist Quakerism among the Hicksites in the Midwest, but in upstate New York, the young John J. Cornell (later a clerk of the yearly meeting) recorded how in 1844 a "heated acrimonious discussion" over abolitionism erupted "before the meeting," causing him to question his belief that the "immediate revelation" of the Holy Spirit was in fact "an unerring guide." After witnessing respected ministers "becoming angry with each other and manifesting that anger in harshness of tone and language," Cornell stopped attending meetings entirely. However, he eventually heard the voice of God tell him: "Though all men else forsake my law, it will not excuse thee." Finding relief in God's spoken word, Cornell soon returned to the Society of Friends.[35] Yet for many others, such happy endings did not occur. What proved to be painful arguments over reform and clerical power clearly shook many meetinghouses to their foundations, and as was so often the case, those demanding change were the ones who suffered most. In September 1843 the Ohio Yearly Meeting discontinued the Green Plain Quarterly Meeting over the objections of abolitionists, which meant that many of the members had been effectively disowned from the Society of Friends.[36]

Commenting on the arguments over clerical authority and reform within the Ohio Yearly Meeting, William Schooley, though not disowned himself, nonetheless believed his yearly meeting had acted in an "illegal" way and had manifested an "unsanctified, unholy spirit" toward the abolitionists. Far from being discouraged by the "signs of the times," however, Schooley believed the "spirit of reformation is on the wing and will never be stayed, till Zion knows an enlargement of her borders and truth triumphs over bigotry and superstition." Schooley continued: "the fundamental principles of the Society of Friends, will never be lost, but will become more and more revealed in its beauty and loveliness till it shall govern the universe of mind."³⁷ Schooley's optimistic take on the situation, however, was not realistic. Those reformers who demanded that religious fellowship be freed from sectarian custom, and from the traditional Quaker distaste for the mixing of religion and politics, were often unable or unwilling to return to the Society of Friends. While it remained unclear what Dugdale's supporters would actually do in the months and years ahead, some clearly desired to create a new society of some kind.³⁸

Pushing forward with their redefinition of Christian community were several Green Plain Friends, most notably Joseph Dugdale and Abraham Brooke, who launched the ephemeral Society of Universal Inquiry and Reform at the American Anti-Slavery Convention of 1843. This society, which met only in 1843, consisted of an entirely free forum for discussion; one attendee referred to it as an excellent example of an organization free from an "aristocratic business committee," "contentions," and "recognitions of color, caste, creed, sect, or sex."³⁹ Many participants in this society went away from it to establish various communitarian experiments in the upper Midwest and Northeast. Such communities epitomized the more ambitious implications of perfectionist "anarchic" Christianity. The preamble to one of the meetings of the universal reformers, for example, declared that "mankind should be regarded as an equal brotherhood, the joint proprietors of the soil and of all the products of human industry." Believing that a "better state of affairs can exist by organizing the social system in accordance with the principles of God's government," the universal reformers sought an "equality of rights and interests . . . secured to all." "We associate together," the document continued, in order "to inquire into our duties in relation to these subjects, and to enable us to perform them."⁴⁰

The meeting of the universal reformers coincided with the proliferation of communitarian socialist groups throughout the United States in the 1840s. Among the best-known communities included Adin Ballou's Hopedale community and the associations at Brook Farm and Northampton—all in Massachusetts. The Northampton Association was founded by the Quaker George Benson and posited the progressive notion that all people had the duty to perform productive labor and possessed an equal right to the fruits of that labor. This community desired that all share in a noncompetitive workplace, and they wanted an intellectual environment where the mind was liberated from the drudgery of conventional society.⁴¹ Scattered throughout the Northeast and Midwest, communities not dissimilar from Northampton attracted those spirits who, though disaffected with nineteenth-century American society, nonetheless possessed an expansive vision of divine transcendence brought about by new forms of human interaction. Those attracted to the communities sought a concrete expression of the government of God on Earth; the very real attempts to share wealth and banish overbearing forms of authority coexisted with a confident, romantic idealism bearing the imprint of mystical Christianity. Human government would be no more, economic competition and private property would vanish, women would be freed from lives of servitude, and education would be a right universally held by all. The communities rejected sectarian, exclusive definitions of Christianity, and they sought no guidance from ministers of any kind.[42]

If the degree of expectation were any measure of success, the communitarians inhabiting their antebellum cities of God would have achieved victory. As it turned out, however, these visionaries could not escape the centrifugal forces of conventional American society. Nor could they avoid personal conflict. John Collins, one of the universal reformers and founder of the Skaneateles community in New York, reported refusals to extend credit to the community, and he feared that one of the members was not a faithful trustee for the shared property. Collins believed his community needed a state charter to truly hold their real estate in common, but he was unable to secure one from the New York state legislature because he and his compatriots were viewed as "fools and fanatics."[43] Other differences occurred over diet, the amount and type of recreation (many Quakers were offended that dancing and card playing took place in the community), and over the form of government (if any). The lure of financial gain (the commune's real estate value had more than doubled, while the actual labor was not especially lucrative) also tempted members away. Perhaps more troubling was how Collins's community could not succeed without his leadership; though communities like Skaneateles were supposedly egalitarian, the fact remained that certain figures were the linchpins for these attempts to usher in God's government. One member later referred to Collins as possessing, "in his practical character, the elements of a perfect tyrant."[44]

Such obstacles facing the communitarian socialists have often caused historians to question the members' actual commitment to class revolution in America. Oftentimes, the similarities drawn between abolitionists and respectable early Victorian culture have obscured the meaning of abolitionism for Protestants often sympathetic to Christian reform. As has been noted, abolitionists and other evangelical Protestant reformers came predominantly from the ranks of prosperous agricultural and professional—if not genteel—white Americans. They subscribed to the moralistic values of middle-class Protestantism; it was not so much capitalism they hated as the abuse of it. The solution to the abuses of capital was not an overthrow of the superstructure, but rather an effort to find an Edenic state where capitalists and laborers were integrally associated in a less competitive economic system. Whatever type of socialism the radical abolitionists supported, it was not the type that sought out proletarian revolution.[45] The valence of Christian socialism moved its adherents toward the hope of spiritual transformation and greatly valued the potency of religious reawakening as the only sure foundation for human progress. In this way, whatever "political" activism the Hicksite reformers engaged in—petitioning legislatures, agitating for suffrage, demanding state-sponsored land reform—always coexisted with the ambiguous desire to elevate the spiritual contingencies of the world the reformers sought to change. Creating new religious institutions to forward God's government therefore occupied a great deal of importance for radical, Hicksite Quakers.

Notwithstanding that most of the cooperative communities founded in the 1840s had failed by the end of that decade, many of their supporters nonetheless moved ahead with other plans for the world's regeneration. The "universal reformers" and other disaffected Friends from the Midwest and Northeast would soon become involved in efforts in the East to create new, "progressive" meetings of Quakers. The "Marlborough Conference," held in Chester County, Pennsylvania, in 1845, debated the question of separation from the Pennsylvania Yearly Meeting. Agreement on this point did not exist even though a "Free Hall" was established for the discussion of reform.[46] By 1848 however, a much more potent experiment in comeouter religion would be advanced by certain members of the Hicksite Genesee Yearly Meeting in upstate New York. Between 1843 and 1848, the Genesee Yearly Meeting had consistently been occupied with calls from Michigan Quarterly Meeting for reform, and they decided in 1848 to "lay down" that meeting on account of its "disregard [for] the injunctions and . . . authority of the church."[47] In response, a number of other Quakers withdrew from the Genesee Yearly Meeting and, along with those from the Michigan Quarter as well as radicals from around the country, established the Congregational Friends at a convention in Waterloo, New York. Here they approved a "Basis of Religious Association," authored by Thomas McClintock, that was intended to be a clarion call to all reformers laboring in repressive ecclesiastical institutions.

"The object of religious association," asserted this document, "may be defined to be, the promotion of righteousness—of practical righteousness—love to God and man—on the part of every member composing the association." If an association is "instrumental to this end," posited the "Basis," then "it is Christian." Even as the Progressive Friends acknowledged their debt to Christianity, they moved the boundaries of Christian fellowship far beyond sectarian organizations; any congregation of individuals seeking "obedience to the evidence of Divine Light" would be included as working toward the kingdom of God.[48] "Christianity," the declaration continued, "respects [the] diversity in men aiming not to undo but further God's will." When man is "sacrificed to the masses in church or state—church or state becomes an offence, a stumbling block in the way of progress, and must end or mend." Progressive Friends believed that "the greater the variety of individualities in church or state, the better is it—so long as all are really manly, humane, and accordant." Disliking what it termed the "despotic power" of churches' "ascending scale of authority," the declaration stated its intention to fully abolish the ministry.[49] This, in theory, meant that any concerned soul would be able to give expression to the revelation of his or her conscience during meetings of these Friends. They would also reject any gender distinctions within meetings; "the equality of women will be recognized . . . so perfectly that in our meetings . . . men and women will meet together and transact business jointly." "Priestcraft" would be thus avoided; no member would receive the title of minister and therefore be viewed as possessing "superior means of Divine knowledge, than others."[50]

A similar declaration from the Pennsylvania Yearly Meeting of Progressive Friends openly denied the special divine illumination contained within Quaker meetings. Calling Friends' claims to sectarian exceptionalism the "acme of superstition and imposture," Progressive Friends decreed that the "claim of organic communion with God lies at the root of many evils in the Churches around us, and hence we desire to make our denial of its validity as emphatic as possible." These Friends asked, "When will the people learn that there is nothing Divine, nothing too sacred for investigation, in the artificial arrangements and prescribed formalities of sects?" By advancing ecumenical spirituality, the Progressive Friends sought not a liberation from religion, but a more inclusive version of it. Rather than define their fellowship in terms of secretive, mystical truths, Progressive Friends sought out that which is holy among all whose greatest "aspiration . . . [is] the world's moral improvement."[51] Christian faith and works were interchangeable for these Quakers, a marked departure from the conventional belief that faith must exist in a Christian antecedent to works. It then followed that the Christian church was not confined to believers of a nominal theology. "Jesus enjoins it upon his hearers to 'seek first the Kingdom of God and His righteousness'; but the popular Church practically tells us, on pains of eternal perdition, to seek first of all the *theology* of that kingdom." It was fallacy to assure Christians "that if [they] only master" a faith in Jesus "that . . . the *righteousness* may safely . . . be left to take care of itself!"

Because churches had misunderstood the very basis of Christianity, to the Progressive Friends it was not surprising that "insatiate Wealth tramples upon lowly Poverty; that War's 'red thunders' reverberate around the world; . . . that Land Monopoly grinds humanity in the dust" and "that immortal beings are driven to their daily toil under the lash . . . when the Church proffers absolution for such crimes upon terms so easy of fulfillment" as acceptance of a creed.[52] Yet the hope of the Progressive Friends lay in their vision of a perfected church that would be the beacon of true spirituality as well as the conveyor of human progress toward the Age of the Spirit. Because they emphasized the potential for humans to bring about the reign of the Prince of Peace, many Progressive Friends united with Andrew Jackson Davis's "Harmonical Philosophy" that anticipated the end of the present era's "ignorance, superstition, fanaticism, and intolerance." In a day not far off, argued Davis, men "shall be as one Body, animated by Universal Love and governed by pure Wisdom." "Man's future," continued Davis, "is glowing with a beautiful radiance."[53] Davis was the leading American spiritualist at the time of the Progressive Friends' founding, and many reformers frequented seances in search of spirit "rappings." Just beneath the visible surface of their present existence, it seemed to these Quakers, the Holy Spirit itself lay in waiting to regenerate a sinful world.

But more than simply waiting on the spirit to mend the world's problems, many of the comeouter Hicksites committed themselves to a political reform of the present age. The meetings of Progressive Friends or Friends of Human Progress were "designed to embrace . . . the various branches of Reform," to create an environment where "every work of Reform" would benefit from a "Universal Unity" to promote the "welfare of mankind," and where worship was "subservient to the progress of practical piety and Philanthropy." Speakers at the meeting need not fear that they would be disciplined or "disowned for no cause save their activity in reformatory associations."[54] By constructing a religious community on the basis of "practical" Christianity, the Progressive Friends opened their fellowship to the supporters of many causes: lectures against slavery, intemperance, capital punishment, and sabbatarianism were common features of the meetings. So too were lectures demonstrating support for the workingman's and women's rights movements.

Because of the commitment of many Progressive or Congregational Friends to communitarian cooperatives, a real interest existed in so-called "land reform." This small movement, which would later find support from George Henry Evans's National Reform Association, advanced the view that "man . . . has the right to land enough to raise a habitation on." "Deprive anyone of these rights and you place him at the mercy of those who possess him."[55] Support existed among land reformers for the distribution of free public lands to actual settlers, for a limitation of the quantity of land held by any one individual, and for an exemption of homesteaders from debt.[56] Many supporters of the Progressive Friends agreed, believing that state-supported land monopoly had deprived poorer citizens of proper avenues to advancement in American society. Lucretia Mott, an attendee at several meetings of Progressive Friends, believed that "Christian democracy" would banish "aristocracy," and she hoped that "monopolies" of both land and business, which allowed the "rich to become richer, and the . . . poor to become poorer and poorer," would soon vanish.[57] Among the many lectures given at various meetings of Congregational or Progressive Friends included those on land reform, and some meetings sent petitions in support of the ten-hour day.[58] Members of the Congregational Friends in Waterloo established a Working Women's Protective Union in 1848.[59] These unions sought to publicize the plight of unskilled female workers and give tentative support for wage demands or other protective legislation before state legislatures. Such labor reform efforts represented a certain degree of cooperation between more propertied women and their lower-class counterparts.

Yet the reform that would later be most associated with the Progressive Friends was women's rights. Forwarding their long-abiding interest in the social and political equality of women, Lucretia Mott and Elizabeth Cady Stanton met in the same locale as the newly formed meeting of Congregational Friends to issue a call for a women's rights convention at Seneca Falls, New York. With the help of Martha Wright and Mary Ann McClintock, this meeting convened on July 19, 1848, and issued its famous "Declaration of Sentiments." The Quaker presence at this meeting was strong: Lucretia Mott, Susan B. Anthony, and Mary Ann McClintock were all Hicksite Friends, and the convention was chaired by Lucretia's husband James. Mary Ann's husband Thomas McClintock, the author of the Progressive Friends' "Basis of Religious Association," also played a prominent role in the proceedings. The 1848 "Declaration of Sentiments" demanded female suffrage, called for an end to coverture, desired more equitable divorce legislation, and decried the closing to women "of all avenues to wealth and distinction which" men consider "most honorable."[60]

Taking note of these proceedings and agreeing with them wholeheartedly, the various meetings of Progressive or Congregational Friends issued their own endorsements of female suffrage and women's rights. As the New York Yearly Meeting of Congregational Friends addressed women in their state, "the idea that God himself has ordained" the degradation of women unites on all sides "to crush her; to bring her so low that the bright sky is shut out from her view, and she is not conscious that were she to throw from her the weight that so crushes her, worlds of light and beauty would break upon her delighted vision."[61] "Her right to the free and full exercise of the Elective Franchise with its duties and responsibilities," continued the meeting, "is based upon the principle of inseparability of representation from taxation, of governments deriving their just powers from the consent of the governed." "To obtain the rights so long denied . . . [women] must send petitions to the Legislature." It was nothing less than a duty for women everywhere to "importune the unjust portion of community until" rights have been restored. Women can "write for the public press, and procure the insertion of useful articles calculated to rectify public opinion." "You," continued the meeting of Friends to female New Yorkers, "can labor with the tongue and pen—'those who would be free, themselves must strike the blow.'"[62]

The purpose of progressive Quakerism was clear: not only would a moral revolution be needed to end coercion in society, but concrete political demands—such as the demand for female suffrage—would also play a crucial role in ushering the millennium. Progressive Quakerism was not simply an attempt to reconstitute Quaker quietism on purer footing; it was a movement that, however hesitatingly, engaged the halls of state power with radically unpopular causes. Along with their ecumenical spirituality, the Progressive Friends' desire to merge political movements with worship signaled a modernization of Quakerism. Seeking after tangible results for sacred worship caused Progressive Friends to reject anything that resembled sectarian "bigotry" and to value religious institutions only to the extent they offered social change. Such a desire possessed only limited similarities with the more orthodox Anti-Slavery Friends because the agenda of Progressive Friends moved far beyond abolitionism and severed most theological ties with Quakerism. The more orthodox Anti-Slavery

Friends had, after all, claimed not to be modifying, but strengthening, the basic tenets of Quakerism in making their anti-slavery testimony more rigorous. Among the Progressive Friends, however, the true and only perfect function of religion was found in uniting with any concerned soul to bring about social and political reform under the aegis of God's government. Unlike the Anti-Slavery Friends, who reunited with the Indiana Yearly Meeting in 1857, many Progressive Friends never returned to Quakerism.

Progressive Friends also attracted non-Quaker membership in far greater numbers than the Anti-Slavery Friends. Abolitionists of no less importance than William Lloyd Garrison, Oliver Johnson, and Theodore Parker attended meetings of Progressive Friends, particularly those at Longwood, Pennsylvania. By drawing in these leading abolitionists, the Progressive Friends demonstrated how marginal definitions of "Quakerism" could be appropriated by certain prominent social activists and used in ways most leading Quakers disliked. Garrison, who as early as 1835 had written to friends that his "religious sentiments" most resembled those of "Barclay, Penn, and Fox," interpreted his struggles against sabbatarianism and a "pro-slavery clerisy" as a latter-day fight on behalf of the early Quakers' unpopular cause of Christian perfection. "This world can never be redeemed," Garrison pronounced, "until it be received into the hearts, and acted out in the lives, of the professed followers of Christ."[63] After having begun to attend meetings of Progressive Friends, Garrison referred to these Quakers as "free and truth-loving spirits," and he hoped they would continue their brave experiment in "practical righteousness; the discovery of truth, and its application . . . to individuals and communities."[64]

Oliver Johnson, a man who had been raised among the "high church party" within Congregationalism, appropriated the image of "one Quaker" shaking the "country for twenty miles around" when he defiantly came out from fellowship with a church that had criticized both female preaching and the lecturing tours of abolitionists. Johnson had grown disgusted with what he termed the "parish popes" of Congregationalism who "would have stopped the mouth of any other person whose humanity impelled him to remember those in bonds as bound with them." For a time, Johnson attended meetings of the Society of Friends, but he found that his views regarding the need for churches to actively pursue the reforms of the age made him unpopular among leading members of the church. In one incident, known in the abolitionist press as the "Marlborough Affair," Johnson was forcibly ejected from a Quaker meetinghouse in Marlborough, Pennsylvania, after two leaders, Humphrey Marshall and Benjamin Parker, deemed his preaching to be of a "disorganizing" character. Johnson was then prosecuted in court by Marshall, Parker, and others for disturbing the peace and was fined by the judge.[65] After having lived under the weight of an oppressive clerisy that included not only Congregationalists but also most leaders of the Society of Friends, Johnson came to the conclusion, as had Garrison, that "nothing was too holy for examination" and that man's own "conviction" must remain "paramount to all human authority."[66] Therefore, Johnson found himself joining with other iconoclast reformers under the banner of free discussion at meetings of the Progressive Friends at Longwood. Quakerism, to men such as Johnson and Garrison, was synonymous with radical social activism. Representing a countercultural experiment where Victorian womanhood, racial prejudice, and class injustice were put under intense scrutiny, the "Quakerism" advanced by men such as Johnson and Garrison proved to be far more oppositional to American society than that of the vast majority of the Society of Friends' leaders.

The two thousand or so attendees of the various meetings of Congregational or Progressive Friends were, therefore, far ahead of their time. Racial equality, land reform, women's rights, opposition to capital punishment, and modernist Christianity were not widely supported in antebellum America. As the meager numbers of Progressive Friends would indicate, the vast majority of Quakers agreed with the *American Republican*'s pronouncement regarding Progressive Friends as an assortment of "long-haired men and short-haired women" who were "plotting revolution" and who would better serve the community in a "snug little asylum."[67] Only making matters worse was the attraction felt by Garrisonian abolitionists for Progressive Quakerism. The work of these abolitionists to usher in a "millennial period" where human society will "shake off its particular prejudices" was referred to by the *Friends Weekly Intelligencer* as a "useless and abortive attempt" to interfere with the existing institution of the Society of Friends. This institution, claimed the editorial, provided the proper restraints on human reason by subjecting all "impracticable schemes of reform" to the scrutiny of divine wisdom.[68] Such "schemes" included the various "communist" communities that, in the eyes of Hicksite leaders, were attempting to uproot "the whole fabric of past and present institutions [by] withdrawing from the individual his principle incentive to labor." Any attempt to usher in a "social millennium" was more or less condemned as un-Christian by the *Friends Weekly Intelligencer*: communism would "subvert the whole design of [the] divine Author" by denying the necessity of creating government for the restraint of "poor, fallen, imperfect, and unregenerate man. . . ."[69]

If men such as Oliver Johnson and William Lloyd Garrison could claim adherence to Quaker doctrines in their support for the abolitionist movement, many other Hicksite Friends also could muster defenses of Quaker quietism solidly rooted in the cosmology of Elias Hicks. Although Hicks died before the creation of the American Anti-Slavery Society, he had been an early opponent of voluntary associations that supposedly operated not out of God's understanding, but out of man's. Many Hicksite leaders in the antebellum era demanded that Quakers attend to the state of their souls and to the spiritual communion of Quaker meetings as the paramount means of leavening the world with the regenerative power of Christ's kingdom.

This rejection of "creaturely" human activity could lead to a type of stance regarding the world that tended toward political conservatism. For Jesse Kersey, Hicksite leaders must speak out against the American Anti-Slavery Society because those Quakers in the organization had "wander[ed] away from the true guide" of Quakerism, God's will.[70] These opinions were further expounded upon by the respected, if outspoken, New York Hicksite George Fox White. In his letters and sermons, White leveled powerful indictments of the Anti-Slavery Society's "worldly" efforts to free slaves. While White demanded that Friends support the free produce movement and that they personally support Christian efforts to keep slaveholders from religious fellowship, White believed that the Anti-Slavery Society had been guilty of "relying upon its own arm for success" instead of that of the Holy Spirit by entering into political debates regarding the means of emancipation in the United States.[71] For White, only "the revealed will of God" constituted a "sure foundation" for bringing about moral change in the world. Evil could not be defeated by "human philanthropy" guilty of using coercion to impose social change on society.[72] Hicksite Quakers such as White doubted that abolitionists could ever hope to legislate morality or otherwise impose an alternative racial order on men and women by entering the political world outside the meetinghouse.

White's fear that Quakers were "depending" upon exogenous social movements for the spiritual sustenance properly provided only by Quaker meetings demonstrates how protests against the "worldliness" of antebellum American society possessed implications for many Hicksites as conservative as those for the Progressive Friends were radical. White's and others' definition of the Quaker cosmology of social change revealed that many Friends—along with hundreds of thousands of other Protestants—disagreed with the theological underpinnings of romantic reform in the nineteenth century. Given that many abolitionist reformers also sought a redefinition of gender roles in American civil society, opposition to abolitionism took on a gendered meaning as well. Many Quaker women expressed displeasure at the radical social experiments devised by certain social activists from within their religious community. Emma Kimber was glad that the leading female Hicksite Quaker Elizabeth Jackson had managed to remain "free from all new-fangledness": "Unitarianism, Anti-Slavery, peace-societies, and Mary Wollstonecraft" extremism.[73] Such "new-fangledness" only worked to the destruction of the Society of Friends. Rachel Hicks reportedly spoke to other Hicksites regarding the "devastation and desolation . . . originating in modern abolition," the "foundation of all other delusions leading to skepticism and infidelity."[74] In her own words, Hicks regretted that "a spirit [seeking] to lay waste to the order and discipline of our Society" tended to "undermine our faith in the teachings of Jesus." It was a great error, in her opinion, for reformers to rely on their "own understanding and human reason" when addressing problems within the Society of Friends.[75] In a much more caustic vein, Edith Smith, writing of radical Friends in New England supportive of nonresistance and "new light" Quakerism, believed that if a certain, unspecified meetinghouse was "to be burnt down, it would help matters greatly."[76]

The voice of institutional reaction against Progressive Quakerism, then, was not only male. The women who denounced the innovations of the Progressive Friends attached paramount importance to the unity and strength of the Society of Friends; the Society was a social movement of its own. Even as other women clamored for changes in gender, class, and ecclesiastical relations among Friends, most female leaders of the Society of Friends rejected movements that sought to denude the distinct sectarian community they had, in many cases, been raised in. Skeptical female Quakers would have agreed with the *Friend*'s view of the gendered nature of their community: "the influence . . . of women on the interests of man and of religion is that of curbing the development of unrestrained reasoning and over-confidence in its powers." Because men were "much more predisposed and fitted for controversial exercise, while simple and unquestioning faith seems to be an easier attainment of women," the rational innovations of reformers were a detriment to the proper restraints of feminine Quaker influence.[77]

It is also worth noting that leading Hicksite Friends disavowed spiritualism, a movement supported by many Quaker women's rights activists, most notably Amy Post, and one that advanced female equality by allowing women to be mediums for the communication of spirits in mixed company. Like communism, spiritualism was accused of being an anti-

Christian and anti-theistic movement: "the attributes of Deity are questioned by a belief in the reality of these performances [and] the omnipresence and omnipotence must be denied the Supreme by the doctrine" of spiritual communion with the dead.[78] By attacking spiritualism and noting that Quaker meetings in no way supported seances, Friends, like many Americans, believed that spiritualism represented that kind of "heathen idolatry" that worked to undermine our "present enlightened and social state." In similar fashion as "Socialism, Free-love-ism, and Mormonism," those who rejected Christianity for spiritualism were in danger of being "debase[d]" to "little better than" brutes.[79] Clearly an association existed in the minds of many Quakers between women's rights and atheism, "demonology, and "witchcraft." Such was the stigma attached to those who worked for a redefinition of accepted understandings of separate gender spheres.[80] Quaker understandings of the purpose of "mothers in Israel" provided powerful resistance to more robust demands for female equality.

By attacking the various forms of religious heresy and social radicalism advanced by the Progressive Friends, leading Hicksite Quakers evinced support for the perceived virtues of an American, Christian republic, and separated respectable religious dissent from "ranterish," "millennial," and potentially treasonous spiritual anarchy. As in "civil polity the worst of all evils is anarchy, so in religion and philanthropy the most dangerous state is ranterism," followed an editorial in the *Friends Intelligencer*. From "ranterism," continued the editorial, proceeds a "disposition to tear down, but not to build up—to uproot and destroy the good and the evil together—to lay waste the labours of past generations and overturn" all "landmarks" of human society. The *Intelligencer* pleaded with Friends to remain within the "kingdom of Christ" and eschew worldly political movements: "Let us labor here [in God's kingdom], and doubtless the harvest will be abundant, without seeking in political turmoil to sow the wind, from which assuredly we shall reap the whirlwind."[81]

The reaction of most Hicksites to the Progressive Friends' interests in a "universal reform" of gender, class, and race relations, as well as to the anarchic implications of their religious community, paralleled that of conservatives throughout the United States. These thinkers included many pro-slavery Southerners, who, in the words of one sympathizer, feared that abolitionism would lead to "Socianism, Universalism, Deism, Socialism, Fouriourism, Millerism" and all other "isms" that strike "at the very vitals of the social compact, and must unhinge the foundations of law and government."[82] The Progressive Friends pushed the egalitarian doctrines of Quakerism to limits that seemed ridiculous to nearly all white Americans; anti-slavery Northerners—Quakers among them—found themselves sounding alarms in like fashion to those who feared for a nation bereft of slavery's social order. The Progressive Friends, to the extent that they supported a strain of anarchism that denounced the evil of all social and legal coercion, represented for most Americans the epitome of irresponsible reform. With this representation, the comeouter Hicksites revealed the limits of Northern anti-slavery sentiment that eschewed attacks on the many accepted inequalities of the American republic.

Hicksite Quakers, in concert with most American Protestants, tended to extol the virtues of their republic when faced with abolitionism, even if they admitted the damaging potential of slavery's existence within that republic. "Universal reform" remained the stuff of "visionary and impracticable schemes," destined to "increase, rather than to diminish, the evils which they are intended to rectify."[83] Hicksite Friends were told to cast their lot with a cohesive American state: "if the allegience [sic] of a peaceful, order-loving, non-resistant body of Christians was ever due any form of civil government, surely it is to one which approaches the nearest to that equality of individuals, the characteristic of the true church of God."[84]

For those who took part in the "universal reform" of Progressive Quakerism, however, hope remained that their intrepid communities would go beyond the perceived equality supposedly extant within the United States to accomplish the true equality of souls promised in God's kingdom. Most of their opponents among the Society of Friends, who placed great importance on the value of social stability and who decried innovations within Quaker communities were, in the opinion of Joseph Post, mistaken: "those who look on the Society of Friends as the ark of truth and safety must feel sad to see it in so shattered a state" because they "feel as though the preservation of every thing good depended on their organization." Post could not understand the sorrow of most Quakers who "seem not to realize that truth and right are spreading among the people."[85] Sarah Thayer of New York also took a more positive view of the divisions among Hicksite Quakers, although her remarks revealed a tinge of anger regarding Friends' skepticism toward her cause: "The economy, sobriety, and habits of diligence which were the legitimate offspring of true christian laws ought to have produced better results [among Friends]. But as all organized relations need to be supplanted by advances—so I for one feel no regret at all." Rather, continued Thayer, "I rejoice . . . that I have lived to see the structure so far demolished, and hope yet to be able to view the ruins where, figuratively speaking, there shall not be one stone left unturned."[86] By "coming out" of older religious institutions, Quaker reformers believed they were supplanting failed churches with ones better equipped to "be in advance of the social ideas of the age." The clergy, in the reformers' opinion, must no longer simply "organize sects, but society."[87] Soon enough, this reorganization of American clerical power would include the very union so often touted by mainstream clergy as in need of preservation from reckless reform. Meetings of Progressive Friends often declared that "No Church, no Government, no Constitution, no Union . . . can have any bearing on our conscience" if those institutions "supported crimes" such as slavery.[88] In their movement to usher in the government of God, many Quaker comeouters would soon boldly attempt to supplant an existing "pro-slavery" American government with one that would indeed herald the perfect freedom promised by Christ's second coming.

# 5

# Quaker Pacifism and Civil Disobedience in the Antebellum Period

The search for new forms of religious community that would serve an abolitionist-led revolution in American race relations encouraged Quaker members of groups such as the Anti-Slavery Friends, Progressive Friends, and Congregational Friends to advance peaceful strategies for civil disobedience against slaveholding government. In many ways, the intractability of antebellum American politicians regarding the slavery issue radicalized the abolitionist movement and forced supporters of immediate emancipation to place their faith in other-worldly transformations of American civil society. The comeouters' mixture of eschatological hope and temporal reform gave institutional expression to the belief that, in the words of James Birney, government "inspired by divine precepts is the only one which will stand."[1] Rooted in their faith in "moral suasion" to reform individual beliefs and behavior, the abolitionists' search for the government of God led them to advocate specific, personal commitments on the part of Christians for the rejection of all legal structures buttressing slaveholding in the United States. By demanding that all Americans refuse to vote for the legislators of a slaveholding government, by publicly encouraging slaves to run away from their masters, and by advising anti-slavery churches to advertise their rejection of a union with slaveholders, Quaker abolitionists challenged the Society of Friends to make its critique of state power embodied in the Quaker peace testimony synonymous with abolitionism.

While all Quakers maintained opposition to war, the implications of their pacifism produced significant conflict among members of the church in the 1840s and 50s. Confronted with controversial uses of pacifism by abolitionist reformers, leaders of the Society of Friends entered into a debate with abolitionists regarding the implications of the Quaker peace testimony for the world's largest slaveholding republic. This evolving dialogue between Quakers and abolitionists regarding the commitment of Christians to immediatism continued to resemble other arguments in early America over the limits of, and necessary restraints on, religious liberty; Friends used language about abolitionists similar to that being mobilized in the popular campaigns against Masons, Catholics, and Mormons in the middle decades of the nineteenth century. By using these ideas prevalent in the culture of American Protestantism to cut off institutional support for the abolitionist movement, Quakers demonstrated how fears about the threats to religious liberty could advance prejudice toward aspects of a pluralistic society. Because there was not yet anything violent about the abolitionists' critiques of the U.S. government in the 1830s and 40s, leading Friends' denunciation of abolitionism provides a notable example of the nearly insurmountable cultural resistance facing those Protestants who advocated immediate emancipation in the antebellum period.

In the two decades before the American Civil War, leaders of the Society of Friends strove to delineate limits around which their followers might search for the kingdom of God, a state of existence—free from man-made instruments and institutions of coercion—that underpinned the Quaker testimony against war. Their church's critique of state power always possessed the implication of an outright rejection of all human authority; the antinomian search for a community guided only by the Holy Spirit could spell the destruction of man-made entities such as the government of the United States. Seeking to prevent the pacifism of the church from being linked to a political movement, the Friend Elisha Bates wrote that the Quaker peace testimony was a private affair that always left "the rest of the world in the quiet possession of their own principles."[2] When confronting the reality of abolitionists flouting laws regarding fugitive slaves or demanding that the American government be superseded by an ambiguous, other-worldly kingdom of God, leading Friends made it clear that Quakers had at that time and had always owed "submission to the mandates of the law."[3] Other leaders of the church, such as Jesse

Kersey, rejected the idea that civil disobedience in the name of Quaker pacifism could in fact be implemented without violent consequences; Kersey believed that the abolitionists' agitation would be likely to advance a "state of warfare," regardless of the intentions of the avowedly peaceful reformers.[4] Using much stronger language, the New York Quaker George Fox White accused abolitionists of "mustering under the crimson banner of treason."[5]

The unconventional desire that Christian perfectionism properly applied could abolish unjust laws and transcend the conventional political process cut across the spectrum of abolitionist commitment, even as the American Anti-Slavery Society split into two factions in 1840 over the diverging movements of "no human government" and the Liberty Party. As Lewis Perry has written, the differences in tactical philosophy between the American Anti-Slavery Society and the American and Foreign Anti-Slavery Society had not obscured the basic commitment of all abolitionists to the belief that the kingdom of God could be established by individual conversion and that the "techniques of universal escape from sin" could be applied "to the moral problem of slavery."[6] In the context of antebellum America, such beliefs definitely had political implications. For the Quaker comeouters studied here, the schism of 1840 had not overshadowed the common characteristic of all abolitionists: they were prophets heralding a new dispensation set in direct opposition to the American state. In their search for the government of God, all comeouters would have agreed with the ideas of Adin Ballou, who wrote that the "millennium and kingdom [of God] must be *within* men, before it can ever be *around* them. Let us have the spirit of the millennium, and do the works of the millennium. Then will the millennium have already come." If men and women learned their proper duties in anticipation of God's kingdom as individuals then there was hope that "finally may all human governments be superseded by the divine government."[7]

Seeking to refashion church communities to make them vehicles of the government described by Ballou, Quaker abolitionists and their allies began to distinguish aspects of the American Anti-Slavery Society's rejection of the conventional political process from the quietism practiced by Friends. In the first place, the simple fact that many members of the Society of Friends voted for candidates for public office who had not denounced the American nation's legal acceptance of slavery revealed to abolitionists how most Quakers failed to apply their church's anti-slavery testimony to American civil society. All abolitionists consistently demanded that leaders of the Society of Friends dissociate themselves from a political system tainted by slavery. For example the *National Anti-Slavery Standard* believed that leaders of the Society of Friends must condemn "its members who dishonor their [anti-slavery] professions by helping to raise to the chief magistracy a slaveholder and a warrior."[8] In the words of the Anti-Slavery Friends, many Quakers had "gone a whoring after the gods of the slaveholders" by having voted for Henry Clay's ascension to "the guardianship of the liberties of the people [as president]." Because they had supported slaveholders and anti-abolitionists for public office, Friends were "guilty of as great an inconsistency as it would be to employ an infidel to preach the gospel."[9] Writing in 1849, after the election of Zachary Taylor as president, Charles Osborn, one of the leaders of the Anti-Slavery Friends, chastised members of the Society of Friends in Indiana for employing their "elective franchise for the elevation of Slavery and War ... in voting for a most incorrigible slaveholder and military chieftain" for president.[10]

Furthering this commitment to reject the laws of a government stained by the "heart's blood of helpless innocents," many abolitionists, Garrisonian and anti-Garrisonian alike, gave support to the illegal liberation of slaves. The so-called "Underground Railroad" had represented the subversive potential of the abolitionist movement for several decades and fed white fears of black rebellion within a slaveholding nation through the destruction of millions of dollars of human private property. But the open allegiance of abolitionists to illegal efforts at emancipation had not been popular with gradualist Quakers; many leaders of the Society of Friends remained fearful of any anti-slavery efforts that smacked of active resistance to the law. In contrast to the American Anti-Slavery Society, the Pennsylvania Abolition Society (an organization officially opposed to immediatism), while going to great lengths to legally free slaves, had nonetheless insisted that freedom for African Americans be achieved within the law. This was seen by immediatists as insufficient. As Amos Phelps believed, "slavery can never be remedied on principles which assume the legitimacy" of the slave owners' property.[11]

The continuing efforts of Quaker abolitionists to personally defeat the claims of slave owners to their property linked their church's anti-slavery testimony to a more robust attack on the federal laws of the American slavepower. The Anti-Slavery Friends, not long after their creation, advised slaves in the South to "obtain your liberty without violence," and declared that slaves were "under no obligation to endure [slavery] one moment longer."[12] The Anti-Slavery Friends also petitioned the governor of Missouri in 1844 when three men were incarcerated in the state prison after having aided fugitive slaves to freedom. Demonstrating their contempt for the fugitive slave law, the petition declared that the imprisonment of individuals who helped self-liberated slaves to freedom was a "violation of just law."[13]

Responding to Quaker opposition to the Underground Railroad, the Anti-Slavery Friends boldly rejected any "man-fearing, popularity-seeking spirit" that sought to appease slaveholding government. Revealing the influence of anarchic ideas on these comeouters, the Anti-Slavery Friends appealed to a higher law than that of the United States government by declaring that slaves were under "no moral obligation" to serve their masters and that all Quakers, by helping slaves escape to freedom, "should obey [God] rather than man, to do unto others as we would [have done] unto us."[14] The sentiments of comeouter groups such as the Anti-Slavery Friends, Progressive Friends, or Congregational Friends proclaimed a belief that the peaceful rejection of human laws upholding the institution of slavery would in fact succeed in advancing a moral revolution among American public opinion. Support for African American freedom by all Christians represented a moral commandment; for "this much injured and hunted race, in this land of boasted freedom, there is no rest to the soles of their feet until they set them on British soil." Anti-Slavery Friends believed that aiding the efforts of slaves to escape bondage should be "embrace[d] as a duty" by all Americans.[15]

The example of the Ohio Friend Richard Dillingham revealed the willingness of certain abolitionists to disobey the legal sanction for slavery and demonstrated the personal sacrifice many activists made during their struggle against the "slaveocracy." While in Tennessee in 1849, Dillingham was caught by authorities while trying to escort three slaves from the state, sentenced to three years in prison (the minimum sentence for "slave-stealing"), then died in jail during a cholera outbreak in Nashville.[16] Though Dillingham had been careful in his trial to emphasize that he had acted alone, his case signaled to many Northerners (and to even more Southerners) the dangers of zealous abolitionism. The words and actions of Thomas Garrett, a Quaker abolitionist in Delaware who claimed to have brought 2,038 slaves to freedom by the mid-1850s, also did not do much to assuage the fears of moderate Northerners regarding the Underground Railroad. When faced with prosecution, Garrett was far more outspoken than Dillingham regarding his intentions to undermine the American slavepower: "I am called an Abolitionist," declared Garrett, "and I now pledge myself, in the presence of this assembly, to use all lawful and honorable means to lessen the burdens of this oppressed people, and endeavor, according to ability furnished, to burst their chains asunder, and set them free." Garrett desired to continue doing so as long as one "slave remains to tread the soil of the state of my adoption—Delaware."[17]

Throughout the 1840s, the attitude of Quaker abolitionists such as these exemplified their growing acceptance of strategies of civil disobedience against a slaveholding state. For example, when speaking before the American Anti-Slavery Society, Thomas Wentworth Higginson extolled the attitude of the "good" Quakers who supported the notion that the only "true law" made the "distinction between the criminal and the slave not in favor of the criminal but the slave." "We want," he continued, "a law which makes escape from slavery not the proof of a crime, but the crowning fact of virtue." Higginson then retold the story of an unnamed Quaker supporter of the Underground Railroad who, when confronted by his neighbors for helping a self-liberated slave "break the law," merely retorted that the slave was "a better man than I thought he was" for having illegally left slavery.[18] This radicalization of Quaker pacifism was unpopular, illegal, and unconstitutional; it also had begun to foster a belief that the American government must end or mend. While hardly all Quaker comeouters supported what came to be known as "disunionism," the logic of those who rejected the authority of the American government had been adhered to by nearly all comeouters.

The ideas behind what came to be called disunion served as another demonstration of the eschatological hopes of abolitionist reformers working for the establishment of the government of God. As a protest against the refusal of national politicians to act to end slavery, many abolitionists began to broadcast their hope that individual Christians begin to reject the legal claim of the United States government to possess any authority over the conscience of American Christians. In many ways, what came to be termed "disunionism" was simply another manifestation of Quaker conscientious objection in times of war; for abolitionists, because of the enslavement of several million human beings, the United States government was already in a state of war with people on its own soil. Perhaps the most articulate proponent of disunionism was Henry C. Wright, who, like his colleague Oliver Johnson, had made the long journey from Congregationalist minister to radical comeouter. Along the way, Wright had been attracted to Quakerism, but he soon found that even this supposedly antislavery body possessed different ideas regarding the abolitionist movement.[19] As a member of the American Peace Society, Wright had grown disillusioned with what he saw as the weak-kneed nature of that society's opposition to war. Because the governing influence within the Peace Society (including many Friends) had instructed Wright to avoid criticizing "specific instances of force such as defensive war, capital punishment, or even slavery," Wright soon found that the Peace Society would not provide the proper support for his conviction that all human force was sinful. Out of the American Peace Society, therefore, would arise the New England Non-Resistance Society in 1837, an organization supported by radical abolitionists and one that, in the words of one of its members, William Lloyd Garrison, "contained all the fanaticism of my head and heart."[20]

In common cause with other radical anti-slavery activists, Henry Wright believed that only by rejecting the temporal political entity of the United States could slavery ever hope to be abolished. Convinced that the U.S. Constitution gave explicit support to slavery, the disunionists advocated the creation of religious communities dedicated to the principle of nonslaveholding government. All Americans must "bring their combined moral and social influence to bear on the Slave-breeding and Slaveholding Government of America, with a view to its destruction," asserted Wright. By "arraying against [the government of the United States] the moral and religious sentiment of mankind [until] every slaveholder shall be branded as a felon," disunionists would succeed in supplanting a government dedicated to slaveholding with one dedicated "to the universal BROTHERHOOD OF MAN." "Human hearts," continued Wright, "should be knit together in brotherly love and sympathy, and we are bound to seek the peaceable overthrow of all human institutions that tend to drive them asunder."[21]

From their founding then, comeouter Quaker meetings of Progressive Friends, Congregational Friends, and Friends of Human Progress boldly announced their commitment to opt out of the American union. A yearly meeting of the Friends of Human Progress in New York declared that the "only rational hope of the principle of the abolition of slavery and of the support of liberty for ourselves and posterity is, in the dissolution of the present American Union, and the formation of a Republic on the principle of *No Union with Slaveholders.*"[22] Similarly, a meeting of the Congregational Friends in Ohio believed that "all who live under the government" had become "kidnappers for Southern tyrants." While others advocated conciliation to the slavepower, these radical Friends declared, "WE GO FOR REVOLUTION, by such instrumentalities as are in accordance with the laws of God."[23] On the heels of such comments, many abolitionists began to send petitions to the United States Congress demanding the "peaceful secession from the American Union."[24]

Throughout the period from the mid-1830s until the eve of the Civil

War, the Society of Friends publicly distanced itself from the anarchic implications of abolitionist agitation often laying claim to a variant of Quaker pacifism. Whether denouncing disunionism or the civil disobedience of the Underground Railroad, the Society of Friends went to considerable lengths to assuage the fears of others in the United States that Quakers sought to link their church's religious testimonies with broader critiques of the American state. This fact soon became clear to abolitionists who had at one time or another belonged to the Society of Friends. In 1839, for example, William Bassett asked the editor of the *Friend* to publish the declaration of sentiments of the New England Non-Resistance Society, a document that made clear Bassett's and others' belief that the oppression of human governments could be overturned if people simply "possessed that faith which overcomes the world." These statements exuding optimism in the peaceful obliteration of temporal authority were rejected by the editor of the *Friend,* however, and no explanation was given for their exclusion from the largest Quaker newspaper in the country.[25] Bassett further claimed that New England Quaker ministers had denounced the doctrines of the Non-Resistance Society as "most pernicious heresy."[26] Upon visiting the New England Yearly Meeting of 1839, Henry C. Wright discovered that several elders, in his words, "regretted my coming," and Wright was unable to get these leaders to meet with him regarding their possible support for the Non-Resistance Society. Making their opposition to Wright and his abolitionist cohort even clearer, the elders of the yearly meeting, according to Wright, "earnestly entreated" young Friends "not to mingle with others in promoting [the] justice and humanity" of nonresistance to the American government.[27]

On the heels of this action, at the next yearly meeting the New England Yearly Meeting issued a public declaration against the doctrines espoused by the New England Non-Resistance Society. Declaring the "necessity of human government in conducting the affairs of men," this yearly meeting recounted how Friends had always manifested their "fidelity to whatever government an overruling Providence might place [them] under." The New England Friends then quoted from the early Quaker leader Robert Barclay, who distinguished the then young Society of Friends from those who "under the pretence of crying up King Jesus and the Kingdom of Christ, either deny or seek to overturn all civil government." The New England Friends stated that their church fellowship was "never . . . willing to throw off" the "salutary restraints" of government on account of "maladministration."[28]

Dating from the late seventeenth century, Quaker leaders had expressed concern that their religious movement predicated upon radical notions of the "Inner Light" might disintegrate from the anarchic impulses of its members. As Robert Barclay wrote in 1676, the "restless Imaginations" of "wandering minds . . . preach[ing] up a higher dispensation" would only turn earnest Quaker souls to "Wickedness and Atheism." Those Quakers who questioned the moral checks placed on them by the larger church fellowship were guilty of "dissolving the very Bond by which they were linked to the Body [of Christ]."[29] Standing in the way of abolitionist efforts to convince Quakers that in fact their interpretation of pacifism would not doom communities such as the Society of Friends, or the larger American state, were fears that those working for the establishment of God's kingdom must not support the destruction of all temporal authority. By equating many abolitionists with early Quaker "ranters" who had declared they had no king but Jesus, leading Friends sought to avoid any insinuation that their church somehow displayed disloyalty to the government of the United States. Because this government included nine slave states in 1840 and was governed by a Constitution that allowed for the recapture of fugitive slaves, the Society of Friends found itself supporting the American union against those who desired uncompromising, unpopular, and unconstitutional support for black freedom.

Besides the New England Yearly Meeting, many other Quakers, over the course of the 1840s and 1850s, denounced the anti-state implications of the abolitionist movement. The *Friends Intelligencer* noted that the Society of Friends did not adopt pacifist principles "to their full extent" and took a skeptical view of the number of Friends who believed that voting was "at variance with the peaceable kingdom of Christ."[30] Among New York City Hicksite Friends, Richard Cromwell, in a meeting for worship, declared that Quakers had always believed that "all power is of God" and that the "powers that be are ordained of God." Cromwell went on to contrast these opinions with those of the "fanatics of the day" who viewed the United States Constitution as a "league with hell."[31] Benjamin S. Jones, though himself a supporter of the Non-Resistance Society, relayed many comments of fellow Quakers mischaracterizing the views of abolitionists supporting various "disunionist" projects by claiming they would "cause a scene of anarchy and desolation, equaled only by the dreadful consequences anticipated by the slavite, from the immediate emancipation of slaves."[32]

When confronting specific acts of civil disobedience made by Quaker abolitionists on behalf of fugitive slaves, leaders of the Society of Friends reminded their flock that it was not "our place to invite slaves to run from their masters."[33] The editor of the *Friends Review* asserted "with the deepest conviction of the inconsistency of slavery with the principles and spirit of the Christian religion" that illegal efforts to secure slaves' freedom were "not the proper method of seeking to redress the evils of this system." The editor went on to claim that "[t]he cause of universal emancipation is too good to court or tolerate alliance with any other than open and honourable means."[34]

Some leaders of the Society of Friends seconded this criticism of the Underground Railroad (even as other ones, like the assistant clerk of the Indiana Yearly Meeting, George Evans, did aid fugitive slaves). According to Walter Edgerton, Indiana ministers Thomas Arnett and Thomas Wells "positively condemned the practice of aiding fugitive slaves," and Edgerton believed that most "weighty" members of the Miami Quarterly Meeting in Indiana were "decidedly and earnestly opposed" to the practice of illegally assisting slaves to freedom.[35] A leader of the Baltimore Yearly Meeting was reputed to have claimed that a local abolitionist had received the "punishment . . . he deserved" after being arrested for aiding slaves escaping from Maryland, and similar comments could be heard within the Hicksite New York Yearly Meeting.[36] In 1844, the North Carolina Yearly Meeting sent out a statement reaffirming its commitment to gradualist measures against slavery that did not challenge the basic legality of slavery. This statement also expressly condemned the practice of aiding fugitive slaves after the unfair prosecution of the North Carolina Quaker Anderson Johnson, who lost all his property on a false charge of aiding a fugitive. Annunciating an extremely cautious view of the Quaker testimony against slavery, the North Carolina Quakers were discouraged from interfering "in the relation between Master and Slave" since to do so would cause Friends to fail in their duties as "law-abiding people."[37] This did not stop many Quakers from continuing to do so, but the fact remains that many Friends feared the consequences of support for the Underground Railroad.

As one historian of the Underground Railroad has maintained, the actual number of self-liberated slaves was quite small in nineteenth-century America—perhaps in the low hundreds per year.[38] The idea of the Underground Railroad—representing more fiction than fact—revealed the considerable force fears of race revolt and slaveholder reprisal had for antebellum Americans (particularly those in the slaveholding and border states). Because so few African Americans succeeded in liberating themselves, the sensitivity of leading Friends to its subversive potential demonstrated at least an implicit agreement with many whites regarding the incapacity for black autonomy within the antebellum United States.

At the same time, the distaste of at least some Quaker leaders for the

Underground Railroad also reflected the personal threats of slave hunters and other vigilantes that preyed on Quakers in the border states. Levi Coffin, for example, relayed many stories of armed "ruffians" raiding his home and the homes of other Friends looking for escaped slaves. The fears of armed violence erupting in their communities and drawing Friends into physical conflict made the abolitionists' principled support for the Underground Railroad unpopular.

Quaker abolitionists, however, would not allow themselves to be cowed into submission by church leaders fearful that activists working for African American freedom would undo both their own religious society and the larger civil society of the United States. In 1848, Elijah Pennypacker rose to speak at a meeting for worship among Philadelphia Hicksite Quakers. In his sermon, Pennypacker laid out the abolitionist complaint that the Society of Friends had sacrificed any commitment to God's higher law out of deference to the mandates of a slaveholding republic. Pennypacker criticized what he saw as the widespread toleration of "legalized and popular crimes" while church leaders "denounce[d] individual sins." Pennypacker continued to declaim the fact that if a man acted as an instrument "of the government to kill, not one man alone, but many" through the extension of slavery "he is honored, and the people seek to promote him to the highest offices of the nation." Pennypacker finally said, "Are we not now putting our organic law above the light of truth?" At this, a leader of the meeting, Clement Biddle, stopped Pennypacker and told him to sit down. James Martin, another leader, backed up Biddle by asking Pennypacker to be silent, and he soon moved to adjourn the meeting for worship.[39] As reported in the abolitionist press, instances such as these provided proof that Friends had long rejected any responsibility for giving unpopular support for the cause of slaves: "Have we any right to expect that these sleek and comfortable people who differ from the world about them in no manner whatsoever . . . should be better than the world?"[40]

Regardless of whether or not the Society of Friends openly supported reform organizations such as the American Anti-Slavery Society, there were, in the opinion of many abolitionists, many ways Quakers could have lent their moral support to the cause of reforming a slaveholding government. Edmund Quincy noted that the Society of Friends supported the "existing government" by voting and holding office and therefore pronounced the Society "false to [its] own principles, in taking part in such governments."[41] The editor of the *National Anti-Slavery Standard,* Sydney Howard Gay, wrote that the Anti-Slavery Society disagreed "with the philosophy of the Quaker[s]" who when appointed to political positions would not hang a man themselves but "would appoint a Deputy that would." "We do not believe," continued Gay, "in appointing Deputies to do what we think to be wrong for ourselves to do."[42] When Gay later learned that many Philadelphia Quakers had voted for Zachary Taylor for president, he simply wrote that "it is as absurd to expect of [Quakers] a life consistent with their professions, as it is to look to Tammany Hall for sympathy with the cause of Anti-Slavery."[43]

Henry Wright echoed these sentiments and was shocked to learn that there were Quaker members of the Massachusetts state legislature, and apparently, even of the Congress: "[I]s it not totally and forever irreconcilable with the principles of Friends, to hold an office which lays them under obligation to raise and support armies—to provide and maintain a navy?" This participation in "human politics," continued Wright, "can never be reconciled with the principles and policy of the Divine government."[44] Drawing attention to the Society of Friends' likeness to other American Protestants, Wright condemned Friends as he chastised the "American Church." Both groups supported the "offices and institutions of government" and both "defend[ed] the prerogative and slaveholding of the State, by her ecclesiastical logic and authority." When reformers called on the church to stand up to the injustices of state power, the "American Church" followed through with the "ex-communication" of those who questioned the "State's divinity."[45]

This attempt to decouple both slavery and the state, as well as "pro-slavery Christianity" from the American government, soon took the form of petitions to state legislatures and the American Congress with the simple yet radical request for the "immediate and peaceful dissolution of the Union."[46] Petitions such as these that attacked the failures of the American union were widely criticized in the press as typifying "fanaticism run mad," and were yet again seen as a "treasonable effort . . . to plunge twenty millions of people . . . into war."[47] Yearly meetings of the Society of Friends largely fell in line with conventional opposition to the abolitionists' attack on slaveholding government. In 1850, a delegation of Friends went to the United States Senate to protest the *African* slave trade (and not the interstate slave trade), but they made clear to Senator William Dayton of New Jersey the desire of Quakers "to disclaim in the most distinct manner any disposition in their Society to favor disunion projects." The delegation further made clear how Friends appreciated "too well the benefits and privileges conferred by and enjoyed under this Government" to advocate disunion.[48] Two years later, upon submitting an address against slavery to the *National Anti-Slavery Standard* that acknowledged the Society of Friends' opposition to slavery but did not state a mode for its abolition, New York Quakers wrote to the editor that this address was written "in the Spirit of the Gospel" and did not engender "strife and discord" as other, abolitionist petitions had supposedly done.[49]

As had been true for the prior two decades, leaders of the Society of Friends sought to align their church with support for the American republic and against the spectacle of religious "ranterism." The popular connection between religious fanaticism and treason had been given greater credence after the germination of many unconventional and heterodox religious beliefs in the early republic, represented by free thinkers, spiritualists, Mormons, Millerites, Oneidan perfectionists, and other "communitist" groups. To many, abolitionism was an equally disreputable movement infused with destructive leveling tendencies. Highly critical of abolitionists' efforts to wage "direct, inveterate warfare against the Constitution and the Union," the editor of the *Democratic Review* wrote in 1850 that "the first and most effectual step in subjugating mankind" begins with "that degree of enthusiasm, which amounts to fanaticism" represented by men like "Joseph Smith and William Lloyd Garrison," who "propound some stupendous dogma, to which they arrogate the sanction of Heaven," then "batter down everything in [their] way."[50] Abolitionists, continued another editorial, not only demonstrated "hostility to the hitherto universally recognized doctrines of Christianity" but were also cooperating "with the socialists" to destroy all "social obligations, the Constitution, the laws, the sanctity of marriage, and the divinity of religion itself."[51]

In antebellum America the connection between religious orthodoxy and social order was embodied legally in sabbatarian and blasphemy ordinances, and according to many leading legal authorities, such as Judge James Kent of New York, the "Christian religion" was synonymous with the "principles of virtue, which helps to bind society together." The "things which corrupt moral sentiment, as obscene actions, prints, and writings, and even gross instances of sedition, have upon [this] principle been held indictable."[52] The prosecutions for blasphemy of such free thinkers as Abner Kneeland and the willingness of judges to enforce laws against cursing, the violation of the sabbath, and the disturbance of worship demonstrated the cultural belief both in the supremacy of orthodox Protestantism and in the notion that religious liberty possessed necessary limits.[53] Many American leaders respected the notion that religion functioned as an instrument conducive to social cohesion, and with men like

Lyman Beecher believed that only with proper Christian instruction could the American republic remain "a safe depository of liberty forever."[54]

In the early 1800s, at least some Protestants still questioned the compatibility of Quakerism with the values of a "Christian nation," and it was often with an eye to dispel such impressions that leaders of the Society of Friends opposed the abolitionists. The Society of Friends, in general, yielded to pressure to frame their theological positions as conventional and nonthreatening. Some controversial works, such as that published by the Methodist Billy Hibbard, condemned Quaker pacifism for its supposed disavowal of God's command to "be subject to the powers that be." Hibbard also believed that many Quakers profaned the sabbath and therefore confused "liberty and licentiousness." Such dangerous views destroyed the "moral obligations" citizens owed to the rest of their society.[55] Making an oblique reference to the disunionist statements certain Quakers propounded the same year, the editor of the *Princeton Review* in 1848 believed that the Society of Friends doctrine of the Inner Light, by representing a "superior" force to all "human laws," could lead to much "crime" caused by men rejecting "all standards but the light within."[56] The Presbyterian minister William Craig Brownlee also viewed the Quakers' "grand tenet of the universal inward light" as destroying "rational and true religion." This willingness "to nurse the monstrous births of heresy" had dire social consequences. For one, the Friends' acceptance of female preaching represented an "outrageous rebellion against the divine order of the house of God!" This rebellion, in Brownlee's opinion, was "more unjust and more tyrannical than that which the female usurps in the domestic circle, when she degrades her husband and seizes the reins of government over the family."[57]

Most likely in an effort to assuage early American leaders that Quakers did in fact respect religious freedom in proper Protestant fashion, many Quakers in the early republic extolled the necessity of Christian civil laws in the face of religious pluralism. The editor of the *Friend,* for example, reminded his readers how "Christianity is the foundation of good government." The "safety of all states depends upon religion; it ministers to social order ... and gives security to property."[58] In 1849, when the Pennsylvania state senate considered amending sabbatarian laws to allow Seventh-Day Baptists (who celebrated Saturday as the sabbath) to open their businesses on Sunday, the *Friend* feared that this potential legislative action represented a first step toward the opening of "the flood gates of licentiousness and infidelity" in the United States. "We need all the aids that now exist," continued this Quaker paper, "to preserve the morals and religious principles of the people."[59]

This language addressing the dangers posed by unwarranted religious change was also employed by the supposedly more liberal Hicksite offshoot of the Society of Friends. Writing in support of the Anti-Masonic Party in the 1830s (a party that according to one historian had been widely supported by Friends), the Hicksite John Gest believed that the Freemasons, by making "sin formidable," had corrupted "the way of the Lord" and had therefore created an institution "obnoxious . . . [to] all the principles of good government, both moral and religious." Although in Gest's mind Masons claimed to be a kind of religious institution, by giving "unrestrained liberty to licentiousness over order," the Masons constituted a grave threat both to "society and government."[60] In the 1850s, Hicksite as well as orthodox Quaker concerns regarding threats to republican religion surfaced again when dealing with the spread of Mormonism and Catholicism. Though they possessed vastly different theological beliefs, Catholic doctrines regarding the spiritual authority of the Vatican and the Mormon acceptance of polygamy each appeared to undermine institutions such as representative government and the American family. For leading Hicksite Quakers, the "Latter-day Saints," as well as other communitarian radicals such as the Oneidans, represented the "many-headed monster which is destroying the church of Christ."[61] The editor of the *Friend* deplored the "fanaticism" of the Mormons that led them "into premeditated treason" against the United States government.[62] Mormon "licentiousness," represented by polygamy, should have automatically prevented them from becoming "amalgamated with the other citizens" of the republic, so that the Mormons' destructive religious ideas not "spread as a leprosy" among the people.[63] Catholics did not fare much better in Quaker journals of the period. When the Vatican proposed to bestow the office of cardinal upon the bishop of Baltimore, the *Friend* asked, "Is there to be an adjunct Pope created for the United States?"[64] The Quakers' fear of "Popish mumery," with its tendency to "enslave and hold in bondage the human intellect," led Friends to believe that "Popery," if left unchecked, would unleash untold social problems for the American republic.[65]

In many ways, the Society of Friends succeeded in making Quaker pacifism or other "peculiar" religious doctrines of their church conform to the values of a slaveholding republic. The church respected the separation of religious sentiments and political action that so many politicians demanded as a necessary bulwark in defense of the union. By 1850, Quaker quietism, at least for some politicians, came to be seen as an acceptance of compromise over the slavery issue. As noted earlier, Pennsylvania Friends submitted a petition to the senate concerning the African slave trade in February 1850 to which they addended their rejection of more radical disunionist petitions submitted by "comeouter" Quaker groups. The senators publicly supported the Friends against the abolitionists, believing Friends' moderation characterized true "benevolence." Senator John P. Hale, in agreement with similar comments made by Preston King and William Drayton, pointed out that a group so "amiable . . . industrious, just, and honorable" would never allow their "peculiar notions" to be mixed up with political radicalism.[66] Yet just after making these comments, the senators voted to reject even the more moderate petition for the abolition of the African slave trade, along with its more radical counterparts submitted by the abolitionist Friends. The only thing thereby accomplished by leading Quakers attempting to assuage the fears of politicians regarding Friends' alliance with abolitionism, in the eyes of abolitionists at least, was success at convincing members of Congress that Friends would not openly object to a political process long reconciled to the legality of slavery.

Later in 1850, the abolitionist belief that Quaker moderation was viewed by politicians as support for compromise with the slavepower appeared to have been borne out when Senator Daniel Webster wrote to a group of constituents in Newburyport, Massachusetts, explaining his support for the Compromise of 1850. Equating Quaker quietism with his type of unionism supposedly needed to preserve the republic, Webster claimed that the Society of Friends "in general" understood "their neighbor's rights" regarding the recapture of liberated slaves. Webster noted with admiration that although Quakers had been opposed to slavery "from the first," they nonetheless had chosen a wise anti-slavery course that "would not . . . overthrow or undermine the constitution of their country." Though there were some misguided members of the church who took a more radical anti-slavery course due to the influence of "puffs of transcendental philosophy," the "great body" of Friends, according to the Massachusetts senator, supposedly approved of his speech of March 7, 1850.[67] In this widely circulated and controversial address, Webster had, in defense of compromise and union, thrown his support behind the strengthening of the fugitive slave code to coerce all Americans into returning self-liberated slaves to their owners.

Even though many states had long asserted their own ability to preserve some semblance of freedom for liberated slaves living in free states, the *Friend* felt it necessary to refer to the Compromise of 1850 as a settlement over which "no true lover of his country" could not "rejoice."⁶⁸ The *Friends Intelligencer* was much more critical of the Compromise of 1850, however, as well as of the imputation that Friends supported concessions to Southerners that undermined the liberty of freed blacks. Yet the paper expressed shock that Webster should have thought that "the course which [we] have pursued on this [slavery] question" would lead the senator to see the Society of Friends as his allies in revoking rights of freed slaves.⁶⁹ Within abolitionist circles, however, there was no surprise that Webster should have assumed that the Society of Friends was an ally. The Compromise of 1850 represented the legitimate fruit of efforts by groups such as the Society of Friends to adopt a nonconfrontational, almost apolitical stance vis-à-vis the slavepower. In Oliver Johnson's opinion, the "solemn self-complacency" of leading Friends had only worked "to discourage and retard the anti-slavery enterprise." Those members of the Society of Friends who had hoped that their more moderate course was far better than those "who would erode the influence" of the Society of Friends "with those in authority by advocating disunion" should have realized the fallacy of their tactics when the Compromise of 1850 made its assault on the rights of self-liberated slaves.⁷⁰ William Goodell echoed these sentiments, chastising Quaker support for the "manstealers and their abettors" who "rule the nation." To Goodell, "earnest and active" opponents of slavery had long been ostracized by the Society of Friends because of those activists' supposedly impolitic demeanor.⁷¹

As has been recognized by historians of the abolitionist movement, the Compromise of 1850 represented a major turning point in the vision of peaceful moral suasion that members of the Anti-Slavery Society had hoped would end chattel slavery in the United States. In the aftermath of this compromise, even supposed pacifists such as Samuel J. May could not help but speak of active resistance to the state. May told his parishioners that theirs was a "holy obligation" to defy the fugitive slave law by force, just as "you are not to lie, steal, and murder."⁷² With increasing frequency, members of the American Anti-Slavery Society, as well as of the American and Foreign Anti-Slavery Society, began to advocate active resistance to the state, thus beginning a process of relinquishing any commitment to peaceful moral suasion. The vision underlying the comeouter hope for a transformed public opinion was becoming clouded by the increasing prospect of slavery's violent end. Abolitionism in the 1850s was a movement not as confident of other-worldly hopes as it was of the use of human force to resist an encroaching slavepower. Besides demonstrating the failure of the abolitionist movement, the period from the Compromise of 1850 until

Abraham Lincoln's decision to make emancipation a war aim in 1862 would test the limits of Quaker pacifism by forcing Friends to choose between liberty for slaves and the preservation of union. In dramatic fashion, the collapse of the viability of peaceful solutions to the problem of slavery's expansion in the 1850s would demonstrate the failure of American churches, like other institutions in the republic, to prevent a nation from descending into civil war.

CONCLUSION
# "Fighting Quakers," Abolitionists, and the Civil War

Since the founding of the American republic, the image of the Quaker has oscillated between representations of virtue and caricatures of hypocrisy. As a religious group vocal in its opposition to things such as slavery, capital punishment, luxuriant living, and war, the Society of Friends has often possessed a presence in American life larger than its numbers. For some writers, the Quakers symbolized all that was good in a society that allowed religious dissent to be channeled into virtuous reform endeavors. The simple life of the Quakers might even be confused with that of the Shakers or the Amish. For others, however, the Society of Friends represented a clan of people who professed one thing and did something quite different, all the while claiming to have a greater concern for the welfare of mankind than those outside the church. More critical accounts of the Friends' character showed little sympathy for the peculiar Quaker dilemma of sometimes having to serve two masters or of being caught between the government of God and that of man. As America descended into the Civil War in the 1850s, the unstable image of the "peculiar people" appeared again when two books each repeated the opposing literary tropes of the "good" Friend or the "fighting" Quaker. One book was the fabulously successful anti-slavery novel *Uncle Tom's Cabin,* by Harriet Beecher Stowe; the other was Herman Melville's seafaring tragedy *Moby Dick.*

In 1852, Harriet Beecher Stowe released *Uncle Tom's Cabin,* a book that did much to awaken the conscience of whites in the free states to the personal horrors of slavery. The book made its debut just as Americans in the free states witnessed the forced re-enslavement of men such as Anthony Burns and Thomas Sims (after Congress strengthened the fugitive slave law), and the book popularized stories of white and black courage in the face of an inhuman slave system. However, Stowe's depiction of saintly Quaker characters such as Simeon and Rachel Halliday were flawed by their author's sentimental style. This became particularly evident with Stowe's portrayal of the Underground Railroad. Through the Hallidays, Stowe communicated a vision of Quaker dissent from conventional society, as well as from the American racial order, that made Friends heroic defenders of black rights at the same time they were divorced from politics. When the liberated slaves Eliza and George Harris make their way to "the Quaker settlement," they are assured of their safety by their white protectors—who, in Stowe's words, exude "peace on earth, good will to men." "For everyone in the settlement is a Friend, and all are watching [out for you]," asserts Simeon Halliday to the former bondsmen. Always peaceful in his rejection of the laws of a slaveholding state, Friend Simeon Halliday tells the escaped slave George Harris not to contemplate violent resistance to slavecatchers for "the leaders of our people taught a more excellent way" than physical force in opposition to human injustice.[1]

Based loosely on noted Quaker abolitionists (such as Thomas Garrett) who aided escaped slaves, Stowe's fictional account of Friends' support for the Underground Railroad was only the beginning of a long series of portrayals of heroic Quaker opposition to slavery that erased the historical dilemma of Friends' opposition to slavery. Representing an uncomplicated picture of how Quaker theology was translated into social and political practice, the enduring symbol of the Quaker Underground Railroad operator has overshadowed the problematic reality facing religious groups opposed to slavery in antebellum America.[2] Even as Stowe intended for her novel to create a more receptive anti-slavery public opinion in the free states, her discussion of the good Friend largely sidestepped the problem of Quaker anti-slavery within a slaveholding republic. Stowe's depiction of Quaker opposition to slavery nonetheless continued in the tradition of viewing the Society of Friends as a group outside the political process and as a church whose religious commitments were easily contained within the private world of personal conscience.

Unlike Stowe's depiction of selfless virtue, Herman Melville's depiction of the "Fighting Quakers" in *Moby Dick* perpetuated the stereotype of Quaker hypocrisy. Released at nearly the same time as *Uncle Tom's Cabin*, Melville's novel met with only a fraction of the success of Stowe's anti-slavery novel, yet, in similar fashion to Stowe, Melville acknowledged a separation between Quaker consciences and the society around them. Unlike Stowe, however, this separation was nothing to be lauded as it led to greed and violence. When writing about the "hard hearted" Quaker Captain Bildad, Melville noted Bildad had "long since come to the sage and sensible conclusion that a man's religion is one thing, and this practical world quite another." Demonstrating this separation of conscience and society, Melville continued that the supposedly peaceable Friends involved in whaling were "the most sanguinary of all sailors and whale-hunters. They are fighting Quakers; they are Quakers with a vengeance."[3] Later in the novel, another Quaker captain, Peleg, allows his desire for profit to cloud his judgment regarding the maniacal ship captain, Ahab, who ultimately takes the Quaker's boat on a futile, fatal quest for the whale, Moby Dick. To Friend Peleg, Ahab was "above the common," and although "stricken" by disease, he had "his humanities."[4]

The decidedly unsentimental "fighting Quakers" depicted in *Moby Dick* followed in a long line of mocking portrayals of thieving and conniving ship captains or slave traders who claimed to belong to the Quaker faith. David Porter's *Journal of a Cruise Made to the Pacific Ocean* relayed an account of being robbed by a Quaker, behavior that "neither agrees with the principles he professes, nor is it such as his sleek coat would lead one to expect."[5] Going back to the eighteenth century, many slave ships possessed names such as *Willing Quaker* or *Friends Goodwill* as a testament to the divided consciences of at least some of those involved in the slave trade.[6] In *The Trippings of Tom Pepper*, when Tom masquerades as a Quaker to avoid a debtor, he is told by a passerby how he had been cheated out of a thousand dollars by a man in a sleek coat claiming to be a Friend.[7]

Between the unfair stereotypes of authors like Melville and the mythic idealizations of Stowe, there was an uneasy existence for those who professed anti-slavery and pacifist beliefs in a society heading toward civil war. The distinct problem facing a religious society that opposed war in all its forms took on nearly tragic proportions by the mid-1850s. By the time Stowe and Melville released their novels, there was nothing peaceful about American abolitionists and the Quakers who supported them; at the same time Quaker pacifism could be allied with support for efforts to save a union increasingly sensitive to the demands of slaveholders.

Try as they might, the Society of Friends could not avoid the troubling implications—be they radical or conservative—following from their opposition to both slavery and war. The dilemma of the Quaker anti-slavery testimony revealed the inability of a group that in many ways represented the vanguard of the white conscience to successfully combine opposition to slavery with support for the union.

In the aftermath of the Compromise of 1850, many Quaker abolitionists began to reconcile their movement, formerly predicated on the transformation of public opinion, with the use of violent force to stop an ever-stronger slavepower. By 1856, the anti-slavery Friend Walter Edgerton acknowledged how "an appalling amount of crime and suffering" had produced among abolitionists a rejection of "that genuine and peaceable" movement "in which we joined years ago."[8] As early as 1851, William Lloyd Garrison, a man who had once claimed that the "great work of national redemption" must be accomplished through "moral power" alone, began publishing sympathetic accounts of anti-slavery meetings that tolerated discussion of "killing all who attempted to re-enslave a fugitive" slave.[9] After the Burns Affair in Boston, during which eight artillery companies took the freed slave Anthony Burns into custody, John Greenleaf Whittier wrote to a fellow abolitionist that "the next attempt to execute the Fugitive Slave law in New England will be resisted to the death—armed, organized revolution."[10] At about the same time, a meeting of abolitionists in Boston passed a resolution stating their intention to oppose the fugitive slave law, quoting the English revolutionary Algernon Sidney: "that which is not just is not law, and that which is not law ought not to be obeyed." The resolution further declared that the "mode of resistance" to be chosen by friends of the slave would be left to an individual's conscience, thus creating an intellectual loophole where belief in the sanctity of one's conscience could justify bloodshed.[11]

On the other side of this dilemma of liberty and union stood the majority of leaders of the Society of Friends, people who articulated skepticism of the abolitionist flirtation with violence by appealing to the Quaker message of peace. However, by so doing, these Friends often adopted an increasingly conservative, unionist tone in the years before the Civil War. In opposition to the statements of men such as Garrison or Whittier, leaders of the Society of Friends spoke out against any excuse to link dissent from the slavepower with violence. At the end of the decade, and after John Brown's raid on Harper's Ferry, the editor of the *Friend* had not given up hope of opportunities to "convince and convert the slaveholders" of the South to release their human property. This would not be possible, claimed the editor, "unless the hearts of speakers and actors are measurably influenced towards" slave owners "by that love which recognizes their claims to brotherhood" and of their right "to be treated with perfect fairness and kind regard."[12] The *Friends Intelligencer* concurred in the opinion that abolitionists had failed in their responsibility to work peacefully for the manumission of slaves. Speaking of slaveholders so often opposed by members of the anti-slavery societies, the editor of this Hicksite paper wrote how "we cannot expect to reform others either by denouncing, or ridiculing them, and it will be found that persuasion is always more available than force in the correction of evil."[13] This insistence by Quaker leaders that some form of moral suasion could still end slavery continued to produce public warnings to slaves and free African Americans on the dangers of active resistance to slave owners. Orthodox Friends in Philadelphia, for example, exhorted slaves to "serve with patience and fidelity while in bondage," while fulfilling "their Christian duties with propriety." Slaves should furthermore "commit their cause into the hands of a merciful and omnipotent Father in heaven."[14] For many African Americans and their abolitionist supporters, this was unrealistic advice that served the interests of slaveholders.

In the wake of the so-called "Christiana Riot" of September 11, 1851, during which freed slaves killed their former master after he had tried to re-enslave them, the Society of Friends demanded that Quakers and their African American associates "guard their minds against being improperly influenced by the excitement occasioned by the event," exhorting them to maintain the "peaceable spirit of Jesus."[15] The Society of Friends felt particularly compelled to reject violent resistance to slavery because one individual involved in the Christiana incident was Castner Hanway, a sometime Progressive Friend who was often misidentified as a Quaker in the local press. Hanway had been accused of treason by the federal government for supposedly inciting the slaves to violence, but no evidence existed to back up the claims, and he was acquitted of treason.[16] Though possessing distaste for the government's prosecution of Hanway, leading members of the Society of Friends nonetheless objected to any compromise with or incitement of black violence against slave masters. It was also "highly important" that Friends of abolition "be on their guard as to the manner in which they attempt to counteract the effects of the excitement." Friends everywhere, "while steadfastly maintaining our well-known views upon the subject of slavery," must "be careful to do it in the peaceable spirit of Jesus." Furthermore, the editor of the *Friend* continued, church members must personally ask African Americans to "give up all idea of attempting to resist by force and violence the laws made against them, however oppressive and unrighteous these laws are, or may continue to be."[17] The Hicksite Philadelphia Yearly Meeting echoed these sentiments when it desired that Friends "imbue" their colored associates with the "Christian spirit of meekness and suffering which becomes the followers of the Lamb," so that African Americans might avoid resisting "injustice or oppression" by "carnal weapons."[18]

For abolitionists, on the other hand, the Christiana affair encouraged greater sympathy for the plight of freed blacks. African Americans, in the words of the *New York Independent,* "however abject . . . have tasted liberty . . . and are ready to defend it." Those politicians who strengthened fugitive slave legislation had "counted upon the utter degradation of the negro race—their want of manliness and heroism—to render feasible its execution."[19] In its coverage of "Pennsylvania Abolitionism" during the Christiana affair, the *Liberator* published many sentiments that demonstrated a growing belief among abolitionists that pacifist principles would not be sufficient in the battle with the slavepower. At a meeting of Congregational Friends in Green Plain, Ohio, in 1851, Henry C. Wright offered his support for a resolution claiming that "RESISTANCE TO TYRANTS IS OBEDIENCE TO GOD" and called on African Americans to resist all "malignant" and "brutal" laws.[20] Speaking before the Pennsylvania Anti-Slavery Society, Samuel Aaron told his fellow abolitionists that he "would not hesitate to strike down any ruffian who should attempt to enslave him or his family" and believed that "those colored men" at Christiana "were only following the example of Washington and the American heroes of '76."[21]

In spite of these sentiments, the official view espoused by prominent Friends in relation to the fugitive slave law was that "righteous means should always be sought by righteous ends." Only those measures that were "regular and constitutional" should be used to combat slavery.[22] Yet the tension facing anti-slavery Americans who desired liberty for slaves without violence simply became more pronounced through the 1850s. Events soon overshadowed the efforts of those who tried to articulate an uncompromised commitment to slavery's peaceful abolition. This fact became particularly evident to Quaker settlers in the Kansas territory. In the 1850s, these Friends experienced firsthand the failure of "popular sovereignty" to create free soil out of the Western territory. Because Quakers were publicly seen by Southerners as anti-slavery, pro-slavery fighters destroyed one of the Friends' missionary schools operated for Shawnee children in Kansas in 1856. Those Quakers who had run the institution "thought it best to return to their homes" to avoid being drawn into guerrilla warfare.[23] In 1857, an unnamed Quaker settler in Kansas reported his trials in the Western territory to a local paper: "On the one hand our neighbors were arming and preparing for defense, and urging us to do the same, whilst on the other the country was invaded by a set of lawless and unprincipled beings." Though many "thefts and robberies" occurred, however, "not a hair on any of our heads was harmed, or a hand laid upon anything of ours. Oh! How we desired that we might be enabled to stand firm in the faith of our religious profession, through any and every trial." This Quaker's "life had been repeatedly threatened, and by persons whom [he] had never seen . . . who reported to the enemy the name of every true anti-slavery man."[24]

Richard Mendenhall, a Quaker resident in Kansas, hoped that members of his church in the territory would "offer another salutary example of the power and efficacy of passive resistance to evil—the martyr's unresistable might of meekness." Yet in seeming contradiction, Mendenhall had to acknowledge that "if defensive warfare could be justified in any case, it would seem to be so in the present one."[25] The bifurcated nature of the Quaker peace testimony affected all members of the church; arguments and recriminations regarding the meaning, uses, and abuses of the Society of Friends' critique of force in American society only continued in the years ahead. Increasingly, abolitionist Friends began to believe that events had turned Quaker pacifism into a kind of conservative unionism inimical to the cause of freedom. At a Quaker meeting in Virginia in 1859, when a male minister preached against the "fanaticism" of abolitionists, Susan B. Anthony sprung to her feet crying, "'Woe unto you scribes and Pharisees, hypocrites that devour wives houses!' Read the New Testament and see if Christ was not an agitator. Who is this among us crying 'peace, peace' when there is no peace!"[26]

For many abolitionists, then, the rejection of pacifism was almost natural and could often be excused because of the actions of slave owners and the American state that, abolitionists believed, wholeheartedly backed them. The continued unfolding of violence surrounding the slavery issue in Kansas presented Friends with the almost superhuman challenge of maintaining their pacifism. Besides the fact that Quaker abolitionist support for emigrant aid societies indirectly backed those settlers' use of force to defend themselves, there were an untold number of Friends, such as Susan B. Anthony's brother Daniel, who took an active part in the guerrilla warfare in Kansas.[27] Similarly, an unknown number of Quakers supported John Brown, who had butchered five unarmed settlers in their beds at Pottawatomie Creek, Kansas. This bloodletting did not satisfy Brown, and he began to plot a slave revolution in the late 1850s. In these efforts, Brown was not an isolated lunatic, but rather was someone who received a fair amount of support from members of the American Anti-Slavery Society.[28]

Brown's attempt to lead a slave revolt failed. The slaves refused to take part, and Robert E. Lee routed Brown's men, who had taken over the federal arsenal. Brown and his fellow fighters were tried and sentenced to death, yet many Quaker abolitionists supported Brown in the days surrounding his execution. Rebecca Buffum Spring, a relative of the anti-slavery Friend Arnold Buffum, upon hearing of the raid on Harper's Ferry, decided to visit the aged revolutionary in Virginia. As a woman who in her own words had "talked against slavery all these years," she was fascinated by a leader who had finally "done something" by attempting to lead a slave revolution in the South. After traveling from Massachusetts to Virginia, and only after receiving a court order, Spring was allowed to meet with John Brown. Spring recalled how the abolitionist revolutionary was a "commanding figure" with a "white halo about his head, on his face a look of peace . . . [t]he slave power seemed stronger that ever . . . but his faith never flinched." A few months later, after Brown's execution, Spring called upon Colonel Thomas Wentworth Higginson to "make a determined effort" to rescue the other of Brown's men who were yet to die, and Higginson did indeed make an unsuccessful attempt to attack the prison holding the men. In a final statement in support for the Harper's Ferry raid, Spring had two of Brown's party buried in her backyard.[29]

Quite likely these two men were Edwin and Barclay Coppoc, brothers from Iowa who had been raised in the Quaker faith but who were in the process of abandoning it along with their pacifism. Though Barclay died during the siege of Harper's Ferry, his brother Edwin was taken prisoner before being executed with Brown in December 1859. In a letter to his uncle from prison, Edwin remained unapologetic: "I had hoped to live see the principle of the Declaration of Independence fully realized. I had hoped to see the dark stain of slavery blotted out from our land. I honestly believe I am innocent of any crime justifying such punishment." In a not-far-off time, stated Coppoc confidently, the "voice of truth will echo through the great army who will follow its banner."[30] Edwin's aunt, Ann Coppoc Raley, also seemed supportive of her nephew's actions. Ann was pleased that her kin did not "surrender to the slave power . . . 'Slane, not conquered, they died free.'" "Who knows," continued Raley, "but that under the present peculiar crisis that some of the best of our flock may be required as a sacrifice for our country and our cause."[31] By emphasizing how the rejection of pacifism represented a "sacrifice," Raley demonstrated another loophole in the logic of abolitionist pacifism—somehow young Quakers were not really to be held accountable for rejecting pacifism when events supposedly forced them to lay down their lives.

In the days and months following John Brown's raid, many Quaker abolitionists exuded little regret that carnal weapons had been used to combat the sin of slaveholding. The leading anti-slavery Friend, Levi Coffin, rather than unequivocally condemn Brown's violent actions, believed that Brown may have been "an instrument in the hands of the Almighty to commence the great work of deliverance of the oppressed. . . ."[32] By claiming that God sanctioned the murderous actions of Brown, Coffin's statements revealed how a belief in a "higher law" than those enacted on earth could be used to condone violence. In words stronger than Coffin's, Susan B. Anthony spoke of John Brown as a man being "crucified for doing what he believed God commanded him to do, 'break the yoke and let the oppressed go free.'"[33]

And as the nation descended into civil war in April 1861, it was not simply Quaker abolitionists or their free soil counterparts in Kansas who took part in armed warfare. Individual Quakers from New England to the Midwest set aside their pacifism in defense of the union by joining the military. As the free states banded together to fight secession, the term "Fighting Quaker" began to be applied to young male Quakers with increasing frequency, and in response to this fact, the *Friend* reprimanded those in the church who applied the term "Fighting Quaker" to themselves. "If a man is a fighting one," declared the editor, "he has not the remotest claim to be a Quaker in principle. . . ." The *Friend* demanded that Quakers "present an unbroken, unyielding front to the world's mighty errors, and with God's armor on" suffer "all things for conscience sake."[34] It may have been that this editorial was in direct response to sentiments such as those expressed by the author of the pamphlet published during the Civil War, in which the claim was made that the "'people called Quakers' have done loyal service heretofore in battles that forever consecrated the soil of our land to freedom." Though the cause of peace was an honorable one, continued the book, "there may come occasions to its followers, when the voice of duty will thrill them as with a trumpet blast, and their souls must leap responsive to the mandate: 'Arise, Go Up To The Battle!'"[35]

By the start of the Civil War, many Friends placed their commitment to American nationalism above pacifist principles. In Philadelphia,

Sarah M. Palmer noted how "Quakers are drilling, contrary to all the peace principles of the sect; indeed from all appearances we may suppose their hopes [to end slavery] are based on war."[36] Daniel Wooten, an Indiana Quaker in the army, wrote his girlfriend that those who "rebell [*sic*] against the law of our country" must be stopped by "any means." Though he acknowledged the traditional Quaker injunction against physical force, Wooten believed that just as God expelled Lucifer from heaven, so must Union soldiers fight to "extinguish" the cause of the Confederacy.[37] A Quaker major in the army from Maine, James Parnell Jones, wrote his family and friends that "now is the time for the country to be thoroughly aroused and strike the final blow for the destruction of the confederacy."[38] These sentiments symbolized a larger trend within Quaker communities; as Jacqueline Nelson discovered in her study of Indiana Quakers, at least 25 percent of eligible Quaker men in Indiana fought for the Union, and because of difficulties ascertaining the faith of any person in nineteenth-century Indiana, Nelson believes that 25 percent represents a significant understatement of service. It is possible that Quaker participation in the military was not much less than the 62 percent of all eligible Indianans who fought in the Civil War.[39] Quaker women also lent considerable support to the war effort, whether as members of aid organizations under the United States Sanitary Commission or as nurses in the army.[40]

With the coming of the Civil War, the transformation from moral suasion to state power as the means of slavery's abolition became nearly complete for abolitionists. Many Quaker abolitionists supported using the Union army as one of liberation and later viewed the federal government as an instrument for transforming race relations in the South. The Quaker Norwood P. Hallowell took an officer position with a regiment of black troops and wrote afterwards that "there was nothing quite so magnificent and, let me add, quite so reliable as the colored volunteer."[41] The young Quaker orator Anna Dickinson told an audience of abolitionists that if the liberation of slaves did not become a war aim, "we have no war-cry, no noble motive. . . . While the flag of freedom waves merely for the white man, God will be against us."[42] Susan B. Anthony wrote Wendell Phillips that although support for the war was "strange," it was "glorious" nonetheless, and along with other female abolitionists, Anthony took part in the Women's National Loyal League's petition to Congress in 1863 demanding that Congress make abolition the law of the land.[43]

Participating in the growing movement among abolitionists to demand that the Union military cause be wedded to emancipation, the Progressive Friends of Longwood, Pennsylvania, wrote to Abraham Lincoln that the only way to end the Civil War was "TO ABOLISH SLAVERY WITHOUT DELAY." This act was "demanded by a due regard for the unity of the country, the safety and happiness of the people, the preservation of free institutions, and by every consideration of justice, mercy, and peace." Rejecting their earlier pronouncements in favor of passive nonresistance, the Progressive Friends encouraged the commander-in-chief to "suppress this treasonable outbreak by all the means and forces at [the army's] disposal," and if not he would "betray the sacred trusts" of the American people. With the backing of William Lloyd Garrison, who had actually written the memorial, Oliver Johnson led a delegation of Progressive Friends to the White House on June 20, 1862, to present Lincoln with the memorial for emancipation. While Lincoln respectfully received the petitioners, he responded to Johnson that an emancipation proclamation would have no effect on the Confederacy since the Constitution was not in force there.[44] Nonetheless, abolitionists would eventually find encouragement in the proclamation of January 1, 1863, that gave freedom to all slaves in states or parts of states in rebellion. Though emancipation had not yet been made final, this act sent a clear signal to abolitionists that the Civil War was evolving into a revolutionary struggle to change the status of African Americans within the United States. This move toward faith in the state to effect social change continued through the 1860s among Quaker abolitionists, as many would later send petitions to Congress demanding African American suffrage and would also support the confiscation of land in the former Confederacy to be redistributed among freed slaves.[45] Quakers who worked for the federal government on behalf of former slaves often acknowledged their dependence on federal military support for the success of their efforts. One such Quaker, Cornelia Hancock, had to concede that she and her fellow Friends "shall all leave when the military does," thus revealing the often precarious nature of Union efforts at advancing racial progress.[46]

In contrast with the abolitionists, meetings of the Society of Friends frequently were skeptical of the revolutionary efforts being unleashed by the Union government and its military. In January 1863, after the Union army began enlisting former slaves, the *Friend* let it be known how Quakers regretted the "invitation to them [former slaves] to enter the army and navy, as they have almost uniformly shown themselves to be a peaceable people and unwilling to engage in war."[47] When an army recruiting station for potential African American soldiers was established in Philadelphia in 1863, George Stearns told his wife how the "Quakers wince" at the prospect of a military camp, and that he had attempted to assure Friends

## Conclusion

that the camp was in fact founded "on peace principles; that is to conquer a lasting peace."[48] Many leading Friends remained unconvinced. The Hicksite *Friends Intelligencer,* after publishing Lincoln's Emancipation Proclamation with the comments of the Prairie Grove Monthly Meeting in Iowa that called on the president to enforce the proclamation "uncompromisedly [sic]," the paper nonetheless warned Friends "to take no part" in the "existing war measures" even if the end of slavery could be served by these means.[49]

Through the end of the war and into Reconstruction, leading Philadelphia Friends continued to remind their readers that Quakers entertained "no allegience [sic] to [either] political party" and wanted little to do with the controversies surrounding radical Reconstruction.[50] The Society of Friends also resisted efforts to bring about lasting social change at the point of a bayonet. The *Friend* stated that even though the "rebellion may be finally crushed, and all the insurgent States be again brought under the jurisdiction of the legitimate government, that cannot restore what has already been lost; it cannot heal the wounds rankling in the hearts of the disloyal or ruined southerner. . . ."[51] In a later edition of the paper, the editor reiterated this view: "[E]ven as superior strength and wealth enabled the government to defeat the insurgents . . . and force them into a sullen submission," the numerous "points of controversy between the North and the South are still undecided." Taking an indirect swipe at the Republicans in charge of the government at the time, the editor of the paper feared that things would remain unsettled in the South until "enlightened reason, justice, and moderation" were able to subdue "vile passions" of politicians interested in protracted "unsettlement and discontent" that the paper feared would only lead to "renewed rebellion and loss of life."[52]

In their insistence that the peaceable kingdom could not be achieved by the revolutions of men, the Society of Friends remained true to their pacifist convictions. Yet before the unfolding of the "second American Revolution," the Society of Friends had allowed the weight of experience with intransigent slaveholders and prejudiced Northerners to block their church's support for more principled condemnations of a slaveholding state. Friends had never been ignorant of the reality of American racism. The interconnectedness between violence, slavery, and racial prejudice had long been recognized by the leaders of the Society of Friends. On many occasions, meetings of Quakers, as well as individual members of the church, published comments that foretold disaster for the United States because of its slaveholding crimes. "Wickedness and oppression are, sooner or later, followed by [God's] just judgements," warned one document from Friends in Philadelphia. "The annals of those that have preceded us furnish abundant evidence that national sins have ever incurred national calamities; and that a course of iniquity and violence . . . has eventually terminated in disgrace and ruin."[53] That recognition, however, possessed a myriad of implications when applied to American civil society in the antebellum period, few of which led to support for the abolitionist movement.

Both before and during the Civil War, the Society of Friends broadcast their skepticism regarding humanity's ability to easily transform race relations and often gave prophetic warnings concerning punishment that also accented human incapacity to shape the future. For Samuel Hughes, a Quaker within the Genesee Yearly Meeting, the Lord would deliver slaves from bondage, but "not by the will, nor according to the time of the wild arguments of men. . . ."[54] The decision of groups such as the Quakers to depict abolitionist efforts to remake American race relations as irresponsible and destructive to Christianity revealed—in general—the Friends' pessimistic assessment of the ability of any American to alter society's racial order. For the Society of Friends, abolitionism had always represented a rejection of peaceful moral suasion by offering a dangerous concoction of religious and political dissent. Yet through this portrayal of the abolitionists, the Friends shared in the kind of moral evasion that has often characterized American race relations. Caught between their belief in the immorality of the American racial order and their own skepticism toward human ability to revolutionize society, the Society of Friends, like the rest of the country, could not banish the lingering shadow of violence from their vision of the peaceable kingdom.

# Notes

### Preface

1. In many cases, histories of the abolitionist movement in the United States have downplayed or ignored just how marginalized the abolitionists were from Northern Protestantism, including the approximately 400,000 Christians who belonged to churches that did not tolerate slaveholding. See, in particular, Thomas Bender, ed. *The Antislavery Debate: Capitalism and Abolitionism as a Problem in Historical Interpretation* (Berkeley, Calif., 1992); Lawrence Friedman, *Gregarious Saints: Self and Community in American Abolitionism* (New York, 1982); Joanne Pope Melish, *Disowning Slavery: Gradual Emancipation and 'Race' in New England, 1780–1860* (Ithaca, N.Y.,1998); and Ronald Walters, *The Antislavery Appeal: American Abolitionism after 1830* (New York, 1978). Although John McKivigan adopted an institutional approach for his landmark study of comeouter abolitionists, he did not explore the anti-slavery churches' relationship to the abolitionists, nor did he examine the American churches' conception of religious liberty as it pertained to abolitionism. See John McKivigan, *The War against Proslavery Religion: Abolitionism and the Northern Churches, 1830–1865* (Ithaca, N.Y., 1984). Other works taking a similar institutional approach to the issues of churches and slavery in the antebellum period include C. C. Goen, *Broken Churches, Broken Nation: Denominational Schism and the Coming of the Civil War* (Macon, Ga., 1985); Donald Mathews, *Slavery and Methodism: A Chapter in American Morality* (Princeton, N.J., 1965). Many historians of the early women's rights movement have addressed some of the issues outlined in this study, but they have not focused on the institutional and religious context in which abolitionism was rejected by otherwise anti-slavery clerical leaders. See Nancy Hewitt, *Women's Activism and Social Change: Rochester, NY, 1822–1872* (Ithaca, N.Y., 1984); and Anna Speicher, *The Religious World of Anti-Slavery Women: Spirituality in the Lives of Five Abolitionism Sisters* (Syracuse, N.Y., 2000). Though no book-length treatment of nineteenth-century Quakers and abolitionists exists, two works do devote some space to the dilemma of Quaker anti-slavery described here. See Thomas Drake, *Quakers and Slavery* (New Haven, Conn., 1950), pp. 133–99; and Peter Brock, *Radical Pacifists in Antebellum America* (Princeton, N.J., 1968), pp. 268–79.

2. Catharine Beecher, *An Essay on Slavery and Abolitionism, with reference to the duty of American females* (Philadelphia, 1837), pp. 127, 137–38.

3. Gilbert McMaster, *The Moral Character of Civil Government* (Albany, N.Y., 1832), pp. 62–63, 64.

4. An excellent recent example of the relationship between ideas about religious liberty and definitions of citizenship is Sarah Barringer Gordon, *The Mormon Question: Polygamy and Constitutional Conflict in Nineteenth Century America* (Chapel Hill, N.C., 2002). For a broader discussion of the meaning of the separation of church and state in the nineteenth and twentieth centuries, see Philip Hamburger, *Separation of Church and State* (Cambridge, Mass., 2002).

5. See Alexander Saxton, *The Rise and Fall of the White Republic: Class Politics and*

*Mass Culture in Nineteenth Century America* (New York, 1990); Michael A. Morrison and James Brewer Stewart, eds., *Race and the Early Republic: Racial Consciousness and Nation-Building in the Early Republic* (Lanham, Md., 2002); Reginald Horsman, *Race and Manifest Destiny: The Origins of American Racial Anglo-Saxonism* (Cambridge, Mass., 1981); Nancy Isenberg, *Sex and Citizenship in Antebellum America* (Chapel Hill, N.C., 1998).

6. For the formulation of the idea of Protestantism's "democratization" in the early decades of the nineteenth century, see Nathan O. Hatch, *The Democratization of American Christianity* (New Haven, Conn., 1989).

7. Stephen S. Foster, *The Brotherhood of Thieves; or a True Picture of the American Church and Clergy: A Letter to Nathaniel Birney* (Boston, 1843), pp. 29–30.

8. Quoted in Douglas M. Strong, *Perfectionist Politics: Abolitionism and the Religious Tensions of American Democracy* (Syracuse, N.Y., 1999), p. 73.

9. The *North Star,* "American Religion and American Slavery," June 27, 1850, p. 2.

10. Robert Abzug has laid out an excellent case for studying the religious mindset of reformers in *Cosmos Crumbling: American Reform and the Religious Imagination* (New York, 1994).

## Introduction

1. As quoted in Drake, *Quakers and Slavery*, p. 129.

2. As quoted in Thomas Hamm, *The Transformation of American Quakerism: Orthodox Friends, 1800–1907* (Bloomington, Ind., 1992), p. 2.

3. Two useful histories of early Quakerism include: Adrian Davies, *The Quakers in English Society, 1655–1725* (London, 1999); Barry Reay, *The Quakers and the English Revolution* (New York, 1985).

4. Frederick Tolles, *Quakers and the Atlantic Culture* (New York, 1960), p. 60.

5. A good account of this process is found in Jean R. Soderlund, *Quakers and Slavery: A Divided Spirit* (Princeton, N.J., 1985).

6. Sydney James, *A People among Peoples: Quaker Benevolence in Eighteenth Century America* (Cambridge, Mass., 1963), pp. 247–50.

7. For the two sides of this tension, see James, *A People Among Peoples,* and Jack Marietta, *The Reformation of American Quakerism, 1748–1783* (Philadelphia, 1984).

8. David Cooper, "A Serious Address to the Rulers of America . . . (1783)," in *Am I Not a Man and a Brother: The Antislavery Crusade of Revolutionary America, 1688–1788,* ed. Roger Bruns (New York, 1977), p. 477.

9. Warner Mifflin, *A Serious Expostulation with the Members of the House of Representatives* (1793) in *The Quaker Origins of Antislavery,* ed. J. William Frost (Norwood, Pa., 1980), p. 265.

10. On the challenges facing anti-slavery reformers in a newly established slaveholding republic, see Gary B. Nash, *Race and Revolution* (Madison, Wisc., 1990), and James D. Essig, *The Bonds of Wickedness: American Evangelicals against Slavery, 1770–1808* (Philadelphia, 1982).

11. Drake, *Quakers and Slavery*, p. 129.

12. Elias Hicks, *Observations on the Slavery of the Africans and Their Descendants* (New York, 1811), pp. 6, 9.

13. Elihu Embree, in the *Emancipator,* May 31, 1820, p. 21. Swarthmore.

14. Addison Coffin, "Early Settlement of Friends in North Carolina: Traditions and Reminiscences," typescript, 1894, p. 102. Guilford College Friends Library.

15. Ruth Ketring Nuermberger, "The Free Produce Movement: A Quaker Protest Against Slavery," *Historical Papers of the Trinity College Historical Society* (Durham, N.C., 1942), p. 61.

16. John S. Tyson, *Life of Elisha Tyson, the Philanthropist* (Baltimore, 1825), p. 84.

17. Alexis de Tocqueville, *Democracy in America,* quoted in Paul Boyer, *The Enduring Vision* (Lexington, Mass., 1996), pp. 294–95.

18. Hatch, *The Democratization of American Christianity.*

19. Two useful though quite different discussions of the rise of an American public sphere include Joyce Appleby, *Inheriting the Revolution: The First Generation of Americans* (Cambridge, Mass., 2000), pp. 194–238; and Charles I. Foster, *An Errand of Mercy: The Evangelical United Front, 1790–1837* (Chapel Hill, N.C., 1960).

20. Bruce Dorsey, "Friends Becoming Enemies: Philadelphia Benevolence and the Neglected Era of American Quaker History," *Journal of the Early Republic* (Fall 1998): pp. 418–19.

21. Elias Hicks, *Extracts from the Letters written by Elias Hicks, to a Friend who had joined an "Association for the Suppression of vice and immorality"* (New York, 1841), pp. 10–11.

22. M. T. C. Gould, ed., *A Series of Extemporaneous Discourses . . . by Elias Hicks* (Philadelphia, 1825), p. 49. Firestone Library.

23. Ibid., p. 48.

24. M. T. C. Gould, ed., *Quaker, or a Series of Sermons, by Elias Hicks* (Philadelphia, 1828), pp. 64–65, 38, 48, 45, respectively.

25. The *Friend,* July 5, 1828, p. 299.

26. The *Friend,* January 10, 1829, p. 102.

27. The *Friend,* April 21, 1832, p. 218.

28. The *Friend,* October 3, 1829, p. 404.

29. The *Friend,* March 31, 1832, p. 199.

30. Dorsey, "Friends Becoming Enemies," p. 412.

31. Gould, ed., *A Series of Extemporaneous Discourses,* pp. 271–73.

32. Ibid., pp. 60, 77.

33. Sean Wilentz, *Chants Democratic: New York City and the Rise of the American Working Class, 1788–1850* (New York, 1984), pp. 158–61. For Quaker communitarian radicalism in the 1820s, see also Anthony F. C. Wallace, *Rockdale: The Growth of an American Village in the Early Industrial Revolution* (New York, 1972), pp. 270–75, 285, 324.

34. *Free Enquirer,* February 6, 1830, p. 118.

35. *Free Enquirer,* November 20, 1830, p. 27, and 1831, October 7, 1829, p. 400, respectively.

36. See the membership lists, respectively, in the *Free Enquirer,* July 8, 1829, pp. 402–404, *The Mechanics Free Press,* April 14, 1830, p. 3.

37. Elias Hicks, *Journal of the Life and Religious Labours of Elias Hicks, Written by Himself* (New York, 1832). Firestone.

38. Dorsey, "Friends Becoming Enemies," p. 419.

39. *Delaware Free Press,* June 18, 1831, p. 3.

40. *Delaware Free Press,* "Sermon, Delivered at Buck's Quarterly Meeting . . . May 26, 1831 by Elizabeth M. Reeder," June 18, 1831, p. 2.

41. Ibid.

42. H. Larry Ingle, "'A Ball That Has Rolled Beyond Our Reach': The Consequences of Hicksite Reform, 1830, as seen in an Exchange of Letters," *Delaware History* (XXI, 1984), p. 131.

43. Quoted in Hamm, *Transformation of American Quakerism,* p. 31.

44. Ibid.

45. For the theory of a "democratization" of American Christianity in this period, see Hatch, *The Democratization of American Christianity.*

46. David Brion Davis estimated that the membership of the three largest manu-

mission societies in the middle period, the Pennsylvania Abolition Society, the New York Manumission Society, and the North Carolina Manumission Society, were 50 to 80 percent Quaker. See Davis, *The Problem of Slavery in the Age of Revolution* (Ithaca, N.Y., 1975), pp. 216–17. Thomas Drake concluded that the Tennessee Manumission Society, a largely Quaker organization, contended with the North Carolina Society as "the most active manumission society" before 1830. Drake also noted the preponderance of Quaker names in the American Convention for Promoting the Abolition of Slavery. See Drake, *Quakers and Slavery*, pp. 129–30. On Quaker leadership in this period of anti-slavery efforts, see also Alice Dana Adams, *The Neglected Period of Anti-Slavery in America, 1808–1831* (Boston, 1908), p. 116.

47. Elizabeth Heyrick, *Immediate, Not Gradual Emancipation* . . . (London, 1824), pp. 2–4.

48. W. E. H. Lecky, quoted in *The Antislavery Debate: Capitalism and Abolitionism as a Problem in Historical Interpretation*, ed. Thomas Bender (Berkeley, Calif., 1992), p. 309.

49. "To the Meetings for Sufferings in America," Casual Correspondence of the London Yearly Meeting for Sufferings, 1834, pp. 204–205. Friends House, London.

50. *The Berean*, October 12, 1824, and continued on November 13, 1824, pp. 234, 274 respectively.

51. Drake, *Quakers and Slavery*, pp. 130–31.

52. Quoted in Drake, *Quakers and Slavery*, p. 132.

53. Coffin, "Early Settlement," p. 80.

54. Ibid., pp. 80, 86.

55. Nathan Mendenhall to Enoch Lewis, December 6, 1830, p. 1. Haverford.

56. Jonas Mace to Nathan Mendenhall, November 3, 1832. Standing Committee Correspondence, no. 118. Guilford Friends Library.

57. North Carolina Yearly Meeting Standing Committee Minutes, January 4, 1826, p. 1.

58. George Swaim to Nathan Mendenhall, June 3, 1832. Guilford Friends Library.

59. Edward Bettle to Nathan Mendenhall, May 21, 183(?). Guilford Friends Library.

60. See Hiram Hilty, *By Land and By Sea: Quakers Confront Slavery and Its Aftermath in North Carolina* (Greensboro, N.C., 1993), pp. 60–66.

61. The *Friend*, December 31, 1831, pp. 95–96.

62. The *Friend*, February 11, 1832, p. 140.

63. The *Friend*, January 28, 1832, p. 121.

64. *National Anti-Slavery Standard*, April 29, 1852, p. 195.

65. Both quotes from Howard Beeth, "Outside Agitators in Southern History: The Society of Friends, 1656–1800" (Ph.D. dissertation, History, The University of Houston, 1984), p. 458.

66. Drake, *Quakers and Slavery*, p. 131.

67. Stephen Weeks, *Southern Quakers and Slavery: A Study in Institutional History* (Baltimore, 1896), pp. 244, 284.

68. As quoted in Daniel Kroupa, "Slave Revolts and North Carolina Quaker Migration" (M.A. thesis, History, Michigan State University, 1997), p. 84.

69. Hamm, *The Transformation of American Quakerism*, p. 13.

70. Coffin, "Early Settlement," p. 113.

71. Jeremiah Hubbard, "Letter from Guilford County, North Carolina, March 4, 1834," p. 5. Guilford Friends Library.

72. Ibid., pp. 4–6.

73. Ibid., p. 5.

74. Casual Correspondence of the London Yearly Meeting for Sufferings, "Epistle

from the Meeting for Sufferings in North Carolina—1834," p. 207. Friends House, London.

75. Ibid., p. 209.

76. Ibid., pp. 209–10.

77. Casual Correspondence of the London Yearly Meeting of Sufferings, "Epistle from Baltimore Yearly Meeting," p. 286. Friends House, London.

78. The *Friend,* December 24, 1831, p. 88.

79. Hubbard, "Letter," p. 3.

80. "Nathan Mendenhall to Enoch Lewis, December 6, 1830," p. 1. Haverford Collection.

### 1. Quaker Gradualists and the Challenge of Abolitionism

1. Quoted in Larry E. Tise, *Proslavery: A History of the Defense of Slavery in America, 1701–1840* (Athens, Ga., 1987), p. 271. On the initial response of the free states to the abolitionist movement, see also Lorman Ratner, *Powder Keg: Northern Opposition to the Antislavery Movement, 1831–1840* (New York, 1968); and Leonard Richards, *"Gentlemen of Property and Standing": Anti-Abolition Mobs in Jacksonian America* (New York, 1970).

2. See, for example, the *Friend,* August 30, 1834, p. 373; February 7, 1835, p. 137; and February 14, 1835, p. 151.

3. "A Quaker Petition against Militia Conscription, 1810," quoted in *Liberty and Conscience: A Documentary History of the Experiences of Conscientious Objectors in America through the Civil War,* ed. Peter Brock (New York, 2002), pp. 85–86.

4. William Evans, *Journal of the Life and Religious Services of William Evans, a Minister of the Gospel in the Society of Friends* (Philadelphia, 1870), p. 32.

5. Quoted in Anonymous, *A Dialogue between Telemachus and Mentor on the Rights of Conscience and Military Requisitions* (Boston, 1818), p. 8.

6. Quoted in Brock, *Liberty and Conscience,* p. 8.

7. John B. Pichard, ed., *The Letters of John G. Whittier, vol.1* (Cambridge, Mass., 1975), "To the Members of the Society of Friends, April 16, 1834," pp. 147–48.

8. Pichard, *Letters of John G. Whittier,* "To Elizur Wright," p. 153.

9. Pichard, *Letters of John G. Whittier,* "To Members of the Society of Friends," p. 147.

10. John Greenleaf Whittier, *Prose Works of John Greenleaf Whittier* (Boston, 1866), p. 25.

11. John Greenleaf Whittier, *Justice, Not Expediency; or Slavery Considered with a View to its Rightful and Effectual Remedy, Abolition* (New York, 1833), pp. 1, 10.

12. As quoted in William Lee Miller, *Arguing about Slavery: John Quincy Adams and the Great Battle in the United States Congress* (New York, 1995), p. 71.

13. Letter to Henry C. Wright, April 16, 1837, in *The Letters of William Lloyd Garrison,* vol. 2, ed. Louis Ruchames (Cambridge, Mass., 1971), p. 258.

14. Whittier, *Justice, Not Expediency,* p. 11.

15. Miller, *Arguing about Slavery,* p. 72.

16. Gerda Lerner, *The Grimke Sisters from South Carolina: Pioneers for Women's Rights and Abolition* (New York, 1967), pp. 124–25.

17. See Paul A. Gilje, *The Road to Mobocracy: Popular Disorder in New York City, 1763–1864* (Chapel Hill, N.C., 1987), pp. 123–288.

18. The *Friend,* May 16, 1835, p. 255.

19. The *Friend,* December 7, 1839, pp. 82–83.

20. "An Address to the Quarterly, Monthly, and Preparative Meetings and the Members Thereof, Composing the Yearly Meeting of Friends, Held in Philadelphia" (New York, 1839), p. 8.

21. The *Friend,* "Address of the Yearly Meeting of Friends for New England . . . (1837)," July 7, 1837, p. 315.

22. Drake, *Quakers and Slavery,* p. 146.

23. The *Friend,* November 5, 1836, p. 40.

24. The *Friend,* November 5, 1836, p. 40.

25. The meetings include New England Yearly Meeting in 1837, Philadelphia (Orthodox) 1837, Indiana (Orthodox) 1837, New York (Orthodox) 1837, New York (Hicksite) 1837, Philadelphia (Hicksite) 1839.

26. Christopher Densmore, "The Dilemma of Quaker Anti-Slavery: The Case of Farmington Quarterly Meeting, 1836–1860," *Quaker History* (Fall 1993): pp. 81–82.

27. "David Irish, Meeting for Sufferings," September 1, 1837. Haviland Records Slavery File, Swarthmore College.

28. See New York Yearly Meeting (Hicksite), Meeting for Sufferings Minutes, 1837. Swarthmore College.

29. William Bassett. *Society of Friends in the United States: Their Views of the Anti-Slavery Question and Treatment of the People of Colour* (Darlington, U.K., 1840), pp. iv, 9–11. Lynn Historical Society.

30. James Birney, *Correspondence Between James G. Birney of Kentucky, and Several Individuals of the Society of Friends* (Haverhill, Mass., 1835), pp. 8, 5.

31. Ruchames, ed., *The Letters of William Lloyd Garrison,* "To Lucretia Mott, April 28, 1840," pp. 590–92.

32. "To the *Liberator,*" September 13, 1832, in *The Letters of William Lloyd Garrison,* vol. 2, ed. Walter Merrill (Cambridge, Mass., 1971), pp. 168–70.

33. The *Liberator,* April 23, 1836, "Refuge of Oppression," p. 1.

34. The *Friend,* December 9, 1837, p. 80.

35. "Sarah Grimke to Sarah Douglass, November 23, 1837," in *The Letters of Theodore Dwight Weld, Angelina Grimke, and Sarah Grimke, 1822–44,* ed. Dwight L. Dumond and Gilbert Barnes (New York, 1941), pp. 480–81.

36. On the Pennsylvania Hall burning, see Henry Mayer, *All on Fire: William Lloyd Garrison and the Abolition of Slavery* (New York, 1998), pp. 243, 245–46.

37. Editorials from the *New York Commercial Advertiser* and the *New York Evening Post* published in the *Liberator,* May 25, 1838, p. 2.

38. "Address of the Yearly Meeting of Friends for New England . . . ," the *Friend,* July 7, 1837, p. 315.

39. The *Palladium,* November 9, 1842, "Society of Friends—Slavery," p. 2.

40. The *Friend,* March 15, 1834, p. 184.

41. New York Yearly Meeting (H) Minutes 1837, p. 3. Swarthmore; "An Address to the Quarterly, Monthly, and Preparative Meetings . . . ," Philadelphia Yearly Meeting 1839, p. 12. Swarthmore Friends Library.

42. New York Yearly Meeting (O) Minutes 1845, "Address to the Quarterly, Monthly, and Preparative Meetings. . . . " Swarthmore Friends Library.

43. Ohio Yearly Meeting (H) Minutes 1840, p. 11. Swarthmore Friends Library.

44. Densmore, "The Dilemma of Quaker Anti-Slavery," p. 84.

45. "Sarah M. Grimke and Theodore Weld to Elizabeth Pease, November 14, 1840," in Dumond and Barnes, ed., *The Letters of Theodore Dwight Weld, Angelina Grimke, and Sarah Grimke,* p. 855.

46. Neurmberger. "The Free Produce Movement," p. 65.

47. Quoted in Thomas Hamm, *The Anti-Slavery Movement in Henry County, Indiana* (New Castle, Ind., 1987), p. 7.

48. *Non-Slaveholder,* January 7, 1846, p. 9.

49. *Non-Slaveholder,* January 7, 1846, p. 7.

50. Charles Osborn, *Journal of Charles Osborn* (Cincinnati, 1854), pp. 458, 443.

51. Ibid., p. 459.

52. Ibid., pp. 466–67, 459.

53. Densmore, "The Dilemma of Quaker Anti-Slavery," p. 84.

54. Minutes of the Indiana Yearly Meeting of Anti-Slavery Friends, 1855, pp. 10–11.

55. The only sociological study of nineteenth-century Quakerism is Robert W. Doherty, *The Hicksite Separation: A Sociological Analysis of Religious Schism in Early Nineteenth Century America* (New Brunswick, N.J., 1967). Focusing on the Philadelphia area during the Hicksite schism, Doherty turned up significant evidence of the material wealth of many Friends, even among the Hicksites, whom Doherty tried to depict as less successful than the wealthier orthodox leaders. (This point is doubtful.) In Chester County, Pennsylvania, Doherty found that around 35 percent of all Quaker households were worth at least $6,000 in the period from 1830 to 1850. Within the city of Philadelphia, moreover, Doherty found evidence of significant wealth, even among Hicksite leaders, 47 percent of whom described themselves, in 1828, as "gentlemen, merchant-importer, professional, or businessmen." Among the Hicksites were included William Wharton, Clement Biddle, and Samuel Noble, all well-to-do gentlemen, as well as the surveyor and conveyancer Benjamin Ferris, who was worth $50,814 at his death in 1867. Among the Orthodox leadership, the statistics of wealth are truly staggering. The median net worth of an orthodox "leader" according to Doherty was $51,214 dollars in and around 1850. Two such leaders, the merchant-importers Thomas and Henry Cope, were worth $1,500,000 and $677,000 at their respective deaths in 1854 and 1865. See Doherty, pp. 56–57, 46, 40–41. Among Indiana Friends, Thomas Hamm also found anecdotal evidence of the rising socioeconomic status of Quakers in that region. See Hamm, *Transformation of American Quakerism,* pp. 37–42.

56. *Non-Slaveholder,* January 7, 1846, p. 7.

## 2. Slavery, Religious Liberty, and the "Political" Abolitionism of the Indiana Anti-Slavery Friends

1. *Review of the 1843 Address of the Indiana Yearly Meeting to the Christian Professors . . . ,* 1843, quoted in Walter Edgerton, *A History of the Separation in the Indiana Yearly Meeting* (Cincinnati, 1856), pp. 201, 205.

2. David Gereau, *Some Thoughts on Slavery, Addressed to the Professors of Christianity, and more particularly to those of the Society of Friends* (New York, 1841), p. 6.

3. Beecher, *An Essay on Slavery and Abolitionism,* pp. 136–37.

4. Calvin Colton, *Abolition, a Sedition* (Philadelphia, 1839), pp. 170–71.

5. "Address of the Baltimore Yearly Meeting of Friends," published in the *Palladium,* November 19, 1842, p. 1.

6. Jesse Kersey, "On the Slave System," undated paper in Kersey Papers, Haverford Collection.

7. *The National Anti-Slavery Standard,* "Letter from E. D. Hudson," November 25, 1841, p. 98.

8. Quoted in Drake, *Quakers and Slavery,* p. 145.

9. *Liberator,* December 30, 1842, pp. 1–2.

10. Quoted in Dorothy Sterling, *Ahead of Her Time: Abby Kelly and the Politics of Antislavery* (New York, 1991), pp. 362–63.

11. Sarah Grimke to Theodore Weld, March 10, 1837, in Dumond and Barnes, ed., *The Letters of Theodore Dwight Weld, Angelina Grimke, and Sarah Grimke,* p. 373.

12. Quoted in Julie Roy Jeffrey, *The Great Silent Army of Abolitionism: Ordinary Women in the Antislavery Movement* (Chapel Hill, N.C., 1998), p. 151.

13. Sarah Grimke to Theodore Weld, March 10, 1837, in Dumond and Barnes, ed., *The Letters of Theodore Dwight Weld, Angelina Grimke, and Sarah Grimke,* p. 373.

14. Bassett, *Society of Friends in the United States,* pp. 18–19.

15. Foster, *The Brotherhood of Thieves*, p. 6.

16. Elizabeth Buffum Chace, *Anti-Slavery Reminiscences* (Central Falls, R.I., 1891), pp. 19–20; Drake, *Quakers and Slavery*, pp. 158–61; Densmore, "The Dilemma of Quaker Anti-Slavery," p. 80.

17. Sarah Grimke to Elizabeth Pease, February 11, 1842, in Dumond and Barnes, ed., *The Letters of Theodore Dwight Weld, Angelina Grimke, and Sarah Grimke*, p. 922.

18. Foster, *The Brotherhood of Thieves*, pp. 6, 28–29, 20.

19. Ibid., pp. 28–29.

20. Quoted in Lewis Perry, *Radical Abolitionism: Anarchy and the Government of God in Antislavery Thought* (Ithaca, N.Y., 1973), p. 65.

21. James Brewer Stewart, *Holy Warriors: The Abolitionists and American Slavery* (New York, 1997), p. 98.

22. James Birney to Lewis Tappan, January 14, 1842, in *Letters of James Gillespie Birney, 1831–1857*, ed. Dwight L. Dumond (New York, 1938), p. 659.

23. James Birney to Lewis Tappan, September 12, 1845, in Dumond, ed., *Letters of James Gillespie Birney*, p. 971.

24. Douglas M. Strong, *Perfectionist Politics: Abolitionism and the Religious Tensions of American Democracy* (Syracuse, N.Y., 1999), p. 73.

25. Quoted in Perry, *Radical Abolitionism and the Government of God*, p. 173.

26. Ibid,, p. 174.

27. McKivigan, *The War against Proslavery Religion*, p. 101.

28. Minutes of the Indiana Yearly Meeting of the Society of Friends (O), 1838, p. 19.

29. Edgerton, *A History of the Separation in the Indiana Yearly Meeting*, p. 45.

30. Minutes of the Indiana Yearly Meeting Minutes (O), 1841, pp. 17–18.

31. Thomas D. Hamm, "'On Home Colonization' by Elijah Coffin," *Slavery and Abolition* (1984): p. 164.

32. See both Hamn, "On Home Colonization," pp. 154–55; and Mary C. Johnson, ed., *The Life of Elijah Coffin* (Cincinnati, 1863).

33. Hamm, "On Home Colonization," pp. 161–62.

34. Hamm, *The Transformation of American Quakerism*, pp. 26–27.

35. Arnold Buffum to Joseph Sturge, April 9, 1839. Boston Public Library.

36. Henry Williams to Samuel Williams, October 3, 1840. Williams Collection, Newport Historical Society.

37. *Liberator*, February 15, 1839, p. 2. In a meeting with Lucretia Mott in 1843, President Tyler told her that abolitionists would surely not want a "flood of blacks moving north" and commended the recent epistle of the Baltimore Yearly Meeting condemning Quaker abolitionism. See Margaret Hope Bacon, *Valiant Friend: The Life of Lucretia Mott* (New York, 1980), p. 105.

38. "Journal of Mahlon Day," April 24, 1840. Haverford Collection.

39. Pichard, *Letters of John G. Whittier*, "Letter to the Pennsylvania Freeman—February 26, 1839," p. 335.

40. *The Free Labor Advocate*, October 15, 1842, pp. 2–4.

41. *The Free Labor Advocate*, October 15, 1842, pp. 2–4.

42. *Liberator*, "From the New York Tribune—Speech of Henry Clay," October 28, 1842, p. 1.

43. *National Anti-Slavery Standard*, "Henry Clay," November 3, 1842, p. 85.

44. *Review of the Declaration of a Meeting of Antislavery Friends*, 1843, p. 7. Earlham College Collection.

45. *Palladium*, October 8, 1842, p. 1.

46. *Review of the Declaration of a Meeting of Antislavery Friends*, 1843, p. 7; Edgerton, *A History of the Separation in the Indiana Yearly Meeting*, pp. 84–86, 139–41.

47. *Review of the Declaration of a Meeting of Antislavery Friends,* 1843, pp. 7–8.
48. Drake, *Quakers and Slavery,* pp. 164–65.
49. Osborn, *Journal,* p. 419.
50. Drake, *Quakers and Slavery,* p. 165.
51. Pichard, *Letters of John G. Whittier,* "Letter to the Pennsylvania Freeman—February 26, 1839," p. 337.
52. Osborn, *Journal,* p. 440.
53. Ibid., p. 445.
54. *Some Observations and Explanations touching the situation of Anti-Slavery Friends . . . ,* published in the minutes of the Indiana Yearly Meeting of Anti-Slavery Friends, 1857, p. 11.
55. *Appeal . . . to all persons everywhere,* published in the Indiana Yearly Meeting of Anti-Slavery Friends Minutes, 1843, pp. 41–42.
56. Minutes of the Indiana Yearly Meeting of Anti-Slavery Friends, 1843, p. 27.
57. Emma Lou Thornbrough, *The Negro in Indiana Before 1900* (Indiana Historical Collection, XXXVII, 1957), p. 173.
58. Minutes of the Indiana Yearly Meeting of Anti-Slavery Friends, 1845, p. 14.
59. Ibid., p. 14.
60. McKivigan, *The War against Proslavery Religion,* pp. 130–31.
61. *Address to the Members of the Society of Friends Throughout the World,* published in the Minutes of Yearly Meeting of Anti-Slavery Friends, 1856, pp. 12–13.
62. *Free Labor Advocate,* "What Churches and Church Members Can Do," May 24, 1841, pp. 154–55.
63. "Some Observations and Explanations touching the situation of Anti-Slavery Friends," Minutes of the Indiana Yearly Meeting of Anti-Slavery Friends, 1857, p. 11.
64. Walter Edgerton, "Appeal of the Indiana Yearly Meeting of Anti-Slavery Friends, held at Newport, Indiana. . . . 1843," p. 47.
65. Sophronia A. Jewett to James Birney, Dayton, Ohio, February 19, 1844, in Dumond, ed., *Letters of James Gillespie Birney,* vol. 11, pp. 780–81, 782–83, 784.
66. Joseph Sturge, *To the Members of the Religious Society of Friends in the United States of America,* 1842, pp. 1–2. Haverford Collection.
67. The *Friend,* September 14, 1844, pp. 401–402.
68. *Liberator,* February 15, 1839, p. 2.
69. William L. Garrison to Helen E. Garrison, May 12, 1838, in *Letters of William Lloyd Garrison,* pp. 358–59.
70. Arnold Buffum to Joseph Sturge, April 9, 1839. Boston Public Library.
71. *To those who have recently withdrawn from Indiana Yearly Meeting of Friends,* published in the *Journal of Charles Osborn,* p. 427.
72. Ruchames, ed., *The Letters of William Lloyd Garrison,* vol. 2, p. 698.
73. Sturge, *To the Members of the Religious Society of Friends in the United States of America.* p. 3.
74. Minutes of the Yearly Meeting of Anti-Slavery Friends, 1844, p. 11.
75. James Porter, *Three Lectures . . . on Come-out-ism . . . That It Is Infidelity* (Boston, 1844), pp. 10, 14. LCP.
76. *Address to the Members of the Society of Friends Throughout the World,* published in the Indiana Yearly Meeting of Anti-Slavery Friends, 1856, p. 13.
77. "Memorial of Newton Stubbs," published in the Minutes of the Indiana Yearly Meeting of Anti-Slavery Friends, p. 12.

### 3. Friends and the "Children of Africa"

1. A good recent account of Quaker egalitarianism regarding race can be found in Thomas D. Hamm et al., "'A Great and Good People': Midwestern Quakers and

the Struggle Against Slavery," *Indiana Magazine of History* (March 2004): pp. 1–25. See also Rufus M. Jones, *The Later Periods of Quakerism* (2 vols., London, 1921), II, especially pp. 559–620; and Emma Lou Thornbrough, *The Negro in Indiana before 1900: A Study of a Minority* (Indianapolis, 1957).

2. The *North Star,* "Plymouth, Weymouth, Schuylerville, Quaker Springs," June 25, 1849, p. 2.

3. *National Anti-Slavery Standard,* "Remarkable Confession," December 16, 1847, p. 114.

4. *National Anti-Slavery Standard,* "Letter from Nantucket," November 17, 1842, p. 94.

5. Nancy Isenberg, "'Pillars in the Same Temple and Priests of the Same Worship': Women's Rights and the Politics of Church and State in Antebellum America," *Journal of American History* (June 1998): pp. 98–99.

6. The *North Star,* "American Religion and American Slavery," June 27, 1850, p. 2.

7. The *North Star,* "The American Religion Pro-Slavery," September 29, 1848, p. 1.

8. My use of the phrase "racial order" is borrowed from the work of George Fredrickson. See his recent book *Racism: A Short History* (Princeton, N.J., 2002), p. 6.

9. *Proceedings of the General Anti-Slavery Convention . . . held in London from June 13th to June 20th, 1843* (London, 1843), pp. 97, 110.

10. Joanne Pope Melish, *Disowning Slavery: Gradual Emancipation and 'Race' in New England, 1780–1860* (Ithaca, N.Y., 1998), p. 3. One important exception to this emphasis on the limits to the abolitionists' racial egalitarianism is John Stauffer, *The Black Hearts of Men: Radical Abolitionists and the Transformation of Race* (Cambridge, Mass., 2002).

11. Quoted in Joseph Willson, *The Elite of Our People,* ed. Julie Winch (University Park, Pa., 2000), p. 30.

12. Leon Litwack, *North of Slavery: The Negro in the Free States, 1790–1860* (Chicago, 1961), p. 130.

13. Zephaniah W. Pease, ed., *The Diary of Samuel Rodman: A New Bedford Chronicle of Thirty-Seven Years 1821–1850* (New Bedford, Mass., 1927), pp. 268–69.

14. George Fox, *Gospel Family Order,* in Frost, ed., *The Quaker Origins,* p. 55.

15. Quoted in Soderlund, *Quakers and Slavery: A Divided Spirit,* p. 183.

16. Henry Cadbury, "Negro Membership in the Society of Friends," *Journal of Negro History,* vol. 21 (April 1936): pp. 154, 158.

17. Quote attributed to Joseph Drinker in Gary Nash, *Forging Freedom: The Formation of Philadelphia's Black Community, 1720–1840* (Cambridge, Mass., 1988), p. 180.

18. Hubbard, "Letter," p. 5.

19. Margaret Hope Bacon, "New Light on Sarah Mapps Douglass and Her Reconciliation with Friends," *Quaker History* (Spring 2001): p. 32.

20. Bassett, *Society of Friends in the United States,* p. 17.

21. Ibid., p. 22.

22. Ida Husted Harper, *Life and Work of Susan B. Anthony,* vol. 1 (Salem, N.H., 1983), p. 39.

23. Sarah Grimke to Elizabeth Pease, April 18, 1840, in Dumond and Barnes, ed., *The Letters of Theodore Dwight Weld, Angelina Grimke, and Sarah Grimke,* p. 829.

24. Quoted in Carolyn Williams, "The Female Antislavery Movement: Fighting Against Racial Prejudice and Promoting Woman's Rights in Antebellum America," in *The Abolitionist Sisterhood: Women's Political Culture in Antebellum America,* ed. Jean Fagan Yellin (Ithaca, N.Y., 1994), p. 167.

25. Emma Kimber to Abby Kimber, November 10, 1839, Robinson Papers, Box XI, Newport Historical Society.

26. Quoted in Katherine Smedley, *Martha Schofield and the Re-Education of the South, 1839–1916* (Lewistown, N.Y., 1987), pp. 116–17.

27. Quoted in Kenneth Ives, ed., *Black Quakers: Brief Biographies* (Chicago, 1991), p. 49.

28. Quoted in Blanche Glassman Hersh, *The Slavery of Sex: Feminist-Abolitionists in America* (Urbana, Ill.1978), p. 127.

29. The *Friend*, "The Society of Friends and Abolition," August 19, 1843, p. 375.

30. Quoted in Cadbury, "Negro Membership in the Society of Friends," p. 169n.

31. The *Friend*, "The Society of Friends and Abolition," August 19, 1843, p. 375.

32. Harper, *Life and Work of Susan B. Anthony*, p. 39.

33. *The British Friend*, "John Candler's Letters on America," April 29, 1843, p. 55.

34. *Free Labor Advocate*, February 11, 1841, p. 18.

35. Elizabeth B. Clark, "'The Sacred Rights of the Weak': Pain, Sympathy, and the Culture of Individual Rights in Antebellum America," *The Journal of American History* (September, 1995): p. 468.

36. Jean Fagan Yellin, ed., *Incidents in the Life of a Slave Girl Written by Herself* (Cambridge, 1987), p. 189.

37. Quoted in Richard Newman, *The Transformation of American Abolitionism: Fighting Slavery in the Early Republic* (Chapel Hill, N.C., 2002), p. 106.

38. Quoted in Litwack, *North of Slavery*, p. 217.

39. Quoted in Williams, "The Female Antislavery Movement," p. 169.

40. Frederick Douglass, *My Bondage and My Freedom* (New York, 1844), pp. 357, 359–60.

41. Bassett, *Society of Friends in the United States*, pp. 24–25, 22.

42. Ibid., p. 25.

43. Ibid., pp. 25–26.

44. See Bacon, "New Light on Sarah Mapps Douglass," pp. 28–29.

45. *National Anti-Slavery Standard*, December 14, 1843.

46. *The Non-Slaveholder*, "The Death of a 'colored' Friend," September 1850, p. 55.

47. Bacon, "New Light on Sarah Mapps Douglass," pp. 33–34.

48. Quoted in Benjamin Quarles, *Black Abolitionists* (New York, 1969), p. 72.

49. The *Liberator*, "Pennsylvania Quakerism," July 4, 1851, p. 108.

50. Weeks, *Southern Quakers and Slavery*, p. 233.

51. *National Anti-Slavery Standard*, "Remarkable Confession," December 16, 1847, p. 114.

52. The *Liberator*, editorial of "Zillah," April 1, 1832, p. 3; see also Marie J. Lindhorst, "Sarah Mapps Douglass: The Emergence of an African-American Educator/Activist in Nineteenth Century Philadelphia" (Ph.D. dissertation, Education, The State University of Pennsylvania, 1995).

### 4. "Progressive" Friends and the Government of God

1. Quoted in Allen C. Thomas, "Congregational or Progressive Friends: A Forgotten Episode in Quaker History," *Bulletin of the Friends Historical Association* (November 1920): p. 22.

2. *Delaware Free Press*, "Frances Wright to the Members of the Society of Friends in Wilmington, Del.," May 22, 1830, p. 3.

3. Thomas Branagan, *The Pleasures of Contemplation* (Philadelphia, 1818), p. 26. Library Company Philadelphia.

4. *Mechanics Free Press,* April 10, 1830, p. 3; September 4, 1830, p. 2.

5. Quoted in Dana Greene, ed., *Lucretia Mott: Her Complete Speeches and Sermons* (New York, 1980), p. 176.

6. Anna Davis Hallowell, *Life and Letters of Lucretia Mott* (Boston, 1884), pp. 73–74.

7. Untitled Document 857, Jesse Kersey Papers, Haverford.

8. *Delaware Free Press,* "Education of Women," November 19, 1831, p. 1. It is also worth noting that many leading Quakers criticized those members of the sect who attended Frances Wright's lectures by saying that the "Fanny Wright men" among their church had "encouraged the dissemination of her principles" tending to the "abrogation of the law of marriage." See *Delaware Free Press,* "Investigation of B. Webb . . . ," November 19, 1831, p. 3, and the letter from Elijah Crane on September 24, 1831, p. 2.

9. *Delaware Free Press,* "To Benjamin Ferris, Letter 5," April 24, 1830, pp. 1–2. Here Owen responded to the accusation of some Quakers that he was advocating the abolition of marriage.

10. Quoted in Hersh, *The Slavery of Sex,* p. 23.

11. Quoted in ibid., p. 9.

12. On Quaker preaching in colonial America, see Rebecca Larson, *Daughters of Light: Quaker Women Preaching and Prophesying in the Colonies and Abroad, 1700–75* (New York, 1999). On women preaching in general before 1830, see Christine Leigh Heyrman, *Southern Cross: The Beginnings of the Bible Belt* (Chapel Hill, N.C., 1997), especially pages 161–205.

13. Margaret Morris Haviland, "Beyond Women's Sphere: Young Quaker Women and the Veil of Charity in Philadelphia, 1790–1810," *William and Mary Quarterly* (July 1994): pp. 419–20.

14. A good treatment of the life of Beecher is contained in Kathryn Kish Sklar, *Catharine Beecher: A Study in American Domesticity* (New Haven, Conn., 1973).

15. Quoted in Greene, ed., *Lucretia Mott: Her Complete Speeches and Sermons,* p. 141.

16. Quoted in Douglass, *The Feminization of American Culture,* p. 116.; see also Abzug, *Cosmos Crumbling,* pp. 195–96.

17. "From a Pastoral Letter, 'The General Association of Massachusetts (Orthodox) to the Churches Under Their Care' (1837)," in *The Feminist Papers: From Adams to de Beauvoir,* ed. Alice S. Rossi (Boston, 1988), pp. 305–306.

18. Sarah Grimke, "Letters on the Equality of the Sexes, XV, (1837)," in Rossi, ed., *The Feminist Papers,* pp. 316–17.

19. Angelina Grimke, "Letters to Catherine Beecher, XII, (1837)," in Rossi, ed., *The Feminist Papers,* p. 322. In making this claim, Grimke was referring both to the male-exclusive nature of the Meeting for Sufferings and that men could make certain disciplinary decisions regarding male members without female approval, but women could not do the same.

20. Sarah Grimke, "Letters on the Equality of the Sexes, I" in Rossi, ed., *The Feminist Papers,* p. 308.

21. *Proceedings of the General Anti-Slavery Convention, Called by the Committee of the British and Foreign Anti-Slavery Society, and Held in London from June 12th to June 23rd, 1840* (London, 1841), pp. 25, 32.

22. Quoted in Ellen Carol DuBois, ed., *The Elizabeth Cady Stanton–Susan B. Anthony Reader* (Boston, 1992), p. 11.

23. Lerner, *The Grimke Sisters from South Carolina,* p. 185.

24. Sterling, *Ahead of Her Time,* p. 64.

25. Amy Post to her sister, November 19, 1844, Post Family Papers, University of Rochester.

26. Joseph Post to Isaac Post, date unknown, letter number 164. See also letter number 158 in Post Family Papers, University of Rochester.

27. Joseph Post to Isaac Post, date unknown, letter number 171, Post Family Papers, University of Rochester.

28. *National Anti-Slavery Standard,* "Hester street Meeting," July 1, 1847, p. 18.

29. Quoted in Hewitt, *Women's Activism and Social Change,* p. 93.

30. Philadelphia Yearly Meeting (H) 1840 Broadside, Robinson Papers, Newport Historical Society.

31. A. Day Bradley, "Progressive Friends in Michigan and New York," *Quaker History,* vol. 52 (1963): p. 101.

32. Evidence of such problems comes from two letters: Peter Macy to Samuel Mott, October 12, 1845, Haverford Collection; and Edith Smith to Daniel Smith, date unknown, in Robinson Papers, Box II, Newport Historical Society.

33. Thomas Hamm, *God's Government Begun: The Society for Universal Inquiry and Reform, 1842–46* (Bloomington, Ind., 1995), pp. 67–68.

34. "An Epistle from Indiana Yearly Meeting . . . to all subordinate Meetings for Discipline; and to Friends generally," Minutes of the Indiana Yearly Meeting (H), 1844, pp. 8–9.

35. John J. Cornell, *Autobiography of John J. Cornell, Containing an Account of his Religious Experiences and Travels in the Ministry* (Baltimore, 1906), pp. 22–23.

36. Hamm, *God's Government Begun,* pp. 70, 197–98.

37. George A. Schooley, ed., *The Journal of Dr. William Schooley: Pioneer Physician, Quaker Minister, Abolitionist, Philosopher, Scholar* (Zanesville, Ohio, 1977), pp. 92–93.

38. Schooley, *Journal of Dr. William Schooley,* pp. 98–99; Hamm, *God's Government Begun,* pp. 197–98, 216–17; Thomas, "Congregational or Progressive Friends," pp. 26, 28.

39. Hamm, *God's Government Begun,* p. 83.

40. Ibid., p. 75.

41. Christopher Clark, *The Communitarian Moment: The Radical Challenge of the Northampton Association* (Ithaca, N.Y., 1995).

42. Arthur J. Bestor, *Backwoods Utopias; the Sectarian and Owenite Phases of Communitarian Socialism in America, 1663–1829* (Philadelphia, 1950).

43. Hamm, *God's Government Begun,* pp. 157–58.

44. Ibid., p. 156.

45. On the differences between abolitionism and the labor movement, see Walters, *The Antislavery Appeal: American Abolitionism after 1830,* pp. 111–28.

46. Albert John Wahl, "The Congregational or Progressive Friends in the Pre–Civil War Reform Movement" (Ph.D. dissertation, Education, Temple University, 1951), p. 37.

47. Quoted in Hewitt, *Women's Activism and Social Change,* p. 130.

48. Thomas McClintock and Rhoda DeGarmo, *Basis of Religious Association, Adopted by the Conference Held at Farmington, in the state of New York, on the Sixth and Seventh of Tenth month, 1848,* pp. 1–2.

49. Ibid., pp. 3–4.

50. Ibid., pp. 5–6.

51. "Exposition of Sentiments Adopted by the Pennsylvania Yearly Meeting of Progressive Friends," in *Proceedings of the Pennsylvania Yearly Meeting of Progressive Friends . . . 1854* (New York, 1854), p. 31.

52. Ibid., p. 32.

53. Nell Irvin Painter, *Sojourner Truth: A Life, A Symbol* (New York, 1996), p. 145.

54. The *North Star,* "Meeting at Waterloo," June 29, 1849, p. 2.

55. Quoted in Wilentz, *Chants Democratic,* p. 336.

56. Ibid., p. 337.

57. Lucretia Mott, "Quarterly Meetings, No Ordinary Occasions," in Greene, ed., *Lucretia Mott: Her Complete Speeches and Sermon*, p. 141.

58. Albert J. Wahl, "The Progressive Friends of Longwood," *Quaker History*, vol. 42, no. 1 (Spring 1953): p. 21.

59. Hewitt, *Women's Activism and Social Change*, p. 130.

60. Quoted in Rossi, *The Feminist Papers*, pp. 416–17.

61. "An Address to the Women of the State of New York from the Yearly Meeting of Congregational Friends, 1850," pp. 13–14. Swarthmore Friends Library.

62. Ibid.," pp. 15, 17.

63. Letter to Mary Benson, November 27, 1835, in Merrill, *Letters of William Lloyd Garrison*, vol. 1, pp. 563–64; Letter to Elizabeth Pease, 1841, and to Elizabeth Pease, July 2, 1842, in Walter M. Merrill, *Letters of William Lloyd Garrison, 1841–49*, vol. 3 (Cambridge, Mass., 1981), pp. 22–23, 90.

64. Letter to Joseph Dugdale, May 19, 1853, in Louis Ruchames, *Letters of William Lloyd Garrison*, vol. 4 (Cambridge, Mass., 1981), pp. 235–36.

65. *National Anti-Slavery Standard*, "Development of Pro-Slavery Quakerism," June 24, 1852, p. 17; and "The Marlborough Affair," July 1, 1852, p. 22.

66. Oliver Johnson, *William Lloyd Garrison and His Times; or Sketches of the Anti-Slavery Movement in America, and of the Man Who Was Its Founder and Moral Leader* (Boston, 1882), pp. 21, 263, 376.

67. Wahl, "The Progressive Friends of Longwood," p. 27.

68. *Friends Weekly Intelligencer*, August 9, 1845, p. 149.

69. *Friends Weekly Intelligencer*, "Communism," November 15, 1851, p. 268; and "Communism," November 1, 1851, pp. 252–53.

70. Jesse Kersey, Untitled Document 856 in the Jesse Kersey Papers, Haverford Friends Collection.

71. Charles Marriott to unknown, December 4, 1849, Marriott Papers, Haverford Friends Collection.

72. George Fox White to Moses Pierce, August 17, 1845, Swarthmore College.

73. Emma Kimber to Abby Kimber, ca. 1845. Robinson Papers, Box II, Newport Historical Society.

74. Joseph Post to Isaac Post, Letter 192, date unknown. Post Papers, University of Rochester.

75. Rachel Hicks, *Memoir of Rachel Hicks* (New York, 1880), pp. 61–62.

76. Edith Smith to Daniel Smith, date unknown. Robinson Papers, Box II, Newport Historical Society.

77. The *Friend*, "Thoughts on 'Women's Rights' Agitation," September 11, 1858, pp. 3–4; see also a similar article in the Hicksite *Friends Weekly Intelligencer*, March 27, 1852, p. 5.

78. *Friends Weekly Intelligencer*, "Spiritual Rappings," April 3, 1852, pp. 12–13; other Quaker objections to the "delusive voices" of the spiritualists can be found in Samuel M. Janney, *Memoirs of Samuel M. Janney* (Philadelphia, 1881), pp. 132–34.

79. William Ramsey, *Spiritualism, a Satanic Delusion and a Sign of the Times* (Providence, R.I., 1861), pp. 17, 120.

80. For a discussion of the connection between spiritualism and women's rights, see Ann Braude, *Radical Spirits: Spiritualism and Women's Rights in Nineteenth Century America* (Bloomington, Ind., 2001).

81. *Friends Weekly Intelligencer*, "Dissolution of the Union," March 16, 1850, pp. 404–405.

82. Quoted in Stephanie McCurry, *Masters of Small Worlds: Yeoman Households*,

*Gender Relations, and the Political Culture of the Antebellum South Carolina Low Country* (New York, 1994), p. 234.

83. *Friends Weekly Intelligencer,* August 9, 1845, pp. 148–49.

84. *Friends Weekly Intelligencer,* "Dissolution of the Union," March 16, 1850, p. 405.

85. Joseph Post to Isaac Post, undated, letter 192. Post Papers, University of Rochester.

86. Sarah E. Thayer to Amy Kirby Post, ca. 1845. Post Papers, University of Rochester.

87. *The National Anti-Slavery Standard,* January 25, 1849, "Politics and the Pulpit," p. 138.

88. *The National Anti-Slavery Standard,* July 5, 1856, "The Progressive Friends," p. 2.

## 5. Quaker Pacifism and Civil Disobedience in the Antebellum Period

1. James Birney to Lewis Tappan, September 12, 1845, in Dumond, ed., *Letters of James Gillespie Birney,* p. 971.

2. Quoted in Brock, *Radical Pacifists in Antebellum America,* p. 279.

3. *Friends Review,* September 27, 1851, p. 24.

4. Jesse Kersey, "On the Slave System," undated and unpublished paper in the Kersey Papers, Haverford Collection.

5. George Fox White to Moses Pierce, May 4, 1842, in George F. White Letters, Swarthmore Friends Library.

6. Lewis Perry, "Versions of Anarchism in the Antislavery Movement," *American Quarterly* (Winter 1968): p. 781.

7. Perry, *Radical Abolitionism,* pp. 132–33.

8. *National Anti-Slavery Standard,* "Orthodox Yearly Meeting of Friends," November 1, 1849, p. 89.

9. *Free Labor Advocate,* September 24, 1842, p. 3.

10. Osborn, *Journal of Charles Osborn,* p. 454.

11. Quoted in Newman, *The Transformation of American Abolitionism,* p. 84.

12. *Appeal to all persons . . . ,* published in the Minutes of the Indiana Yearly Meeting of Anti-Slavery Friends, 1843, pp. 45–46.

13. Minutes of the Indiana Yearly Meeting of Anti-Slavery Friends, 1844, p. 29.

14. *Address to the Society of Friends on the American Continent,* published in the Minutes of the Indiana Yearly Meeting of Anti-Slavery Friends, 1844, pp. 6–7.

15. *Free Labor Advocate,* July 24, 1841, p. 1; *Appeal to all persons . . . ,* pp. 45–46.

16. A. L. Benedict, *Memoir of Richard Dillingham* (Philadelphia, 1852), pp. 2–29. Haverford Collection.

17. Quoted in Harriet Beecher Stowe, *Key to Uncle Tom's Cabin* (Boston, 1853), p. 55.

18. *National Anti-Slavery Standard,* "Speech of T. W. Higginson," May 16, 1857, pp. 2–3.

19. See Lewis Perry, *Childhood, Marriage, and Reform: Henry Clarke Wright, 1797–1870* (Chicago, 1980).

20. Quoted in Mayer, *All on Fire,* p. 251.

21. Henry C. Wright, *The Dissolution of the American Union, Demanded by Justice and Humanity, as the Incurable Enemy of Liberty . . .* (Glasgow, 1845), pp. 3–5.

22. *National Anti-Slavery Standard,* "Slavery and the Churches," November 17, 1855, p. 1.

23. Quoted in Drake, *Quakers and Slavery,* p. 175.

24. See, for example, the *Liberator,* "Dissolution of the Union," January 25, 1850, p. 15.
25. Brock, *Radical Pacifists in Antebellum America,* p. 98.
26. *The Non-Resistant,* June 15, 1839, p. 2.
27. *The Non-Resistant,* July 6, 1839, pp. 2–3.
28. New England Yearly Meeting, *View of the Society of Friends in Relation to Civil Government* (Providence, 1840), pp. 6, 9–10.
29. Robert Barclay, *The Anarchy of the Ranters And Other Libertines . . .* (London, 1676), pp. 17, 21, 50.
30. *Friends Intelligencer,* "Non-Resistance," August 21, 1847, pp. 164–65.
31. *National Anti-Slavery Standard,* "Lucretia Mott in New York," November 17, 1855, p. 2.
32. *The Non-Resistant,* February 16, 1839, p. 3.
33. *The Friend,* October 12, 1850, p. 31.
34. *Friends Review,* May 13, 1848, p. 538.
35. Edgerton, *History of the Separation in the Indiana Yearly Meeting,* p. 34, 239–41.
36. *National Anti-Slavery Standard,* "Philadelphia Yearly Meeting of Friends," March 23, 1848, p. 170; Drake, *Quakers and Slavery,* p. 187.
37. Hiram Hilty, "North Carolina Quakers and Slavery" (Ph.D. dissertation, Duke University, 1968), p. 201.
38. Larry Gara, *Liberty Line: The Legend of the Underground Railroad* (Lexington, Ky., 1961).
39. *National Anti-Slavery Standard,* "Outrage in Friends' Meeting," October 5, 1848, p. 74.
40. *National Anti-Slavery Standard,* "The Taylorite Quakers," November 23, 1848, p. 102.
41. Quoted in Brock, *Radical Pacifists in Antebellum America,* p. 278.
42. *National Anti-Slavery Standard,* "No Voting and Disunion," August 14, 1851, p. 46.
43. *National Anti-Slavery Standard,* "The Taylorite Quakers," November 23, 1848, p. 102.
44. *The Non-Resistant,* "To Friends—Human Politics," June 15, 1839, pp. 1–2; see also *The Non-Resistant,* "War and Quakerism," February 16, 1839, p. 1.
45. *The Non-Resistant,* "American Church and State," February 9, 1842, p. 4.
46. See, for example, *The Congressional Globe . . . of the first session of the 31st Congress* (Washington, D.C., 1850), p. 319.
47. *Philadelphia Public Ledger,* February 18, 1850, p. 2.
48. *National Anti-Slavery Standard,* "Friends," February 28, 1850, p. 159; *The Congressional Globe . . . of the first session of the 31st Congress* (Washington, D.C., 1850), p. 362.
49. *National Anti-Slavery Standard,* "Address of Friends," November 4, 1852, p. 93.
50. *Democratic Review,* "The Conspiracy of Fanaticism," May 1850, p. 391.
51. *Democratic Review,* "Abolition v. Christianity and the Union," July 1850, p. 4.
52. Quoted in Sarah Barringer Gordon, "Blasphemy and the Law of Religious Liberty in Nineteenth Century America," *American Quarterly* (December 2000): p. 685.
53. See Mark Hanley, *Beyond a Christian Commonwealth: The Protestant Quarrel with the American Republic* (Chapel Hill, N.C., 1994), pp. 41–48, 157–63.
54. Daniel Walker Howe, *The Political Culture of the American Whigs* (Chicago, 1979), pp. 156–57.
55. Billy Hibbard, *An Address to the Quakers* (New York, 1811), pp. 114, 129; see also Asa Rand, *Two Sermons on Christian Fellowship* (Portland, Maine, 1817).

56. *The Princeton Review,* "The Doctrine of the Inner Light," July 1848, pp. 378–80.

57. William Craig Brownlee, *A Careful and Free Inquiry into the True Nature and Tendency of the Religious Principles of the Society of Friends, Commonly Called Quakers* (Philadelphia, 1824), pp. 295, 195, 201, 206. See also Samuel Cox, *Quakerism Not Christianity, or Reasons for Renouncing the Doctrine of Friends* (New York, 1833).

58. The *Friend,* January 10, 1829, p. 102.

59. The *Friend,* February 10, 1849, p. 168; see also the *Friend,* February 2, 1850, p. 160.

60. John Gest, *A Brief Defence of John the Baptist, Against Foul Slander and Wicked Libel of Freemasons . . .* (Philadelphia, 1834), pp. 13, 15. On Quaker support for the Anti-Masons, see Paul Goodman, *Towards a Christian Republic: Antimasonry and the Great Transition in New England, 1826–36* (New York, 1988), pp. 75–79, 92–93, 136–37, 178–79, 186–87.

61. *Friends Weekly Intelligencer,* "Millennial," October 9, 1852, p. 228.

62. The *Friend,* November 21, 1857, p. 87.

63. The *Friend,* December 29, 1855, p. 127.

64. The *Friend,* May 26, 1849, p. 296.

65. The *Friend,* July 21, 1849, p. 352; and the *Friend,* "Episcopacy and Popery," December 7, 1850, p. 95.

66. The Congressional Globe . . . of the first session of the 31st Congress, pp. 363, 364.

67. *Friends Weekly Intelligencer,* "Daniel Webster and the Society of Friends," June 8, 1850, pp. 85–87.

68. Quoted in Drake, *Quakers and Slavery,* p. 181.

69. *Friends Weekly Intelligencer,* "Daniel Webster and the Society of Friends," June 8, 1850, p. 86.

70. The *Pennsylvania Freedmen,* March 28, 1850, p. 3.

71. Quoted in Drake, *Quakers and Slavery,* p. 177.

72. Quoted in Stewart, *Holy Warriors,* p. 157.

## Conclusion

1. Harriet Beecher Stowe, *Uncle Tom's Cabin* (New York, 1966), pp. 141, 188.

2. The myth of the Quaker-led Underground Railroad has been discussed in Gara, *The Liberty Line,* pp. 164–94. See also Glenn Nelson Cummings, "Exercising Goodness: The Antislavery Quaker in American Writing" (Ph.D. dissertation, English, University of Virginia, 1996). Many modern-day popular depictions of the Underground Railroad have also been influenced by accounts such as Stowe's in making Quakerism synonymous with work on behalf of black freedom. See, for example, Ann Hagedorn, *Beyond the River: The Untold Story of the Heroes of the Underground Railroad* (New York, 2002) as well as the website of the National Underground Railroad Freedom Center at www.freedomcenter.org; the website of the Public Broadcasting System, "Africans in America" at www.pbs.org, and the Underground Railroad heading at the website for the National Register of Historic Places, www.cr.nps.gov/nr/travel/underground.

3. Herman Melville, *Moby Dick* (London, 1851: reprint, 1927), pp. 74–75, 73.

4. Ibid., pp. 96–7.

5. David Porter, *Journal of a Cruise Made to the Pacific Ocean, by Captain David Porter . . .* (Philadelphia, 1815), p. 144.

6. For these ships, see Mitra Sharafi, "The Slave Ship Manuscripts of Captain Joseph B. Cook: A Narrative Reconstruction of the Brig *Nancy*'s Voyage of 1793," *Slavery and Abolition* (April 2003): p. 78.

7. Charles F. Briggs, *The Trippings of Tom Pepper; or the Results of Romancing* (New York, 1847), p. 108.

8. Walter Edgerton, *Address to the Members of the Society of Friends Throughout the World,* published in the Minutes of the Indiana Yearly Meeting of Anti-Slavery Friends, 1856, pp. 13–14.

9. Mayer, *All on Fire,* p. 120; the *Liberator,* "Rhode Island A. S. Society," November 14, 1851, p. 187.

10. To Robert Charles Winthrop, June 10, 1854, in Merrill, *Letters of John Greenleaf Whittier,* p. 264.

11. The *Liberator,* "Great Meeting in Faneuil Hall," June 2, 1854, p. 86.

12. The *Friend,* December 1859, pp. 111–12; see also June 23, 1860, pp. 335–36.

13. *Friends Intelligencer,* December 24, 1859, pp. 648–49.

14. Quoted in Drake, *Quakers and Slavery,* p. 194.

15. The *Friend,* September 27, 1851, p. 16.

16. See Thomas P. Slaughter, *Bloody Dawn: The Christiana Riot and Racial Violence in the Antebellum North* (New York, 1991), p. 67.

17. The *Friend,* September 27, 1851, p. 16.

18. Philadelphia Yearly Meeting, "At a Meeting of the Representative Committee, or Meeting for Sufferings, held 1st month, 31st, 1851, p. 1. Haverford College.

19. Quoted in Slaughter, *Bloody Dawn,* p. 67.

20. The *Liberator,* "Death to Slavehunters—Treason to the U.S. Government a Duty to God and Man," November 28, 1851, p. 92.

21. The *Liberator,* "Pennsylvania Abolitionism," October 24, 1851, p. 170.

22. *Friends Review,* September 27, 1851, p. 24.

23. The *Friend,* September 20, 1856, p. 16.

24. Unspecified newspaper article from 1857, Samuel Allinson Scrapbook, p. 14, Haverford College.

25. *The National Era,* "Friends in Kansas," September 4, 1856, p. 2.

26. Quoted in Mary D. Pellauer, *Toward a Tradition of Feminist Theology: The Religious Social Thought of Elizabeth C. Stanton, Susan B. Anthony, and Anna Howard Shaw* (New York, 1991), p. 200.

27. For evidence of support for emigrant aid societies, see *Friends Review,* December 13, 1856, pp. 222–23; for Daniel Anthony, see Jennifer L. Weber, "'If Ever War Was Holy': Quaker Soldiers and the Union Army," *North and South* (April 2002): pp. 68–69.

28. A good account of Brown's activities is Stephen Oates, *To Purge This Land With Blood* (New York, 1970).

29. Eve Lewis Perera and Lucille Salitan, eds., *Virtuous Lives: Four Quaker Sisters Remember Family Life, Abolitionism, and Woman's Suffrage* (New York, 1994), pp. 122–24.

30. Edwin Coppoc to his uncle, Harper's Ferry, December 13, 1859, in Errol Elliot file, Haverford College.

31. Ann Coppoc Raley to Mary Ball, 1859, in Errol Elliot file, Haverford College.

32. Levi Coffin to Daniel Huff, December 1, 1859, Huff Family Papers, Earlham College.

33. Quoted in Pellauer, *Toward a Tradition of Feminist Theology,* p. 197.

34. The *Friend,* "Fighting Quakers," November 18, 1862, pp. 52–53.

35. A. J. H. Duganne, *The Fighting Quakers: A True Story of the War For Our Nation* (New York, 1866), p. 28.

36. Quoted in Weber, "'If Ever War Was Holy,'" p. 66.

37. Quoted in Jacqueline S. Nelson, "Civil War Letters of Daniel Wooton: The Metamorphosis of a Quaker Soldier," *Indiana Magazine of History and Biography* (March

*Notes to pages 131–134*

1989): pp. 50–52, 57; see also the letter from Ethan Foster to William H. S. Wood, February 22, 1881, William H. S. Wood Collection, Haverford College.

38. Quoted in Weber, "'If Ever War Was Holy,'" p. 65.

39. Jacqueline Nelson, *Indiana Quakers Confront the Civil War* (Indianapolis, Ind., 1991), pp. 20–23, 96.

40. See Henretta Stratton Jaquette, ed. *South After Gettysburg: Letters of Cornelia Hancock* (New York, 1937); Smedley, *Martha Schofield and the Re-Education of the South*; Jacquelyn Nelson, "Military and Civilian Support for the Civil War by the Society of Friends in Indiana," *Quaker History* (Spring 1987): p. 58.

41. Norwood P. Hallowell, *The Negro as a Soldier in the War of the Rebellion* (Boston, 1897), pp. 9–10, 16.

42. Wendy Hamand Venet, *Neither Ballots nor Bullets: Women Abolitionists and the Civil War* (Charlottesville, Va., 1991), p. 39; for the biography of Anna Dickinson, see Giraud Chester, *Embattled Maiden: The Life of Anna Dickinson* (New York, 1951).

43. Venet, *Neither Ballots nor Bullets*, pp. 34, 39, 109.

44. *Proceedings of the Yearly Meeting of Progressive Friends held at Longwood, Chester county, PA, 1862*, "Memorial to the President," pp. 11, 13, 16.

45. See Richard L. Morton, "'Contrabands' and Quakers in the Virginia Peninsula, 1862–69," *Virginia Magazine of History and Biography* (October 1953): p. 425; and *Friends Intelligencer,* "The Negro Question," April 9, 1864, p. 77.

46. Letter from Cornelia Hancock to her mother, March 18, 1866, in Jaquette, ed. *South After Gettysburg,* p. 223.

47. The *Friend,* January 10, 1863, p. 151.

48. Quoted in James McPherson, *The Struggle for Equality: Abolitionists and the Negro in the Civil War and Reconstruction* (Princeton, N.J., 1964), p. 192.

49. The *Friends Intelligencer,* March 14, 1863, pp. 6, 8.

50. The *Friend,* November 21, 1868, p. 103.

51. The *Friend,* April 9, 1864, p. 255.

52. The *Friend,* February 23, 1867, p. 207.

53. Philadelphia Yearly Meeting of the Society of Friends (O), "The Appeal of the Religious Society of Friends, to their Fellow-Citizens of the United States, on behalf of the Colored Race" (1859), pp. 2, 13. Earlier examples of similar comments can be found in New England Yearly Meeting, "Testimony of the Religious Society of Friends Against Slavery" (Boston, 1847), pp. 6–7; and Philadelphia Yearly Meeting (O), "Address of the Representatives of the Religious Society of Friends, Commonly Called Quakers . . . to the Citizens of the United States" (1837), p. 4.

54. Quoted in Densmore, "The Dilemma of Quaker Anti-Slavery," p. 88.

# Bibliography

### Primary Sources

*Archival Materials*

Friends Collection, Earlham College (Richmond, Ind.)—Huff Family Papers
Friends Collection, Guilford College (Guilford, N.C.)
Friends Library (London, U.K.)
Newport Historical Society (Newport, R.I.)—Williams Collection, Robinson Papers
Rush Rhees Library, University of Rochester (Rochester, N.Y.)—Post Family Papers
The Quaker Collection, Haverford College (Haverford, Pa.)—Errol Elliot File, William H. S. Wood Collection, Jesse Kersey Papers.
The Friends Historical Library, Swarthmore College (Swarthmore, Pa.)—George Fox White File, Haviland Records Room File.

*Books, Edited Collections, and Pamphlets*

Barclay, Robert. *The Anarchy of the Ranters And Other Libertines.* . . . London, 1676.
Bassett, William. *Society of Friends in the United States: Their Views of the Anti-Slavery Question and Treatment of the People of Colour.* Darlington, U.K., 1840.
Benedict, A. L. *Memoir of Richard Dillingham.* Philadelphia, 1852.
Birney, James. *Correspondence Between James G. Birney of Kentucky, and Several Individuals of the Society of Friends.* Haverhill, Mass., 1835.
Beecher, Catharine. *An Essay on Slavery and Abolitionism, with reference to the duty of American females.* Philadelphia, 1837.
Branagan, Thomas. *The Pleasures of Contemplation.* Philadelphia, 1818.
Brownlee, William Craig. *A Careful and Free Inquiry into the True Nature and Tendency of the Religious Principles of the Society of Friends, Commonly Called Quakers.* Philadelphia, 1824.
Bruns, Roger, ed. *Am I Not a Man and a Brother: The Antislavery Crusade of Revolutionary America, 1688–1788.* New York, 1977.
Chace, Elizabeth Buffum. *Anti-Slavery Reminiscences.* Central Falls, R.I., 1891.
Colton, Calvin. *Abolition, a Sedition.* Philadelphia, 1839.
Cornell, John J. *Autobiography of John J. Cornell, Containing an Account of his Religious Experiences and Travels in the Ministry.* Baltimore, 1906.
Douglass, Frederick. *My Bondage and My Freedom.* New York, 1844.
DuBois, Ellen Carol, ed. *The Elizabeth Cady Stanton–Susan B. Anthony Reader.* Boston, 1992.
Dumond, Dwight L., and Gilbert Barnes, eds. *The Letters of Theodore Dwight Weld, Angelina Grimke, and Sarah Grimke, 1822–1844.* New York, 1941.
Dumond, Dwight L., ed. *Letters of James Gillespie Birney, 1831–1857.* New York, 1938.
Edgerton, Walter. *A History of the Separation in the Indiana Yearly Meeting.* Cincinnati, 1856.
Evans, William. *Journal of the Life and Religious Services of William Evans, a Minister of the Gospel in the Society of Friends.* Philadelphia, 1870.

Foster, Stephen S. *The Brotherhood of Thieves; or a True Picture of the American Church and Clergy: A Letter to Nathaniel Birney.* Boston, 1843.
Frost, J. William. *The Quaker Origins of Antislavery.* Norwood, Pa., 1980.
Gereau, David. *Some Thoughts on Slavery, Addressed to the Professors of Christianity, and more particularly to those of the Society of Friends.* New York, 1841.
Gould, M. T. C., ed., *Quaker, or a Series of Sermons, by Elias Hicks.* Philadelphia, 1828.
———, ed. *A Series of Extemporaneous Discourses . . . by Elias Hicks.* Philadelphia, 1825.
Greene, Dana, ed. *Lucretia Mott: Her Complete Speeches and Sermons.* New York, 1980.
Hallowell, Anna Davis. *Life and Letters of Lucretia Mott.* Boston, 1884.
Heyrick, Elizabeth. *Immediate, Not Gradual Emancipation.* London, 1824.
Hibbard, Billy. *An Address to the Quakers.* New York, 1811.
Hicks, Elias. *Extracts from the Letters written by Elias Hicks . . .* New York, 1841.
———. *Journal of the Life and Religious Labours of Elias Hicks, Written by Himself.* New York, 1832.
———. *Observations on the Slavery of the Africans and Their Descendants.* New York, 1811.
Hicks, Rachel. *Memoir of Rachel Hicks.* New York, 1880.
Johnson, Oliver. *William Lloyd Garrison and His Times; or Sketches of the Anti-Slavery Movement in America, and of the Man Who Was Its Founder and Moral Leader.* Boston, 1882.
McClintock, Thomas, and Rhoda DeGarmo. *Basis of Religious Association, Adopted by the Conference Held at Farmington, in the state of New York, on the Sixth and Seventh of Tenth month, 1848.* New York, 1848.
McMaster, Gilbert. *The Moral Character of Civil Government.* Albany, N.Y., 1832.
Merrill, Walter M., ed. *The Letters of William Lloyd Garrison.* Vols. 1, 3. Cambridge, Mass., 1971.
Osborn, Charles. *Journal of Charles Osborn.* Cincinnati, 1854.
Pease, Zephaniah W., ed., *The Diary of Samuel Rodman: A New Bedford Chronicle of Thirty-Seven Years 1821–1850.* New Bedford, Mass., 1927.
Perera, Eve Lewis, and Lucille Salitan, eds. *Virtuous Lives: Four Quaker Sisters Remember Family Life, Abolitionism, and Woman's Suffrage.* New York, 1994.
Pichard, John B., ed. *The Letters of John G. Whittier,* vol. 1. Cambridge, Mass., 1975.
Porter, James. *Three Lectures . . . on Come-out-ism . . . That It Is Infidelity.* Boston, 1844.
Rand, Asa. *Two Sermons on Christian Fellowship.* Portland, Maine, 1817.
Rossi, Alice S., ed. *The Feminist Papers: From Adams to de Beauvoir.* Boston, 1988.
Ruchames, Louis, ed. *The Letters of William Lloyd Garrison.* Vols. 2, 4. Cambridge, Mass., 1971.
Schooley, George A., ed. *The Journal of Dr. William Schooley: Pioneer Physician, Quaker Minister, Abolitionist, Philosopher, Scholar.* Zanesville, Ohio, 1977.
Stowe, Harriet Beecher. *Key to Uncle Tom's Cabin.* Boston, 1853.
Sturge, Joseph. *To Members of the Religious Society of Friends in the United States of America* London, 1842.
Tyson, John S. *Life of Elisha Tyson, the Philanthropist.* Baltimore, 1825.
Whittier, John Greenleaf. *Justice, Not Expediency; or Slavery Considered with a View to its Rightful and Effectual Remedy, Abolition.* New York, 1833.
———. *Prose Works of John Greenleaf Whittier.* Boston, 1866.
Wright, Henry C. *The Dissolution of the American Union, Demanded by Justice and Humanity, as the Incurable Enemy of Liberty. . . .* Glasgow, 1845.

## Minutes and Proceedings

Minutes of the Baltimore Yearly Meeting of the Religious Society of Friends (Swarthmore College)
Minutes of the Indiana Yearly Meeting of the Religious Society of Friends (O) (Earlham College)

## Bibliography

Minutes of the Indiana Yearly Meeting of the Religious Society of Friends (H) (Earlham College)
Minutes of the Indiana Yearly Meeting of Anti-Slavery Friends (Earlham College)
Minutes of the New York Yearly Meeting of the Religious Society of Friends (O) (Haverford College)
Minutes of the New York Yearly Meeting of the Religious Society of Friends (H) (Swarthmore College)
Minutes of the North Carolina Yearly Meeting of the Religious Society of Friends (Swarthmore College)
Minutes of the Ohio Yearly Meeting of the Religious Society of Friends (O) (Swarthmore College)
Minutes of the Ohio Yearly Meeting of the Religious Society of Friends (H) (Swarthmore College)
Minutes of the Pennsylvania Meeting of the Religious Society of Friends (O) (Swarthmore College)
Minutes of the Pennsylvania Meeting of the Religious Society of Friends (H) (Swarthmore College)
The Congressional Globe . . . of the first session of the 31st Congress. (Washington, D.C., 1850)
Proceedings of the General Anti-Slavery Convention, Called by the Committee of the British and Foreign Anti-Slavery Society, and Held in London from June 12th to June 23rd, 1840. (London, 1840)
Proceedings of the General Anti-Slavery Convention . . . held in London from June 13th to June 20th, 1843 (London, 1843)
Proceedings of the Pennsylvania Yearly Meeting of Progressive Friends . . . 1854 (New York, 1854)

### Newspapers

Delaware Free Press (Wilmington, Del.)
Free Enquirer (New York, N.Y.)
Friends Intelligencer (Philadelphia, Pa.)
Friends Review (Philadelphia, Pa.)
Mechanics Free Press (Philadelphia, Pa.)
National Anti-Slavery Standard (New York, N.Y.)
Non-Slaveholder (Philadelphia, Pa.)
The Berean (Philadelphia, Pa.)
The British Friend (London, U.K.)
The Friend (Philadelphia, Pa.)
The Emancipator (Mufreesboro, Tenn.)
The Free Labor Advocate (Newport, Ind.)
The Liberator (Boston, Mass.)
The Non-Resistant (Boston, Mass.)
The North Star (Rochester, N.Y.)
The Palladium (Richmond, Ind.)
The Pennsylvania Freedman (Philadelphia, Pa.)

## Secondary Sources

### Books and Articles

Abzug, Robert. *Cosmos Crumbling: American Reform and the Religious Imagination.* New York, 1994.
Adams, Alice Dana. *The Neglected Period of Anti-Slavery in America, 1808–1831.* Boston, 1908.

# Bibliography

Appleby, Joyce. *Inheriting the Revolution: The First Generation of Americans.* Cambridge, Mass., 2000.
Bacon, Margaret Hope. "New Light on Sarah Mapps Douglass and Her Reconciliation with Friends," *Quaker History* 32 (Spring 2001).
———. *Valiant Friend: The Life of Lucretia Mott.* New York, 1980.
Bender, Thomas, ed. *The Antislavery Debate: Capitalism and Abolitionism as a Problem in Historical Interpretation.* Berkeley, Calif., 1992.
Bestor, Arthur J. *Backwoods Utopias; the Sectarian and Owenite Phases of Communitarian Socialism in America, 1663–1829.* Philadelphia, 1950.
Billington, Ray. *The Protestant Crusade, 1800–1860: A Study of the Origins of American Nativism.* New York, 1938.
Bradley, A. Day. "Progressive Friends in Michigan and New York," *Quaker History* 52, 1963.
Braude, Ann. *Radical Spirits: Spiritualism and Women's Rights in Nineteenth Century America.* Bloomington, Ind. 2001.
Brock, Peter, ed. *Liberty and Conscience: A Documentary History of the Experiences of Conscientious Objectors in America through the Civil War.* New York, 2002.
———. *Radical Pacifists in Antebellum America.* Princeton, N.J., 1968.
Cadbury, Henry. "Negro Membership in the Society of Friends," *Journal of Negro History* 21 (April 1936).
Clark, Christopher. *The Communitarian Moment: The Radical Challenge of the Northampton Association.* Ithaca, N.Y., 1995.
Clark, Elizabeth B. "'The Sacred Rights of the Weak': Pain, Sympathy, and the Culture of Individual Rights in Antebellum America," *The Journal of American History* (September 1995).
Davies, Adrian. *The Quakers in English Society, 1655–1725.* Oxford, 1999.
Davis, David Brion. *The Problem of Slavery in the Age of Revolution.* Ithaca, N.Y., 1975.
Densmore, Christopher. "The Dilemma of Quaker Anti-Slavery: The Case of Farmington Quarterly Meeting, 1836–1860," *Quaker History* (Fall 1993).
Doherty, Robert W. *The Hicksite Separation: A Sociological Analysis of Religious Schism in Early Nineteenth Century America.* New Brunswick, N.J., 1967.
Dorsey, Bruce. "Friends Becoming Enemies: Philadelphia Benevolence and the Neglected Era of American Quaker History," *Journal of the Early Republic* (Fall 1998).
Douglas, Ann. *The Feminization of American Culture.* New York, 1977.
Drake, Thomas. *Quakers and Slavery.* New Haven, Conn., 1950.
Duganne, A. J. H. *The Fighting Quakers: A True Story of the War For Our Nation.* New York, 1866.
Essig, James D. *Bonds of Wickedness: American Evangelicals against Slavery, 1770–1808.* Philadelphia, 1982.
Foster, Charles I. *An Errand of Mercy: The Evangelical United Front, 1790–1837.* Chapel Hill, N.C., 1960.
Fredrickson, George. *Racism: A Short History.* Princeton, N.J., 2002.
Friedman, Lawrence. *Gregarious Saints: Self and Community in American Abolitionism.* New York, 1982.
Gara, Larry. *Liberty Line: The Legend of the Underground Railroad.* Lexington, Ky., 1961.
Gilje, Paul A. *The Road to Mobocracy: Popular Disorder in New York City, 1763–1864.* Chapel Hill, N.C., 1987.
Goodman, Paul. *Towards a Christian Republic: Antimasonry and the Great Transition in New England, 1826–36.* New York, 1988.
Goen, C. C. *Broken Churches, Broken Nation: Denominational Schism and the Coming of the Civil War.* Macon, Ga., 1985.
Gordon, Sarah Barringer. "Blasphemy and the Law of Religious Liberty in Nineteenth Century America," *American Quarterly* (December 2000).

# Bibliography

———. *The Mormon Question: Polygamy and Constitutional Conflict in Nineteenth Century America.* Chapel Hill, N.C., 2002.
Hallowell, Norwood P. *The Negro as a Soldier in the War of the Rebellion.* Boston, 1897.
Hamburger, Philip. *Separation of Church and State.* Cambridge, Mass., 2002.
Hamm, Thomas. *God's Government Begun: The Society for Universal Inquiry and Reform, 1842–46.* Bloomington, Ind. 1995.
———. "Moral Choices: Two Indiana Quaker Communities and the Abolitionist Movement," *Indiana Magazine of History* (June 1991).
———. "'On Home Colonization' by Elijah Coffin," *Slavery and Abolition* (September 1984).
——— *The Transformation of American Quakerism: Orthodox Friends, 1800–1907.* Bloomington, Ind., 1995.
Hanley, Mark. *Beyond a Christian Commonwealth: The Protestant Quarrel with the American Republic.* Chapel Hill, N.C., 1994.
Harper, Ida Husted. *Life and Work of Susan B. Anthony.* 2 vols. Salem, N.H., 1983.
Hatch, Nathan O. *The Democratization of American Christianity.* New Haven, Conn., 1989.
Haviland, Margaret Morris. "Beyond Women's Sphere: Young Quaker Women and the Veil of Charity in Philadelphia, 1790–1810," *William and Mary Quarterly* (July 1994).
Hersh, Blanche Glassman. *The Slavery of Sex: Feminist-Abolitionists in America.* Urbana, Ill., 1978.
Hewitt, Nancy. *Woman's Activism and Social Change: Rochester, NY, 1822–1872.* Ithaca, N.Y., 1984.
Heyrman, Christine Leigh. *Southern Cross: The Beginnings of the Bible Belt.* Chapel Hill, N.C., 1997.
Hilty, Hiram. *By Land and By Sea: Quakers Confront Slavery and Its Aftermath in North Carolina.* Greensboro, N.C., 1993.
Howe, Daniel Walker. *The Political Culture of the American Whigs.* Chicago, 1979.
Ingle, H. Larry. "'A Ball That Has Rolled beyond Our Reach': The Consequences of Hicksite Reform, 1830, as seen in an Exchange of Letters," *Delaware History* (XXI, 1984)
———. *Quakers in Conflict: The Hicksite Separation.* Knoxville, Tenn., 1986.
Isenberg, Nancy. "'Pillars in the Same Temple and Priests of the Same Worship': Women's Rights and the Politics of Church and State in Antebellum America," *Journal of American History* (June 1998).
Ives, Kenneth, ed. *Black Quakers: Brief Biographies.* Chicago, 1991.
James, Sydney. *A People among Peoples: Quaker Benevolence in Eighteenth Century America.* Cambridge, Mass., 1963.
Jaquette, Henretta Stratton, ed. *South After Gettysburg: Letters of Cornelia Hancock.* New York, 1937.
Jeffrey, Julie Roy. *The Great Silent Army of Abolitionism: Ordinary Women in the Antislavery Movement.* Chapel Hill, N.C., 1998.
Jordan, Ryan. "The Indiana Separation of 1842 and the Limits of Quaker Anti-Slavery," *Quaker History* (Spring 2000).
Kroupa, Daniel. "Slave Revolts and North Carolina Quaker Migration" (M.A. thesis, History, Michigan State University, 1997).
Larson, Rebecca. *Daughters of Light: Quaker Women Preaching and Prophesying in the Colonies and Abroad, 1700–75.* New York, 1999.
Lerner, Gerda. *The Grimke Sisters from South Carolina: Pioneers for Women's Rights and Abolition.* New York, 1967.
Litwack, Leon. *North of Slavery: The Negro in the Free States, 1790–1860.* Chicago, 1961.
McCurry, Stephanie. *Masters of Small Worlds: Yeoman Households, Gender Relations, and the Political Culture of the Antebellum South Carolina Low Country.* New York, 1994.

McKivigan, John. *The War against Proslavery Religion: Abolitionism and the Northern Churches, 1830–1865.* Ithaca, N.Y., 1984.

McPherson, James. *Battle Cry of Freedom: The Civil War Era.* New York, 1988.

———. *The Struggle for Equality: Abolitionists and the Negro in the Civil War and Reconstruction.* Princeton, N.J., 1964.

Mayer, Henry. *All on Fire: William Lloyd Garrison and the Abolition of Slavery.* New York, 1998.

Marietta, Jack. *The Reformation of American Quakerism, 1748–1783.* Philadelphia, 1984.

Mathews, Donald. *Slavery and Methodism: A Chapter in American Morality, 1780–1845.* Princeton, N.J., 1965.

Melish, Joan Pope. *Disowning Slavery: Gradual Emancipation and 'Race' in New England, 1780–1860.* Ithaca, N.Y., 1998.

Miller, William Lee. *Arguing about Slavery: John Quincy Adams and the Great Battle in the United States Congress.* New York, 1995.

Nash, Gary. *Forging Freedom: The Formation of Philadelphia's Black Community, 1720–1840.* Cambridge, Mass., 1988.

———. *Race and Revolution.* Madison, Wisc., 1990.

Nelson, Jacqueline S. "Civil War Letters of Daniel Wooton: The Metamorphosis of a Quaker Soldier," *Indiana Magazine of History and Biography* (March 1989).

———. *Indiana Quakers Confront the Civil War.* Indianapolis, Ind., 1991.

Newman, Richard. *The Transformation of American Abolitionism: Fighting Slavery in the Early Republic.* Chapel Hill, N.C., 2002.

Nuermberger, Ruth Ketring. "The Free Produce Movement: A Quaker Protest against Slavery," *Historical Papers of the Trinity College Historical Society.* Durham, N.C., 1942.

Oates, Stephen. *To Purge This Land With Blood.* New York, 1970.

Painter, Nell Irvin. *Sojourner Truth: A Life, A Symbol.* New York, 1996.

Pellauer, Mary D. *Toward a Tradition of Feminist Theology: The Religious Social Thought of Elizabeth C. Stanton, Susan B. Anthony, and Anna Howard Shaw.* New York, 1991.

Perry, Lewis. *Childhood, Marriage, and Reform: Henry Clarke Wright, 1797–1870.* Chicago, 1980.

———. *Radical Abolitionism: Anarchy and the Government of God in Antislavery Thought.* Ithaca, N.Y., 1973.

———. "Versions of Anarchism in the Antislavery Movement," *American Quarterly* (Winter 1968).

Quarles, Benjamin. *Black Abolitionists.* New York, 1969.

Ramsey, William. *Spiritualism, a Satanic Delusion and a Sign of the Times.* Providence, R.I., 1861.

Reay, Barry. *The Quakers and the English Revolution.* New York, 1985.

Sassi, Jonathan D. *A Republic of Righteousness: The Public Christianity of the Post-Revolutionary New England Clergy.* New York, 2001.

Sklar, Kathryn Kish. *Catharine Beecher: A Study in American Domesticity.* New Haven, Conn., 1973.

Slaughter, Thomas P. *Bloody Dawn: The Christiana Riot and Racial Violence in the Antebellum North.* New York, 1991.

Soderlund, Jean R. *Quakers and Slavery: A Divided Spirit.* Princeton, N.J., 1985.

Speicher, Anna. *The Religious World of Anti-Slavery Women: Spirituality in the Lives of Five Abolitionism Sisters.* Syracuse, N.Y., 2000.

Stewart, James Brewer. *Holy Warriors: The Abolitionists and American Slavery.* New York, 1997.

Sterling, Dorothy. *Ahead of Her Time: Abby Kelly and the Politics of Antislavery.* New York, 1991.

Stauffer, John. *The Black Hearts of Men: Radical Abolitionists and the Transformation of Race.* Cambridge, Mass., 2002.

Strong, Douglas. *Perfectionist Politics: Abolitionism and the Religious Tensions of American Democracy.* Syracuse, N.Y., 1999.

Smedley, Katherine. *Martha Schofield and the Re-Education of the South, 1839–1916.* Lewistown, N.Y., 1987.

Thomas, Allen C. "Congregational or Progressive Friends: A Forgotten Episode in Quaker History," *Bulletin of the Friends Historical Association* (November 1920).

Tolles, Frederick. *Quakers and the Atlantic Culture.* New York, 1960.

Venet, Wendy Hamand. *Neither Ballots nor Bullets: Women Abolitionists and the Civil War.* Charlottesville, Va., 1991.

Wahl, Albert J. "The Progressive Friends of Longwood," *Quaker History* 42, No. 1 (Spring 1953).

Walters, Ronald. *The Antislavery Appeal: American Abolitionism after 1830.* New York, 1978.

Wallace, Anthony F. C. *Rockdale: The Growth of an American Village in the Early Industrial Revolution.* New York, 1972.

Weber, Jennifer L. "'If Ever War Was Holy': Quaker Soldiers and the Union Army," *North and South* (April 2002).

Weeks, Stephen. *Southern Quakers and Slavery: A Study in Institutional History.* Baltimore, 1896.

Wilentz, Sean. *Chants Democratic: New York City and the Rise of the American Working Class, 1788–1850.* New York, 1984.

Willson, Joseph. *The Elite of Our People.* Edited by Julie Winch. University Park, Pa., 2000.

Yellin, Jean Fagan, ed. *The Abolitionist Sisterhood: Women's Political Culture in Antebellum America.* Ithaca, N.Y., 1994.

——, ed., *Incidents in the Life of a Slave Girl Written by Herself.* Cambridge, 1987.

# Index

*Page numbers in italics refer to illustrations.*

Aaron, Samuel, 127
Abbe Raynal, the, 4
abolitionists/abolition movement: challenges facing, 14–15, 70–71; compared to revolutionary movements, 60–61; countercultural church communities, xi, 39–40, 98; emigrant aid societies, 128, 152n27; founding and rise of, 2, 5, 51; and institutional religion, 45; marginalization of, 28, 42, 135n1; opposition to, 28–32, 99, 101, 111–14, 116, 142n37; political involvement, 49–51, 119; resistance to, 17, 19–20, 33, 43, 133–34, 153n53; response to, 24–25, 83, 88–89, 90, 100, 139n1; sedition accusations, 43; tactics/strategy, 43–45, 104–105, 125, 126–27. *See also* civil disobedience; comeouters/comeouter movement; disownment; immediatism; pacifism; Underground Railroad; women's rights
African Americans: abolition movement participation, 75–78; access to public sphere, 69; black autonomy, 113; library companies, 8; military recruitment of, 132–33; Quaker membership, 72–73, 78; rights/status of, 7–8, 18, 42, 50, 68, 79, 132–34; uplift programs, 56–57; Victorian assumptions of, 70. *See also* free blacks; stereotypes
Allen, Richard, 71
Allen, William, 15, 87
Alton, Ill., 34–35
"amalgamation," 53
American and Foreign Anti-Slavery Society, 47, 106, 120–21

American Anti-Slavery Convention, 90
American Anti-Slavery Society: conflict within, 47–48, 106; founding and rise of, 16, 26, 27–30, 44–45; Higginson speech, 109; national reaction to, 28–30, 34, 47; petition and postal campaigns, 24, 30–32, 63; Quaker opposition to, ix–x, 28–32, 41, 42, 59, 81, 99–100; rejection of quietism, 106–107; women's role, 86–88
American Baptists Free Mission Society, 48
American Bible Society, 9
American Colonization Society, 6, 18, 20–21
American Convention for Promoting the Abolition of Slavery, 137n46
American Convention of Abolition Societies, 16
American Free Produce Association, 38
American Peace Society, 109–10
American Protestantism: democratization of, 9–12, 136n6, 137n45; gender inequality, 86; middle-class moralistic values, 91–92; and race relations, 134; reaction to Quakers, 117–18; response to abolition movement, 45, 83; theological orthodoxy, 9–12; threats to, 118; white cultural symbols, 80. *See also* Christianity; comeouters/comeouter movement; Negro pew
*American Republican,* 98
American Revolution, 4–5
Amish community, 3
anarchy/anarchic Christianity, 10, 35, 47, 90–91, 101–102, 111
Anthony, Daniel, 128

# Index

Anthony, Susan B.: abolition petition to Congress, 131; fanaticism of abolitionists, 128; on John Brown, 130; Negro pew, 72; racial segregation, 74; women's rights, 84, 95
anti-clericalism, 9–12, 15, 48, 59, 82–83, 88–90, 97
Anti-Masonic Party, 118
Anti-Slavery Almanac (1839), 63, 64
anti-slavery churches, 26, 57–61
anti-slavery conventions: American Anti-Slavery Convention (1843), 90; American Convention for Promoting the Abolition of Slavery, 137n46; American Convention of Abolition Societies, 16; British and Foreign Anti-Slavery Convention, 59; Convention of the Church Anti-Slavery Society, 57; New England Anti-Slavery Convention, 75–76; World Anti-Slavery Convention, 61, 69, 79, 86–87
Anti-Slavery Friends: actions/beliefs, 55–60, 62, 107–109; Clay presidential campaign, 107; disbanding, 61; founding of, 41–42, 55–56; fugitive slave law petition, 107–108; marginalization of, 59, 61; and Progressive Friends, 96–97
anti-slavery lectures, 43–44, 49, 59, 61, 87
anti-slavery movements: disagreements within, 14–15; petition campaigns, 25, 30–32, 52–53, 63, 87, 131; prophetic style, 33–34, 106; Quaker leadership, 41–43, 102, 114–16, 137n46. *See also* abolitionists/abolition movement; comeouters/comeouter movement
anti-slavery publications: Anti-Slavery Friends, 56; Bassett defense of abolitionists, 44; "Brutus" pamphlet, 19–20; *Champion of Freedom*, 39; on colonization, 49; *Free Labor Advocate and Anti-Slavery Chronicle*, 49; *Friends Review*, 112–13; the *Liberator*, 45, 127; *National Anti-Slavery Standard*, 45, 77–78, 107, 114–15; *New York Independent*, 127; *Non-Slaveholder*, 38–39, 78; the *Palladium*, 54; *Protectionist*, 49; on treatment of free blacks, 74; from yearly meetings, 31, 32, 49, 140n25. *See also* the *Friend*
Arch Street Meeting House, 65
Arnett, Thomas, 113
atheism, 101

Ballou, Adin, 90, 106
Baltimore, Md., 16, 43
Baltimore Yearly Meeting(s), 22, 36, 113, 142n37
Barclay, Robert, 111–12
Barney, Nathaniel, 68–69
"Basis of Religious Association," 92–93
Bassett, William: Anti-Slavery Society campaign, 27, 32–33; censure/disownment, 43, 45; S. M. Douglass correspondence, 76–77; on Negro pew, 72, 76; New England Non-Resistance Society, 111
Bates, Elisha, 105
Beard, William, 49
Beecher, Catharine, x, 42, 85
benevolent empire theology, 9, 11, 14
Benezet, Anthony, 4, 6, 36
Benson, George, 90
the *Berean*, 16
Bettle, Edward, 18
Bible burning, 13
Bible Societies, 9
Biddle, Clement, 114, 141n55
Birney, James, 33, 47–48, 58, 104
black code legislation, 70
blacks, fear of, 50, 71–73, 113, 142n37
Blatchly, Cornelius, 39; *Some Causes of Popular Poverty*, 12
Blaugdon, Barbara, 79–80
Boston, Mass., Burns Affair, 125
boycott movements, 36–40, 49. *See also* Free Produce movement
Britain: abolition of slavery, 15, 21, 60; comeouter movement, 42, 59–61; immediatism, 15–16, 21–22, 26, 41, 61. *See also* London
British and Foreign Anti-Slavery Convention, 59
British and Foreign Bible Society, 11
British Society of Friends, 2–3, 42, 59–61
Brook Farm community, 90
Brooke, Abraham, 90

# Index

brotherly love ideal, 3
Brown, John, 125–30
Brown, Nicholas, 68
Brownlee, William Craig, 117
"Brutus" pamphlet, 19–20
Buffum, Arnold: anti-slavery lectures, 60; on institutionalized racism, 68, 69; Liberty Party, 51; New England Anti-Slavery Society, 26; *Protectionist,* 49; on treatment of free blacks, 74, 79
Burke, Edmund, 4
Burns, Anthony/Burns Affair, 123, 125

Caln (Pa.) Quarterly Meeting, 30, 88
Campbellites, 9
Candler, John, 74
capitalism, 92
Capron, Effingham, 26
Catholicism, 118
censure. See disownment
Chace, Elizabeth Buffum, 44–45
Chandler, Elizabeth, 84
Chapman, Maria Weston, 84
Charleston, Va., 19–20
Chartists, 60
Chester County, Pa., 92
Child, Lydia Maria, 84
Christian anarchism. See anarchy/anarchic Christianity
Christian socialism, 91–92. See also socialism
Christiana Affair, 126–27
Christianity: anarchic movements, 10, 35, 47, 90–91, 101–102, 111; egalitarianism, 71, 77, 79; L. Mott on Christian democracy, 95; mystical Christianity, 91; pro-slavery status, 115; prophetic tradition, 55, 106; and race relations, 68–69, 134; rationalist Christianity, 10; romantic idealism, x, 9, 90–92, 97, 106, 116; social Christianity, 58. See also American Protestantism; Negro pew
church and state relations, xi, 11, 43, 118–19
Cincinnati, Ohio, 57
citizenship, and religious beliefs, 25, 57–59, 90–92, 135n1
civil disobedience, 104–21; abolitionists, 107–109; defiance of fugitive slave law, 120–21; official Quaker position on, 112–14; opposition to, 111
Civil War, 121, 130–34
Clay, Henry, 6, 42, 51, 52–54, 60, 107
Coffin, Addison, 17, 20
Coffin, Elijah, 20, 50–54
Coffin, Levi, 49, 54, 55, 56, 114, 130
Coffin, William C., 75–76
Collins, Isaac, 79
Collins, John, 91
colonization movement: African American response to, 7, 22; Hubbard defense of, 20–23, 26, 50–51; *Julius Pringle* saga, 18; opposition to, 17, 19, 49, 55; practice of, 6, 16–19, 29; Southern Quakers' support of, 20–22
Colton, Calvin, 43
comeouters/comeouter movement: and abolitionists, 55, 83, 135n1; "Basis of Religious Association," 92–93; in Britain, 42, 59, 61; comeouter communities, 48, 79, 81; goals/agenda, 46–50, 102–105; Hicksite Quakers, 79, 81, 92–94, 102; legacy, 62; marginalization of, xi–xii, 2, 57–59, 61; role as prophets, 106. See also abolitionists/abolition movement
Committee on the Concerns of the People of Color, 49
Committee(s) for Vigilance, 20
communitarian societies/communism, 11–12, 90–92, 98, 116–18, 137n33
commutation fines, 25
Compromise of 1850, 119–20, 125
Confederacy, 131–32
Congregational Friends, 83, 96, 98, 108, 127; "Basis of Religious Association," 92–93
Congregationalists, 24, 86, 97, 98
Connecticut, 70
conscientious objection, 25, 109. See also civil disobedience; pacifism
conservatism, 101
consumerism, 40
Continental Congress, 5
Convention of the Church Anti-Slavery Society, 57

## Index

Cooper, David, 5
cooperative communities, 90–92, 95
Cope, Thomas, and Henry Cope, 141n55
Coppoc, Barclay, and Edwin Coppoc, 129
Cornell, John J., 89
Cornwall (N.Y.) Quarterly Meeting, 88
cotton/cotton trade, 38–39
countercultural church communities, xi, 39–40, 98
Crandall, Prudence, 34, 64, 70
Cromwell, Oliver, 2
Cromwell, Richard, 112
Cropper, James, 15

Davis, Andrew Jackson, 94
Davis, David Brion, 137n46
Day, Mahlon, 51–52
Dayton, William, 115
Declaration of Independence, 53, 129
Declaration of Sentiments, 27, 95–96, 111. *See also* anti-slavery publications; Minute(s)
deism, 83, 101
Delaware, 108–109
*Delaware Free Press,* 12, 13, 84, 146n8
democratic evangelism, 9–12
*Democratic Review,* 116
deportation of freed slaves. *See* colonization movement
Dickinson, Anna, 131
Dicks, Zachariah, 20
Dillingham, Richard, 108
Disciples of Christ, 9
discipline: decisions regarding, 146n19; disciplinary code, 3–4, 37, 49; Hicksite reformation of, 3–4, 49, 81–83, 88, 89–90; quietism as, 24, 81, 99
disownment: for anti-slavery lectures, 43–44, 87; Quaker principle of, 3, 4, 37; threats/actions of, 12, 13, 43, 45–46, 54, 55, 87–91, 153n53
dissent/religious dissent, 25, 41–42, 79
District of Columbia, anti-slavery campaigns, 30–32, 47, 63
disunionism, 109–12, 115–16
Doherty, Robert W., 141n55
Douglass, Charles, 77
Douglass, Frederick, xi, 68, 69, 75–76, 87
Douglass, Grace Bustill, 72, 76–78

Douglass, Sarah Mapps, 72, 73, 76–80
Drake, Thomas, 137n46
Drayton, William, 119
Dugdale, Joseph, 88, 90

Edgerton, Walter, 49, 62, 78–79, 113, 125
education: integration of, 70; Quaker missionaries, 127–28; universal public education, 12, 84; of women, 84, 146n8
egalitarianism, 42, 71, 79, 129, 143n1, 144n10
emancipation: and civil war, 121; demands for, ix–x, 15, 132–33; institutional religion, xi; and institutionalized racism, 68; legal efforts, 107; practical concerns over, 17; Whittier on, 26. *See also* manumission
Emancipation Proclamation, 132, 133
Embree, Elihu, 6; *Emancipator,* 7
emigrant aid societies, 128, 152n27
emigration of freed slaves. *See* colonization
England. *See* Britain
the Enlightenment, 4
equality. *See* egalitarianism
evangelical Protestantism, 8–9, 14, 47–50, 91–92
Evans, George, 95, 113
Evans, Jonathan, 10
Evans, William, 25

Farmington (N.Y.) Quarterly Meeting, 32
female education. *See* women's rights
Female Society for the Encouragement of Free Labor, 7
female speech. *See* women's rights
Ferris, Benjamin, 13–14, 141n55
"fighting" Quaker, 122, 124, 130–32
Forrest, Thomas, 1–2
Foster, Abby, 87
Foster, Stephen, xi, 44, 46, 48
Fox, George, 2–3, 54, 71
Frances Wright Hall of Science, 12
Franklin, Benjamin, 5
Fredrickson, George, 144n8
Free African Society, 71
free blacks: Christiana Affair, 126–27; education programs for, 57, 68;

## Index

treatment of, 18, 71, 74–75, 78–79, 113, 119–20, 142n37. *See also* African Americans
Free Produce movement, 36–40, 49, 99
free soil movement, 127–30
free speech: abolitionists, 45; for women, 35, 86–87, 146n12
free thinkers, 116
Freemasons, 118
Freewill Baptists, 9, 46
French and Indian War, 4
the *Friend:* anti-Hicks editorials, 10–11; anti-slavery petition campaign, 30–31; Christianity and government, 117; "Defense of American Friends," 59–60; Fighting Quakers, 130; interracial worship, 73–74, 77; John Brown's Harpers Ferry Raid, 125–26; Lovejoy murder, 35; Mormonism, 118; position on military, 132–33; Reconstruction, 133; support for colonization, 29; treatment of freed blacks, 119–20, 126–27; women's role, 83–88, 100
the *Friends Intelligencer:* abolitionist movement, 111, 126; Compromise of 1850, 120; Emancipation Proclamation, 133
Friends of Human Progress, 83, 94–95, 110
*Friends Review,* 112–13
*Friends Weekly Intelligencer,* 98, 101
frontier Methodism, 8
Fugitive Slave Act, 62, 107–108, 112, 119, 120–21, 123, 125, 127
fugitive slaves, aid for, 17–18, 113

gag rule, 30, 51
Garrett, Thomas, 66, 108–109, 123
Garrison, William Lloyd: American Anti-Slavery Society, 26, 27, 47; and Christian comeouters, 58–59, 61; demands for emancipation, 132; "fanaticism" of, 116; *Genius of Universal Emancipation,* 7; immediatist movement, 15, 60, 99; Longwood Progressive Friends Yearly Meeting, 66, 97; New England Non-Resistance Society, 47, 110; Quaker anti-slavery pamphlets, 33; rejection of high church practices, 98; use of violent force, 125
Gay, Howard, 114–15
gender relations/gender equality, 47, 86, 88, 93, 100–101
Genesee (N.Y.) Yearly Meeting(s), 37, 45, 88, 92, 134
Gest, John, 118
"good friend," 122–23
Goode, Mr. (abolition skeptic), 19
Goodell, William, xi, 48, 120
government of God, notion of, 47, 48, 90–92, 97, 109–12
"grabocratic" capitalism, 39
Gracestreet Church Meeting (London), 59
gradualism: concepts, 5, 6, 15, 22; and emancipation, 107; practice of, 16, 18–19, 29–30, 36; quietism theology, 24, 81, 99; racial segregation, 75; support of, 42, 113
Great Migration, 20, 23
Green, Beriah, 48
Green, Jacob, 60
Green Plain (Ohio) Quarterly Meeting(s), 88–90, 127
Grimke, Angelina: African American stereotypes, 73; American Anti-Slavery Society, 47; anti-abolition violence, 35; disownment threats, 45–46; immediatism, 28; treatment of free blacks, 74, 75; wedding, 46; women's rights, 85–87
Grimke, Sarah: censure/disownment threats, 44–46; fear of free blacks, 72–73; "Letters on the Equality of the Sexes and the Condition of Women," 86; Lovejoy murder, 35
guerrilla warfare, 128–30
Gurney, Joseph John, 14, 60
Gurney, Samuel, 15

Haiti, 5, 17, 20, 36
Hale, John P., 119
Hallowell, Benjamin, 25
Hallowell, Norwood P., 131
Hamm, Thomas, 141n55, 143n1
Hancock, Cornelia, 132
Hanway, Castner, 126
"Harmonical Philosophy" (Davis), 94
Harper's Ferry, Va., 125–26, 129–30
Haviland, Margaret Morris, 85

# Index

Heyrick, Elizabeth, 15
Hibbard, Billy, 117
Hicks, Edward, paintings of, 1–2
Hicks, Elias: anti-clericalism, 9–12, 15; comeouterism, 81; Free Produce movement, 36; *Observations on the Slavery of the Africans and their Descendants,* 7; preaching of, 8, 12–13; Quaker quietism, 99; Trenton sermon, 11–12
Hicks, Rachel, 100
Hicksite Quakers: anti-slavery views, xii, 127, 140n25; disciplinary code reforms, 3–4, 41, 49, 81–83, 88–90; divisions within, 13–14, 61, 102, 141n55; opposition to, 10–11, 14–15; Pennypacker speech (Philadelphia), 114; political conservatism, 99–101; response to abolitionists, 88–90, 99–100; separation from orthodox Quakers, 8, 13, 28, 88–89; views on orthodoxy, 9–12, 82–84; women's rights campaigns, 61. *See also* comeouters/comeouter movement; immediatism; Orthodox Quakers; Quakers
Higginson, Thomas Wentworth, 109, 129
*History of the People Called Quakers* (Sewell), 79–80
Hopedale Community, 90
Hopper, Isaac, 45, 88
House of Representatives. *See* United States Congress
Howitt, William, 61
Hubbard, Jeremiah, 20–23, 26, 50–51, 71
Hughes, Samuel, 134
Hunt, John, 20

Imlay, Maria, 12, 13
immediatism: abolitionists/abolition movement, 40, 75–78, 132–33; British movement for, 15–16, 21–22, 27, 59; challenges faced by, 15, 105; demands for racial equality, ix–x, 15, 44–45; and Hicksite Quakers, 29–30, 42, 81; Hubbard on, 21; Liberty Party support of, 47–48; reaction to, ix–x, 24; rejection of, 21–22, 28–32, 35, 36, 40–43, 60–61; religious institutions, xi, 21–22, 26, 57–61; rise of, 2, 25–29, 84; views on colonization, 16; Whittier on, 26; women's role, 86–87; Yearly Meeting positions on, 32
Indiana: anti-slavery lectures, 49; commitment to preservation of Union, 131; material wealth of Quakers, 141n55; passage of black laws, 50; Quakers on state legislature, 50–51; racial prejudice, 78–79; Whig Party rally, 52–54
Indiana Yearly Meeting of Anti-Slavery Friends, 54–55
Indiana Yearly Meeting(s): abolitionist membership, 48–49, 54; Clay visit, 52–54; denunciation of slavery, 31, 140n25; disownment actions, 54; London delegation meeting, 61; Mote painting, 65; positions on anti-slavery societies, 49–50; positions on immediatism, 41, 88–89. *See also* Hicksite Quakers
Indians. *See* Native Americans
Inner Light doctrine, 3, 10, 112, 117
institutional religion, xi, 45, 46, 48
integration, 35, 71–80
intermarriage, fears of, 22, 71, 72
interracial education, 64
interracial worship, 72–73, 78
Irish, 73
Irish, David, 32
Irish Repealers, 60
Isaiah (prophet), 55
Isenberg, Nancy, 69

Jackson, Elizabeth, 100
Jacobs, Harriet, 75
Jesus, 10, 128
John Brown's raid, 129–30
Johnson, Anderson, 113
Johnson, Oliver, 63, 97–99, 109, 120, 132
Johnson, Phebe, 13
Jones, Absalom, 71
Jones, Benjamin S., 112
Jones, James Parnell, 131
*Journal of a Cruise Made to the Pacific Ocean* (Porter), 124
*Julius Pringle* saga, 18

# Index

Kansas Territory, 127–30
Kelly, Abby, 44, 45, 87
Kent, James, 116
Kersey, Jesse, 83, 99, 106
Kimber, Abby, 63
Kimber, Emma, 73, 100
King, Preston, 119
kingdom of God, search for, 105
Kneeland, Abner, 116

land reform/redistribution, 92, 95, 132
Lay, Benjamin, 36
Lee, Robert E., 129
Leonard, Rachel, 7
the *Liberator,* "Pennsylvania Abolitionism," 127
Liberia, 6, 17, 18, 21, 22
Liberty Party, 44, 47–52, 106
Lincoln, Abraham, 121, 131–32, 133
literary portraits of Quakers, 122–24
London: British and Foreign Anti-Slavery Convention, 59; Gracestreet Church Meeting, 59; London Yearly Meeting(s), 15–16, 21–22, 61; World Anti-Slavery Convention, 61, 69, 79, 86–87. *See also* Britain
Longwood (Pa.) Progressive Friends, 66, 97–98, 131–32
Lovejoy, Elijah, murder of, 34–35
Lundy, Benjamin, 7, 35; *Genius of Universal Emancipation,* 16, 84
Lynn, Mass., Anti-Slavery Society campaign, 27

Mabbett, Lorenzo, *Champion of Freedom,* 39
Mace, Jonas, 17
Macon, Nathaniel, 19
manumission: Continental Congress debates, 5; Henry Clay petition, 52–53; manumission societies, 137n46; Southern laws for, 17–18, 20, 21. *See also* emancipation
Marlborough Affair, 97–98
Marlborough Conference (Pa.), 92
marriage, 22, 71, 72, 82–84, 146nn8–9
Marriott, Charles, 45
Marshall, Humphrey, 97
Martin, James, 114
Martineau, Harriet, 84

martyrdom, 128
Massachusetts, 86, 90–91
Massachusetts Anti-Slavery Society, 75–76
May, Samuel J., 120
McClintock, Mary Ann, 95
McClintock, Thomas, 92–93, 95
McKimmey, William, 89
McMaster, Gilbert, x
Meeting for Sufferings committees: Clay Midwest visit, 54; immediatism, 32; modifying Quaker discipline, 49; role of women, 83, 146n19
Melville, Herman, *Moby Dick,* 124
Mendenhall, Hiram, 52–53
Mendenhall, Nathan, 17, 20
Mendenhall, Richard, 128
Mennonite community, 3
mercantilism, 39
Miami (Ind.) Quarterly Meeting, 113
Michigan, 92–93
Midwest, Clay visit to, 42, 51–54
Mifflin, Warner, 5–6
military/militia, 3, 20, 25, 131–34
millennium, anticipation of, 96, 98, 106. *See also* utopian idealism
Millerites, 116
Minute(s): on colonization, 49; response to anti-abolitionists, 88. *See also* anti-slavery publications; petition campaigns
miscegenation, fears of, 22, 71, 72
missionary unions, 9
Missouri, 107–108
Missouri Compromise, 1–2, 6
mob violence/"mobocracy," xii, 28, 34–35
*Moby Dick* (Melville), 124
moral suasion, 104, 120, 126, 131–34
morality, legislation of, 99
Mormons/Mormonism, 9, 116, 118
"mothers in Israel," 84–85, 101
Mott, James, 63, 95
Mott, Lucretia: as abolitionist, 17, 33; on Christian democracy, 95; Free Produce movement, 37, 38; meeting with President Tyler, 142n37; photograph, 63; on Quaker reformation, 81–83; women's rights, 84, 85, 95

# Index

Nat Turner insurrection, 18, 19
*National Anti-Slavery Standard*, 107, 114–15
National Reform Association, 95
National Underground Railroad Freedom Center, 151n2
nationalism, commitment to, 130–31
*Nationalist Anti-Slavery Standard*, 77–78
Native Americans: education, 127; forced relocation, 50; Penn treaty with, 1
Needles, Edwin, 75
Negro pew, 67–80; American Protestantism, 67–71; S. B. Anthony on, 72; Arch Street Meetinghouse, 65; W. Bassett on, 72, 76; Quaker Meetings, 67, 71–73, 76–77, 78
Nelson, Jacqueline, 131
New Bedford (Mass.) Lyceum, 70
New England: abolition movement, 24, 26–30; anti-slavery convention, 75–76; anti-slavery lectures, 43–44; institutionalized racial prejudice, 68–69
New England Anti-Slavery Society, 26
New England Non-Resistance Society, 47, 110, 111
New England Yearly Meeting(s): anti-slavery lectures, 43; anti-slavery position, 30, 32, 111, 140n25, 153n53; disownment actions, 43, 45
New Light Presbyterians, 9
New Light Quakers, 88, 100
New Model Army, 2
New Testament, 77, 86, 128
New York, 31, 34, 91–93
*New York Independent*, 127
New York Manumission Society, 137n46
New York Society for Promoting Communities, 12
New York Yearly Meeting(s): aiding fugitive slaves, 113; anti-slavery petition campaign, 31–32; anti-slavery publications, 140n25; Congregational Friends, 96; discipline reforms, 88; disownment actions, 45; Free Produce movement, 37. *See also* Hicksite Quakers
Newport, Ind., 54, 56
Noble, Samuel, 141n55

Non-Resistance Society, 44, 47, 110, 111
*Non-Slaveholder*, 78
North Carolina: anti-slavery movements, 16–18; colonization movement, 17, 22; fears of slave revolts, 17–18, 20–23, 50; manumission laws, 17–18, 20, 21; military taxes, 20
North Carolina Manumission Society, 7, 15–18, 20, 137n46
North Carolina Yearly Meeting(s), 17–18, 22, 34, 113
Northampton Association, 90–91
Northwestern Territories, 18, 50

Ohio Yearly Meeting(s), 37, 61, 88–89
Oneidan perfectionists, 116, 118
Orthodox Quakers: anti-slavery publications, 140n25; disownment actions (Philadelphia), 45–46; interest in politics, 50–51; material wealth, 141n55; opposition to immediatism, 29; reaction to Progressive Friends, 98; and religious dissent, 10, 41–42; role of women, 83–88; support of Whig Party, 50–52; treatment of freed blacks, 126. *See also* Hicksite Quakers; Quakers
orthodoxy, challenges to, 9–12, 116
Osborn, Charles, 6, 14, 39, 49, 55, 107
Owen, Robert Dale, 12, 13, 82–83
Owenite socialists, 11, 13

pacifism, 104–21; achievement of peaceable kingdom, 133–34; American Revolution, 4–5; bifurcation of peace testimony, 32–33, 38–40, 124–29, 133–34; condemnation and rejection of, 117, 126–27; controversial uses of, 105–106; French and Indian War, 4; non-Quaker response to, 25; and political practice, xii, 105–106; Quaker ethic of, 3–4, 25, 43, 132–33; rejection of, 128–34; and taxation, 3; and values of slaveholding republic, 118–19
pamphlets/pamphleteers, 9, 19–20, 33. *See also* anti-slavery publications
Parker, Benjamin, 97
participatory culture, 9

passive resistance, 128
peace testimony. *See* pacifism
"Peaceable Kingdom," visions of, 1–2, 80, 133–34
Pemberton, James, 4
Penn, William, 1, 3
Pennsylvania: founding of, 3, 4; *Liberator* article on "Pennsylvania Abolitionism," 127; Longwood Progressive Friends Yearly Meeting, 66, 97–98; Marlborough Affair, 97–98; material wealth of Quakers, 141n55; Penn treaty with Native Americans, 1; Quaker reformation in, 4, 81–83; State Senate, 117–18
Pennsylvania Abolition Society, 107, 137n46
Pennsylvania Anti-Slavery Society, 35, 63, 127
Pennsylvania Free Produce Societies, 37–38
Pennsylvania Hall, 35, 64, 87
Pennsylvania Society for Promoting the Abolition of Slavery, 5, 15
Pennsylvania Yearly Meeting(s), 92, 93
Pennypacker, Elijah, 114
People's Hall, Philadelphia, 12
perfectionism: Christian ideal of, x, 11, 90–92, 97, 106, 116; and civic institutions, xi, 48
Perry, Lewis, 106
petition campaigns: anti-slavery, 25, 30–32, 52–53, 63, 87, 131; on conscience, 25; disunionism, 110, 115–16; gender equality, 88; status of African Americans, 132–34
Phelps, Amos, 107
phenotype identity, 79
Philadelphia: African American attendance at Quaker meetings, 72, 78; anti-slavery violence, 34; Arch Street Meeting House (1866), 65; "benevolent empire" theology, 9; Bible Society, 9; interracial worship, 71, 73–74; material wealth of Quaker households, 141n55; Pennypacker speech, 114; racial prejudice, 78; Reconstruction era, 133; recruitment of African American soldiers, 132–33; Society for the Relief of Free Negroes Unlawfully Held in Bondage, 5; Tract Association of Friends, 9, 11; treatment of freed blacks, 18, 71, 126; workingman's movements, 12
Philadelphia Female Anti-Slavery Society, 76
Philadelphia Yearly Meeting(s): anti-slavery publications, 140n25; anti-slavery views, 29–30, 127, 133–34; disownment actions, 43, 45–46, 153n53; gender equality petition, 88; Hicksite separation from, 13; Reeder sermons, 13. *See also* Hicksite Quakers
Phillips, Wendell, 87, 131
plain life ethic, 3, 4
police forces, creation of, 28
political abolitionists, 47–50, 53
politics and religion, blending of, 58, 89–90, 94–96, 134
Porter, David, *Journal of a Cruise Made to the Pacific Ocean*, 124
Porter, James, 62
Post, Amy, 75, 82, 84, 87, 100–101
Post, Isaac, 75, 82
Post, Joseph, 87, 102
Pottawatomie Creek, Kansas, 129
Prairie Grove (Iowa) Monthly Meeting, 133
prejudice, ethnic, 73. *See also* racial prejudice/racism
Princeton, N.J., 71
*Princeton Review*, 117
Progressive Friends, 92–103; and Anti-Slavery Friends, 96–97; beliefs/goals, 93–94, 96–98, 102–103, 108; Christiana Riot, 126–27; emancipation delegation to White House, 132; founding of, 83, 92–94; gender equality campaign, 93; Longwood, Pennsylvania, 66, 97–98, 131–32; membership of, 63, 94–95, 97–99; reaction to, 98–103; social activism, 94–95; women's rights campaigns, 95–96, 100–101
Protestantism. *See* American Protestantism
public sphere, 69, 75–78
Pugh, Sarah, 63
Purvis, Robert, 70

Quaker abolitionists. *See* abolitionists/abolition movement

Quakers: and American Protestantism, 117–18; American Revolution, 4–5; anti-slavery reforms, 102, 114–16; bifurcation of peace testimony, 32–33, 38–40, 124–29, 133–34; Civil War, 131–34; conservatism, 105, 125–26; images and literary tropes of, 122–24; integration of Meetings, 71–80; material wealth of, 141n55; missionary activities, 127–28; Negro pew, 67, 71–73, 76–78; New Light Quakers, 88, 100; Quaker ethics, 3–4; slave ownership by, 3–5, 29; and social change, 99–100; Southern attitudes toward, 19–23; theological disputes, 10–14; women's role, 83–88, 100, 146n19. *See also* Great Migration; Hicksite Quakers; Orthodox Quakers; pacifism; Society of Friends

quietism: collapse of, 87–91, 106; as discipline, 24, 81, 99; Elias Hicks on, 99; and slavery issue, 118–20

Quimby, Daniel, 87

Quincy, Edmund, 114

race relations: antebellum America, 67–70, 144n8; and Christianity, 134; fear of race revolt, 5–6, 17–18, 20–23, 50, 113, 128–29; Hubbard on, 22; racial equality, x, xi, 53, 56–57, 143n1, 144n10; racial stereotypes, 70, 73–74; Southern states, 22, 131–34. *See also* Negro pew

racial prejudice/racism: abolitionists/abolition movement, 74–75; Edgerton on, 78–79; fear of blacks, 50, 70–73, 113, 142n37; institutionalized, 68–69, 133–34; Quakers, 22, 67–73, 77–79. *See also* Negro pew

radicalism, xii, 13–14, 50, 98, 100, 109, 119, 137n33. *See also* American Anti-Slavery Society

Raley, Ann Coppoc, 129–30

Randolph, John, 19

ranterism, 101, 112, 116

Reconstruction era, 133–34

Reeder, Elizabeth, 13

religion: abolitionism as religious duty, 44–45; institutional religion, 45; religious dissent, x, 45; search for consensus, 14–15; social activism and religious freedom, 59, 87–88. *See also* Negro pew

religious liberty: anti-abolitionism, x–xi; anti-clericalism, 82–83; and citizenship, 25, 135n1; comeouter movement, 135n1; limitations of, x, 10, 105, 116; and political practice, x, 25, 34, 117–19, 134. *See also* comeouters/comeouter movement

religious sectarianism, 53

Religious Society of Friends. *See* Society of Friends

Republican Party, 42

Republican Political Association of Working Men, 12

Revelation, Book of, 45

Rhoads, Samuel, *Non-Slaveholder,* 38–39

Rhode Island, 4–5, 14

Richmond, Ind., 42, 52–54

riots/mob violence, 24, 28, 34–35

Rochester, N.Y., 88

Rodman, Samuel, 70

sabbatarianism/anti-sabbatarianism, 9, 47, 50, 97, 116–18

Salem (Mass.) Quarterly Meeting, 32

Santo Domingo, 5, 20

Schofield, Martha, 73

Schooley, William, 89–90

schools: burning of, 64; racial prejudice, 68–69. *See also* education

sectarian exceptionalism, 30

sects, 8

sedition, accusations of, 43

segregation, 67–71, 74, 75. *See also* Negro pew

Seneca Falls, N.Y., 95

Seventh-Day Baptists, 9, 117–18

Sewell, William, *History of the People Called Quakers,* 79–80

Shawnee Indians, 127–28

Sidney, Algernon, 125

Sims, Thomas, 123

Skaneateles community, N.Y., 91

slave insurrections: fears of, 5–6, 17–18, 20–23, 50, 113; Nat Turner, 18, 19; Santo Domingo, 5, 20

slave narrative genre, 75

slave owners, 3–5, 22, 23, 29
slave states: admission to union, 30, 47. *See also* Missouri Compromise
slave trade: and American Revolution, 4–5; banning of interstate, 47; petition to Senate to abolish, 115, 119; Quaker participation in, 3
slavery: abolition of, 15–16, 21, 32, 37, 60; condemnation of, 31–32, 133–34; District of Columbia antislavery campaigns, 30–32, 47, 63; freedom for children of slaves, 17; ideals of the Enlightenment, 4; institutional religion, 46, 48; Quaker views on, ix–x, 2–5, 31, 118–20; and state government, 115–16; United States Constitution, 5, 26, 46, 53, 110, 112. *See also* emancipation; free blacks; manumission
slave ships, 124
Smith, Adam, 4
Smith, Edith, 100
Smith, Gerrit, 27, 47
Smith, Joseph, 116
social activism: gendered nature of, 86–87; Quaker cosmology of, 99–100; radicalization of, 98; religious authority, 57–59, 87–88; social testimonies, 14; universal reformers, 90–91
socialism, 11, 13, 90–92, 116. *See also* communitarian societies/communism
Society for the Protection of Free People of Color, 16
Society for the Relief of Free Negroes Unlawfully Held in Bondage, 5
Society of Friends: attempts to modernize, 96–97; beliefs and principles, ix–x, 2–5, 31, 37, 133–34; cosmology, 104–107; founding of, 2–3; positions on abolition, 27, 69, 111–14, 126; racial prejudice, 67–73, 79. *See also* Quakers
Society of Universal Inquiry and Reform, 90
socioeconomics: boycott movements, 36–40, 49; economic dislocation and emancipation, 50; Quaker wealth, 141n55
sociopolitical reform movements, 8–9

Southampton County, Va., 18, 19
Southern states, abolitionist movements, 16–23
Spartanburg, Ind., 57
spiritualism, 10, 100–101, 116, 148nn78,80
Spring, Rebecca Buffum, 129
St. George's Methodist Episcopal Church (Philadelphia), 71
Stacey, George, 87
Stanton, Benjamin, 42, 49; *Free Labor Advocate and Anti-Slavery Chronicle,* 49
Stanton, Elizabeth Cady, 87, 95
Stanton, Henry, 47
Stauffer, John, 144n10
Stearns, George, 132–33
stereotypes: African Americans, 70, 73–74, 79; Quakers, 122–24
Stowe, Harriet Beecher, 151n2; *Uncle Tom's Cabin,* 123
Stubbs, Newton, 62
Sturge, Joseph, 59–60, 61
suffrage: African Americans, 132; women, 95–96
Sunday school unions, 9, 12
Swain, George, 18

Tallack, William, 74
Tappan, Arthur, 15, 27
Tappan, Lewis, 27, 34
taxation, 3, 20
Taylor, George, 37
Taylor, Zachary, 107, 115
temperance movement, x, 50
Tennessee, 108
Tennessee Manumission Society, 137n46
Texas, 30
Thayer, Sarah, 102
theology: benevolent empire, 9, 11, 14; Inner Light doctrine, 3, 10, 112, 117; Progressive Friends, 93–94; racial stereotype assumptions, 74; religious dissent, 41–42; response to abolitionism, 24–25, 29–30, 32–33, 36–37; "revealed" nature of, 99. *See also* discipline; quietism
Thompson, George, 87
Tocqueville, Alexis de, 8
tract associations, 9, 12
Trenton, N.J., 11–12
Turner, Nat, 18

Tyler, John, 51, 142n37
Tyson, Elisha, funeral of, 7

*Uncle Tom's Cabin* (Stowe), 123
Underground Railroad: depictions of, 123, 151n2; founding, 107–109, 111, 151n2; Quaker opposition to, 108, 113–14
Union Church, 48
Union government, 131–33
Union Literary Institute, 57
Unitarianism, 100
United States Congress: African slave trade protest, 115, 119; anti-slavery petition campaigns, 30–31, 131; disunion petitions, 110; gag rule, 30, 51; Missouri Compromise debates, 1–2
United States Constitution: drafting of, 5; position on slavery, 26, 46, 53, 110, 112; rights of free blacks, 70
United States Sanitary Commission, 131
universal emancipation, 113
universal public education, 12, 84
universal reforms, 90–92, 102
universal salvation, 10
Universalists, 9
utopian idealism, x, 9, 90–92, 97, 98, 106, 116

Van Buren, Martin, 34, 51
Victorian society assumptions, 70, 73–74, 79, 86
vigilante actions, xii, 28, 34–35, 114
violence/violent force, use of, 125–27, 133–34
Virginia, 4, 18–19, 25, 128
Virginia Yearly Meeting(s), 18–19
voluntary associations, 8–9, 41–42, 99

Walker, David, 17, 19
war: American Revolution, 4–5; Civil War, 121, 130–34; defensive war, 110, 128; French and Indian War, 4; guerrilla warfare, 128–30; opposition to, 105, 125; Quakers as "warmakers," 19. *See also* pacifism
Ward, Samuel Ringgold, 78
Warder, John, 9
Ware, William, 86
Washington, George, 25

Waterloo, N.Y., 51, 92, 95
Webb, Benjamin, 12, 13
websites, Underground Railroad, 151n2
Webster, Daniel, 119–20
Weld, Theodore, 46
Wells, Thomas, 113
Wesleyan Methodist Connection, 48
West Indies, 15–16, 21, 32
Westtown Boarding School, 13
Wharton, William, 141n55
Wheeler, Daniel, 60
Whig Party, 42, 50–54, 60
White, David, 18
White, George Fox, 37, 88, 99, 106
White House, emancipation delegation, 132
Whittier, John Greenleaf: Anti-Slavery Society campaign, 27–28, 35; Burns Affair, 125; on emancipation, 26; on gradualists, 52, 54–55; *Justice, Not Expediency*, 26
Wilbur, John/Wilburite controversy, 14, 15
Wilburite Quakers, 29
Williams, Henry, 51
Wilmington, Del., 12, 13, 16, 82
Wilmington Monthly Meeting, 13–14
Wilmington Society for the Encouragement of Free Labor, 37–38
Wollstonecraft, Mary, *Vindication of the Rights of Women*, 84, 100
women: Congregationalist pastoral letter on, 86; interest in education and philanthropy, 85, 146n8; literary associations, 8; notions of role in society, 85–86; participation in Civil War, 131–32; role in orthodox Quakerism, 83–88; social activism, 7, 44–45, 100; status of, in Anti-Slavery societies, 87–88
Women's National Loyal League, 131
women's rights: abolitionist support of, 35, 61, 83–88, 100–101, 135n1; "Declaration of Sentiments," 95–96; education, 83–85; free speech, 35, 86–87, 146n12; gender equality petitions, 88; opposition to, 86–87, 100; Progressive Friends, 95–96, 100–101; spiritualism, 148n80; suffrage, 95–96

Woolman, John, 4, 36
Wooten, Daniel, 131
Working Women's Protective Union, 95
workingman's movement, 11–12, 84, 95

World Anti-Slavery Convention (London), 61, 69, 79, 86–87
Wright, Frances, 12, 82–84, 146n8
Wright, Henry C., 109–11, 115, 127
Wright, Martha Coffin, 84, 95

**Ryan P. Jordan** is visiting lecturer at University of California–San Diego.